Sukuk and Islamic Capital Markets

A Practical Guide

Consulting Editor **Rahail Ali**

Consulting editor
Rahail Ali

Publisher
Sian O'Neill

Editors
Carolyn Boyle, Jo Moore

Marketing manager
Alan Mowat

Production
John Meikle, Russell Anderson

Publishing directors
Guy Davis, Tony Harriss, Mark Lamb

Sukuk and Islamic Capital Markets: A Practical Guide
is published by
Globe Law and Business
Globe Business Publishing Ltd
New Hibernia House
Winchester Walk
London SE1 9AG
United Kingdom
Tel +44 20 7234 0606
Fax +44 20 7234 0808
Web www.globelawandbusiness.com

Printed by Antony Rowe Ltd

ISBN 978-1-905783-42-7

Table of contents

Preface

Rahail Ali
Hogan Lovells (Middle East) LLP

This book is designed to provide a practical understanding of the Islamic capital market or, as it is often called, the *sukuk* market. It also explores the regulation and standardisation of the *sukuk* market, and affords a practical insight into treasury and liquidity management products for Islamic financial institutions. No discussion on treasury products would be complete without an understanding of the much used (and criticised) *tawarruq* or commodity *murabaha* transactions. Invariably, a discussion on the form and substance of some contemporary Islamic finance products is compulsory for a proper appreciation of Islamic finance and its application in different markets.

This book is organised into four sections. Part I provides an overview of Islamic capital and money markets and related products and structures; Part II analyses the roles that key participants play in the *sukuk* market; Part III considers the regulation, standardisation and listing of *sukuk*; and Parts IV and V look to the future for the *sukuk* market.

The book is aimed at people who work in the finance, asset management and treasury sectors. This, of course, includes those involved in researching, developing, originating and executing Islamic finance transactions and products, as well as risk management personnel and professionals such as accountants and lawyers. For those with career aspirations in the Islamic finance sector, this book will provide a practical understanding of a subject whose foundation is Islamic jurisprudence and whose overriding concern is ethical financing.

Rahail Ali is the global head of Islamic finance at Hogan Lovells. He is an acknowledged expert on Islamic finance, reflected in numerous accreditations from leading industry and legal journals, as well as his top-tier rating in various directories. Mr Ali has worked on many of the most innovative and high-value Islamic finance transactions closed to date, including 'jumbo' syndicated financings and inaugural sukuk issuances for sovereigns, IFC (World Bank Group), Emirates and Petronas ("Rahail Ali is arguably the leading figure in the *sukuk* market" – Legal 500 EMEA*). Mr Ali is regularly consulted by leading publications as well as banks, governments and regulatory authorities, and is a member of Her Majesty's Treasury's Islamic Finance Experts Group.*

An overview of the *sukuk* market

Rahail Ali
Hogan Lovells (Middle East) LLP

---

1. Origins of the *sukuk* market

The *sukuk* market is at a seminal point in its development, following unprecedented growth in the Islamic finance industry in recent years. In fact, the terms 'Islamic capital market' or '*sukuk* market' would have been meaningless a decade ago, aside from a general desire for the Islamic finance industry to raise capital on a long-term basis using the efficiency and transparency of the capital markets. Provision of Islamic finance from the bank and syndication markets was well established before the advent of the first global *sukuk*: the Malaysian sovereign *sukuk* issued in 2002. The Malaysian *sukuk* was not the first *sukuk* ever issued, but it was the first to gain widespread coverage, as were the GE Capital and International Finance Corporation (IFC) *sukuk* issuances in November 2009. Those *sukuk*s were issued in the midst of the global financial crisis and drew attention to the *sukuk* market's opportunities. For a multilateral institution such as IFC to issue a *sukuk* demonstrates how far the *sukuk* market has come. The development of the *sukuk* market has resulted in increased sophistication, but innovation has also brought some controversy. This chapter provides an overview of the *sukuk* market and those developments, primarily by reference to the structures and documentation involved.

Capital markets

A 'capital market' is a market for issuance and sale of bonds, stocks or similar securities to raise long-term capital. The maturity of securities distinguishes debt capital markets from the 'money market', where trading is in short-term debt instruments with a tenor of less than one year or so. Capital markets are divided into debt capital markets and equity capital markets. The *sukuk* market falls into the debt capital markets arena because contemporary *sukuk* are structured to produce a fixed-income return for *sukuk* holders. Capital markets are also classified into primary markets and secondary markets. In the primary market an investor buys securities which are issued for the first time. Existing securities are purchased and sold in the secondary market. Primary capital markets are important for capital development of an economy.

2. Nature of *sukuk*

Derived from the term '*sak*' in classic Arabic, the term '*sukuk*' (the plural of '*sak*') as used today is synonymous with 'Islamic bond'. However, *sukuk* are not IOUs or debt instruments like conventional bonds. Accordingly, while *sukuk* are commonly termed Islamic bonds, this description actually serves to confuse. Contemporary *sukuk* (in the commercially understood, fixed-income 'Islamic bond' sense) would be better explained as *Sharia*-compliant certificates:

- whose (fixed) income return derives from ownership (on a *pro rata* and undivided basis) of *Sharia*-compliant assets, including contractual rights, held on trust for *sukuk* holders – no *sukuk* holder can claim a specific part of the assets as its own, as they are co-owned with other *sukuk* holders *pro rata*; and
- whose redemption (or principal 'repayment', to use loosehand terminology) on maturity or following default results from an obligation to purchase those assets by a corporate, bank or sovereign (commonly called the 'obligor') whose creditworthiness is the economic rationale for investing in the *sukuk*.

The term 'asset based' is sometimes used as shorthand to distinguish *sukuk* structurally as fixed-income securities from actual asset-backed securities. The distinguishing feature is that the recourse to the assets underpinning the *sukuk* should not form the commercial decision to invest in the *sukuk*. This is because, ordinarily, *sukuk* holders cannot sell them in the market or to third parties – only the obligor can and will be obliged to purchase them, because that is the commercial deal. This is also because of the nature of the assets or the practical and legal issues in endeavouring to obtain custody or possession of those assets. By the obligor assuming an obligation to pay for those assets, this creates a debt, and therefore a base economic characteristic to that of a conventional bond. This does not mean that the *sukuk* is an IOU or that *pro rata* ownership of the assets underpinning the *sukuk* is devoid of substance. Instead, it is a reflection of the commercial nature of contemporary *sukuk* as fixed-income securities, with the underlying *sukuk* assets being used to structure a *Sharia*-compliant instrument. While the economic results may be the same, the means by which they are obtained is the key difference between a conventional bond and a *sukuk* – the former is *haram*, or prohibited, and the latter is permissible.

3. *Sukuk* documentation and structures

Sukuk are structured instruments. With any structured product, understanding its structural and documentary components is key to understanding it – and *sukuk* are no different. *Sukuk* documentation is often split into what are colloquially called '*Sharia* transaction documents' and 'capital markets documents'. The designation is, of course, imprecise because all *sukuk* documents must be *Sharia* compliant and they can also all be said to be capital markets documents, given the nature of the instrument being issued. However, the terminology does serve to split *sukuk* documentation understanding into documents which should follow capital market norms relating to custody, payment and administration generally, and documents which form the core of a *Sharia*-compliant transaction (ie, contractual provisions required to provide a periodic return and pay the face amount of the *sukuk* to *sukuk* holders in a *Sharia*-compliant manner).

3.1 *Sukuk* documentation standards

There have been a few ill-fated attempts to standardise *sukuk* documentation. The lack of success is predictable. This is because *sukuk* are structured instruments and, as such, several considerations invariably arise when structuring *sukuk*. They also need to be *Sharia* compliant and pronounced as such by (eminent) *Sharia* scholars, who can have different views on what is and is not permissible. The core principles of Islamic finance are universal and very simple, but more peripheral or detailed application of those core principles requires knowledge of Islamic jurisprudence or *fiqh*. Islamic jurisprudence derives much from (and in fact embraces) intellectual opinions because, through genuine striving for knowledge, consensus can be achieved and knowledge increased. To the uninitiated, divergent opinions present discord. But much in the same way as there are medical, legal and other expert differences of opinion, varying views on what are, in reality, issues of detail and not core *Sharia* compliance concerns should not be overstated. This, controversial as it may sound, also applies to the Accounting and Auditing Organisation for Islamic Financial Institutions (AAOIFI) ruling on *sukuk*, because in its most basic form, the AAOIFI ruling was and remains a question of form versus substance – or holistically, the direction or purpose of the Islamic finance market. At a micro level, is it right to use a *musharaka* or *mudarabah* structure, but negate a genuine assumption of investment risk for one partner by its ability to 'put' its interest in the *musharaka* or *mudarabah* to the other partner or obligor? At a macro level, should the Islamic finance market engage in financial engineering to economically replicate conventional products? The simple response would be that there is nothing wrong with providing the same return as a conventional product in a *Sharia*-compliant or ethical manner.

At a transaction-specific level, the controversies engendered by the AAOIFI ruling were perhaps confusing to some because the use of diminishing *musharaka* (which involves one party to the *musharaka* periodically buying out the other party's interest in the *musharaka*) is a widely used structure, particularly for home financing, so why limit its use for *sukuk*? The view that *sukuk* should not be distinguished is strengthened by the commercial nature of the instrument being issued – namely, a fixed-income security and not one giving an equity upside return. However, the controversies surrounding the AAOIFI ruling are essentially as much to do with the Islamic finance market continuing to wrestle with profound issues which go to its very nature and which continue to cause confusion (eg, the often-repeated insistence on the need for a profit-and-loss sharing system), without appreciating that the provision of retail and corporate finance in a *Sharia*-compliant manner is no less important to meet socio-economic needs and has no less value in proper *Sharia* analysis.

Asset ownership due diligence considerations

Interposing asset ownership into any financing structure, including *sukuk*, requires early due diligence considerations for deal viability. Considerations that need to be addressed include whether there are any security interests on other third-party rights over assets. What regulatory consents, approvals and so on are required for any sale? Are the assets *halal*? If so, can they be effectively excluded from any sale? Do documents need to be registered, recorded or filed at any public office or registry? Are any notarial or other fees payable? Registration fees will be payable in most jurisdictions when the asset being conveyed is land. What taxes could in principle be charged on the sale? Are there any capital gains, value added tax, sales or other local taxes such as stamp or other documentary taxes that could be charged by a sale of the assets or even a disposal of the *sukuk*? If significant taxes or fees are chargeable (eg, because they are linked to the value of the assets), what can be done to mitigate them?

The AAOIFI *sukuk* ruling

In November 2007 Sheikh Taqi Usmani, one of the world's leading *Sharia* scholars and chairman of the AAOIFI Board of *Sharia* Scholars, said that 80% of *sukuk* are not *Sharia* compliant, mainly because their method for redemption incorporates a purchase undertaking (a promise that the 'obligor' will redeem the *sukuk* by repurchasing the underlying assets at a price representing the face amount of the *sukuk* at maturity or following an event of default). Sheikh Usmani's view was that this promise violated the principle of risk and profit-sharing on which such *sukuk* should be based. The AAOIFI brought together its Board of *Sharia* Scholars to clarify the issues raised by Sheikh Usmani and to form a consensus among the *Sharia* scholars. After much discussion, the AAOIFI Board of *Sharia* Scholars published a six-point paper in 2008 outlining their position on *sukuk*, which included a ruling that purchase undertakings at face value for *musharaka* and *mudarabah sukuk* structures are no longer permissible.

Mudarabah* and *Musharaka

A *mudarabah* is a partnership (akin to a non-discretionary investment management arrangement) between a capital provider and a person that applies its skill and expertise in investing that capital. Put differently, one partner – the *rab-ul-maal* (or the investor) – contributes capital; and the other – the *mudarib* (or investment trustee) – invests its time and skill with a view to generating profit on that capital.

A *musharaka* is a partnership which differs from *mudarabah* because each party to the venture must contribute capital, unlike a *mudarabah*, where the *mudarib* invests its time and skill only.

4. Money market impetus for *sukuk*

Debate and discussion have often failed to acknowledge the most obvious and glaring points: Islamic finance operates in a conventional debt finance regulatory environment, where trading in debt is the means by which banks make margins – the ubiquitous IOU, in all its guises, is the mainstay of the conventional banking world and its ultimate weakness. 'Renting money' is prohibited by Islamic finance, because making money out of money serves no societal benefit as money is merely a medium of exchange. A discussion on banking regulation is beyond the scope of this chapter, but it is the backdrop against which the *sukuk* market evolved and must therefore be borne in mind.

In many respects, the *sukuk* market owes its origins to the money market. The need for a solution to the perennial difficulties that Islamic financial institutions face in transforming their short-term liabilities (ie, deposits) into long-term assets (ie, receivables) provided the conceptual impetus to the *sukuk* market. Bank deposits, from a conventional accounting and regulatory perspective, are treated as liabilities because the bank 'owes' the money to the customer.

The notion that as tradable investment instruments, *sukuk* could be used to assist

Table 1: Commodity *murabaha*

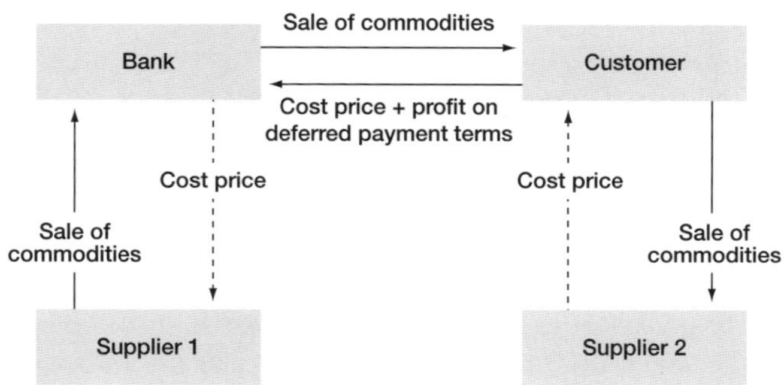

Commodity *murabaha*

- The bank buys commodities from Supplier 1.
- The bank sells the commodities to the customer under a *murabaha* contract with deferred payment terms.
- To realise cash, the customer sells (usually through the bank as agent) the commodities at cost price to Supplier 2.
- Result: the customer gets financing, the bank gets a *murabaha* contract receivable (and the suppliers are paid a commission).
- Commercial cash flow achieved through netting and transfer of rights.

In a commodity *murabaha* the parties' interest does not lie in the objects to be bought and sold (so it is a *tawarruq* transaction), but rather their cash realisable value by immediately selling them. *Tawarruq* derives from the classical Arabic *'wariq'*, meaning silver. In the historical context, the purchaser in a *tawarruq* transaction was buying only the object of the sale for cash or dinars (originally, silver coins). This type of transaction is the subject of a substantial *Sharia* scholarly debate. Some scholars take the view that it is acceptable, drawing authority from the general meaning of "whereas Allah [S.W.T.] has permitted trading" in the *Quran*. Further support for the legitimacy of this type of transaction is that there is no intent to charge or receive *riba*, or interest, and it helps people to satisfy their financial needs. Scholars taking a contrary view assert that because the object of the sale is wholly irrelevant to the intended purpose of the transaction, intermediating an object for sale does not legitimise the result of the transaction: extension of credit. The Prophet Muhammad (pbuh) said: "actions are but by intentions, and each man will have but that which he intended." There is a third view that *tawarruq* is permissible, but only if certain conditions are satisfied (eg, the person is in financial need and cannot meet that need by other *Sharia*-compliant means).

development of an Islamic money market by Islamic banks buying and selling *sukuk* to house or manage excess liquidity temporarily, instead of *tawarruq* or commodity *murabaha* treasury products (see Table 1), gained much interest – not least because commodity *murabaha*, while appeasing many, fails to satisfy all. In summary, the desire for a better short-term money market liquidity or treasury management product grew with the rapid increase in Islamic deposits. That growth was driven by the desire of retail banking customers to deposit or invest funds in a manner consistent with their beliefs. Sovereign interest, from Malaysia in particular, and general demand for (cheap) finance, buoyed by the real estate boom in the Gulf, accelerated the advent of *sukuk* from a conceptual (short-term) money market product to a (longer-term) capital market instrument.

5. *Sukuk* structures

The earliest and predominant structure of *sukuk* issued to date has been the *sukuk al-ijara* (see Table 2). Its prevalence can be explained by the need to present investors with familiar structures; a sale and leaseback structure is easily understood, even by those unfamiliar with Islamic financing. While there is no such thing as a 'cookie-cutter' *sukuk*, repeat structures, following the earliest *sukuk al-ijara*, reflect a market seeking to create benchmark structures and yield curves.

Other *sukuk* structures, primarily *musharaka* (see Table 3 overleaf) and *mudarabah* (see Table 4 overleaf), were developed to overcome the disadvantages of the *sukuk al-ijara* structure – namely, that the *sukuk* issue amount cannot be justified if the value of the assets (which will be the subject of the sale and leaseback structure) do not approximate to the issue amount. Put differently, a *sukuk* cannot be issued for $100 million if its proceeds are to buy only $50 million from the obligor. Other disadvantages include *sukuk* structural inflexibility to accommodate commercial points such as periodic redemptions and the obligor's commercial need to dispose of or deal with the assets immediately if they are on lease.

Those drawbacks gave rise to the first *musharaka sukuk* structure: the 2005 $200 million Dubai Multi-Commodities Centre (DMCC) *sukuk*. A sale and leaseback structure was not viable as the land available for the *sukuk* was undeveloped and consequently did not have a value to justify the targeted issue amount. While the DMCC *sukuk* received widespread acclaim for a number of reasons (it was the first international *sukuk* to employ a *musharaka* structure and the first rated *sukuk* coming out of Dubai), the DMCC *sukuk* was also notable for the fact that its proceeds were to be used to finance construction projects.

The DMCC *sukuk* demonstrated that construction projects could be funded using a *musharaka* structure, rather than the usual *istisna/ijara* or forward lease route, avoiding complications that those structures face in generating acceptable periodic returns during the construction phase.

However, in hindsight, the DMCC *sukuk* was most noteworthy because it was the first to offer investors an option for settlement in commodities (in that case, gold) rather than cash. Settlement flexibility is, of course, vital for equity-linked *sukuk* offerings such as convertible and exchangeable *sukuk* offerings. A *sukuk* structure must accommodate the commercial deal where the *sukuk* may be redeemed in the

Table 2: ***Sukuk al-ijara***

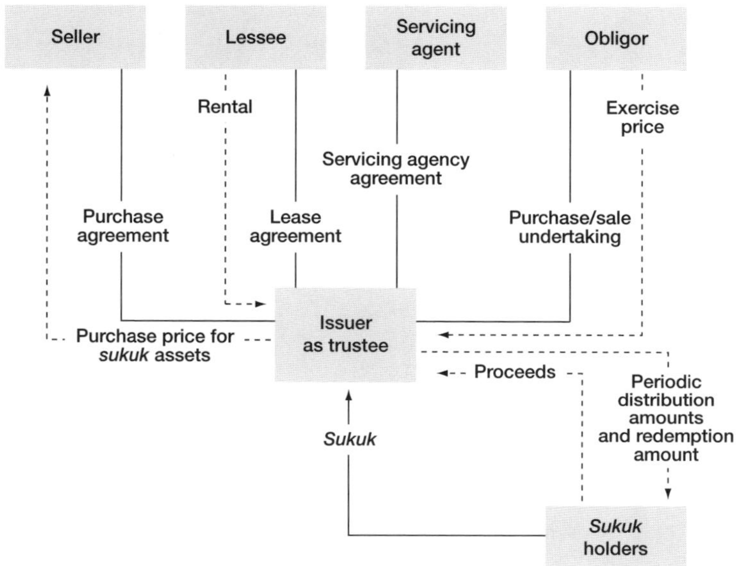

Sukuk al-ijara structure highlights:

- The issuer is a special purpose vehicle (SPV).
- The issuer issues *sukuk*.
- The issuer applies the proceeds of the *sukuk* to buy assets from the seller, which will be leased to the obligor, acting as lessee, pursuant to the lease agreement.
- Under the servicing agency agreement, the obligor acts as the lessor's agent to discharge obligations which the lessor cannot contract out for *Sharia* compliance, (eg, major maintenance of the leased assets).
- The issuer distributes rental to *sukuk* holders as periodic distribution amounts.
- The obligor executes a purchase undertaking in favour of the issuer (as trustee for *sukuk* holders). *Sukuk* redemption at maturity or following default is achieved by *sukuk* assets being 'put' to the obligor and the obligor paying for them.
- A sale undertaking is typically used for tax redemption. Redemption is achieved by the obligor 'calling' for the *sukuk* assets and the obligor paying for them to fund redemption.

Note: The seller, lessee, servicing agent and obligor are the same person in a sale and leaseback structure.

same commercial and tax scenarios as a conventional convertible equity-linked bond (eg, voluntary redemption, change of control, elective tax redemption). *Sukuk al-musharaka* and *sukuk* al-mudarabah accommodate structural flexibility by structurally permitting 'puts' and 'calls' without many limitations. Flexibility is important to accommodate innovation and development. At present, the *sukuk* market is in a state of flux following the AAOIFI ruling because, beyond *sukuk al-ijara* or *ijara* portfolio asset-managed *sukuk* structures, there is no clear structure which has gained general *Sharia* market acceptability.

Table 3: ***Sukuk al-musharaka***

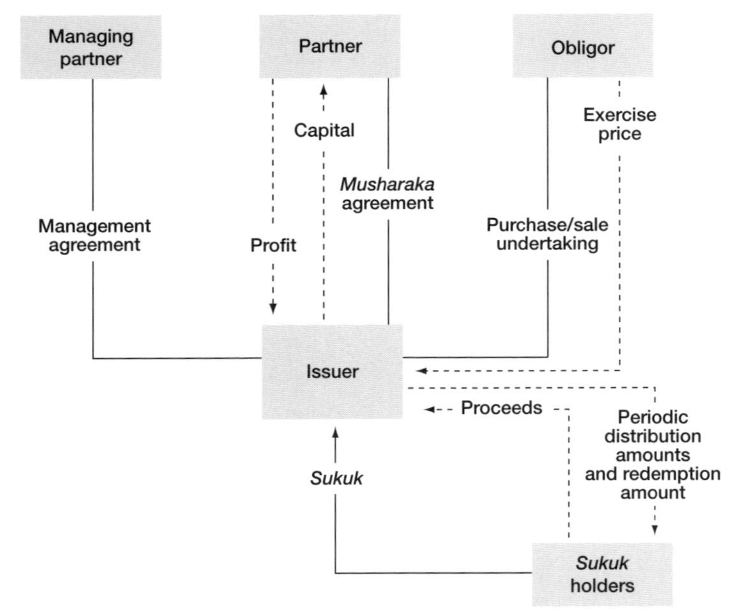

Sukuk al-musharaka structure highlights:

- The issuer is an SPV.
- The issuer issues *sukuk.*
- The issuer contributes the proceeds of the *sukuk* to the *musharaka.*
- The obligor makes a contribution in kind to the capital of the *musharaka* and manages the *musharaka* as managing partner.
- Profit generated from the *musharaka* is distributed between the issuer and the obligor in pre-agreed proportions, with profit in excess of periodic distribution amounts paid to the obligor as incentive fees for its management of the *musharaka.*
- The issuer distributes profits to sukuk holders as periodic distribution amounts.
- The obligor executes a purchase undertaking in favour of the issuer (as trustee) for *sukuk* redemption at maturity or following default.
- A sale undertaking is typically used for tax redemption.

6. *Sukuk* documents

As mentioned earlier, *sukuk* documentation is often split into *Sharia* transaction documents and capital markets documents.

6.1 Mandates

Preceding entry into the *Sharia* transaction documents and the capital markets documents is the signing of mandate documents.

Table 4: ***Sukuk al-mudarabah***

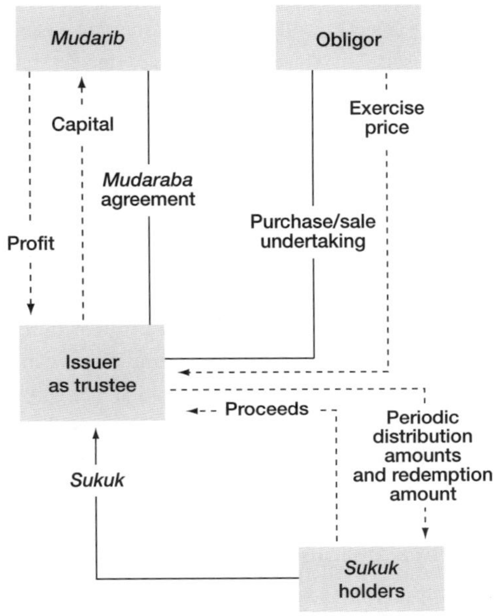

Sukuk al-mudarabah structure highlights:

- The issuer is an SPV.
- The issuer issues *sukuk.*
- The issuer contributes the proceeds of the *sukuk* as capital of the *mudarabah.*
- Profit generated from the *mudarabah* is distributed between the issuer and the *mudarib* in pre-agreed proportions, with profit in excess of periodic distribution amounts paid to the *mudarib* as incentive fees.
- The issuer distributes profits to *sukuk* holders as periodic distribution amounts.
- The obligor executes a purchase undertaking in favour of the issuer (as trustee) for *sukuk* redemption at maturity or early redemption following default.
- A sale undertaking is typically used for tax redemption.

6.2 Lead managers' mandate letter

This is a letter setting out the agreement between the obligor and the financial institutions acting as lead managers of the *sukuk*. The SPV issuer is not a party because it is usually established later. The letter will set out the roles of the managers and responsibilities for the prospective *sukuk* including, if not already determined, the structure of the *sukuk* (eg, *sukuk al-ijara*). Their role, if so agreed, may involve the managers underwriting the *sukuk* issuance or, more typically, a 'best efforts' arranging function. In any case, this letter will include the *sukuk*'s high-level deal details, including fees or commissions to be paid to the managers on issuance or closure of the *sukuk* and provisions for costs, expenses and indemnities.

6.3 Mandate with *Sharia* scholars and *fatwa*

The lead managers usually select the *Sharia* scholars who will issue the *sukuk fatwa* (pronouncement). If the lead managers have their own *Sharia* boards, they will typically make a selection on a common scholar basis, as well as on the profile and seniority of the scholar. The managers may decide that there will be a *Sharia* panel comprising three scholars. Three is a good number to present to investors, as the *Sharia* scholars will ordinarily be selected in consideration of the banks and financial institutions of which they are panel members, and so that a majority view can prevail on points which are open for intellectual consensus.

6.4 Mandate with paying agents and other service providers

One of the lead managers usually invites fee proposals from prospective paying agents, delegates and service providers, without which payment, administration and enforcement of the *sukuk* terms and conditions cannot properly be carried out, bearing in mind that the issuer is usually an SPV specifically incorporated to issue the *sukuk* and to act as trustee for the *sukuk* holders. The obligor will typically decide whom to appoint after being presented with competing proposals, and will sign a mandate on the service provider's standard engagement terms.

7. Capital markets documents

7.1 Prospectus

The prospectus or offering document is the key document for *sukuk* investors (and for listing, if any) because it discloses all material information that an investor needs to know to decide whether to invest in the *sukuk*. There are legal and regulatory requirements to protect investors against false or misleading statements, such as the EU Prospectus Directive (2003/71/EC) and, if listed, the rules of the relevant stock exchange, all of which mandate the level of disclosure required. The offering document is not a contract between the obligor, the issuer and the *sukuk* investors. It is nonetheless a legal document because it is primarily a legal and regulatory mandated disclosure document whose contents cannot be 'puffed up' – investors should be able to rely on its contents to make an informed decision as to whether to invest.

The obligor will be responsible for the contents of the offering document, as will the SPV issuer. But remember that the issuer is usually an SPV – the worth of the SPV's responsibility is only as good as the obligor's ultimate responsibility. The managers and all service providers and paying agents will always disclaim responsibility or liability for the contents of the offering document. If things go wrong, disclaimers will not provide a universal exclusion on claims – they will fall to be considered to establish who is liable. Therefore, managers are understandably aware of the need to ensure that the offering document is true and accurate and does not omit anything which could make it misleading. Due diligence is carried out to provide the appropriate degree of comfort. The extent of the due diligence depends on the obligor, the market and what the diligence exercise itself throws up for further review, consideration, analysis and disclosure.

7.2 Global certificate

Sukuk are invariably not issued as individual *sukuk* certificates, but are represented by a global certificate. The use of a global certificate is driven by the role of clearing systems (eg, Euroclear and Clearstream). Clearing systems remove settlement risk by payment being made against simultaneous delivery through accounts in the clearing system and settlement instructions. A global certificate accommodates trading through Euroclear and Clearstream by the global certificate being delivered to a common depository on behalf of Euroclear and Clearstream. The securities account of each *sukuk* holder will be credited with the face amount of the interest in the global *sukuk* purchased by each *sukuk* holder. If an investor does not hold an account in the clearing system, it can appoint an account holder as its custodian through a custodian arrangement between them.

7.3 Declaration of trust

A declaration of trust is required because the *sukuk* must create an undivided *pro rata* interest in the assets that the *sukuk* represents for the holders of the *sukuk*. 'Undivided' means that no *sukuk* holder can point to any part of the *sukuk* assets and claim them as exclusively its own – the interest of each *sukuk* holder is indivisible and *pro rata* according to the face amount held by the *sukuk* holder. The declaration of trust achieves this through the creation of a trust over the *sukuk* assets by the issuer declaring a trust over them in favour of the trust beneficiaries (ie, the *sukuk* holders). It sets out the relationship between the *sukuk* holders with regard to those assets. Pursuant to the declaration of trust, the issuer, as trustee, will hold the *sukuk* assets for the *sukuk* holders *pro rata* according to the face amount of *sukuk* held by each *sukuk* holder. The issuer also agrees to distribute all income from the trust assets in accordance with the terms and conditions of the *sukuk*. This document is entered into by the obligor, the issuer (as issuer and trustee) and a service provider typically acting as a delegate of the trustee. The governing law for the declaration of trust is usually English law. The unique feature of a *sukuk*, as compared to a conventional bond or conventional structured note, is that the issuer of the *sukuk* is also the trustee, but the issuer has no obligation independent of the *sukuk* assets to pay because the *sukuk* is not an IOU – payment comes from the obligor under the *Sharia*-compliant contracts it signs with the issuer as trustee. The declaration of trust will set out its duties and responsibilities and will seek to exclude general, non-applicable provisions of English law generally relating to trustees.

If a *sukuk* must be structured in circumstances where the use of an English law declaration of trust is not valid to confer the undivided, *pro rata* interest in the *sukuk* assets of the *sukuk* holders (eg, the *sukuk* is a pure civil jurisdiction transaction in which the SPV issuer must be incorporated locally) an agency declaration can be considered to create a relationship of principal and agent, as opposed to trustee and beneficiaries, between the SPV and the *sukuk* holders.

7.4 Paying agency agreement

The issuer is required to carry out numerous functions under the *sukuk*. As the issuer is an SPV, it is not in a position to carry out these functions. These functions include payment of the redemption amount and periodic distribution amounts when payable under the terms and conditions of the *sukuk*. Therefore, the issuer will appoint a service provider to act as paying agent. Other service provider appointments will be to act as:

- a replacement agent (ie, for the issuance of replacement *sukuk* certificates in place of those which have been lost, stolen, mutilated, defaced or destroyed if individual *sukuk* certificates are ever issued because the clearing system operating through a global *sukuk* certificate ceases to function);
- a transfer agent, to transfer individual certificates; and
- a calculation agent, to determine the periodic distribution amount payable to the *sukuk* holders.

A registrar will keep a record of information relating to the outstanding face amount of *sukuk*, all transfers and changes of ownership of individual *sukuk*, the names and addresses and account details of *sukuk* holders and all cancellations or replacements of *sukuk*. Provided that no individual *sukuk* certificates are issued, the holder of the global *sukuk* certificate will be the common depository of the clearing systems. In practice, a single corporate service provider or its affiliate is usually appointed to perform these functions and the parties to the paying agency agreement are that entity or its affiliate, the obligor and the issuer. Again, the governing law for the paying agency agreement is typically English law.

7.5 Cost undertaking

Because the issuer is an SPV and will not have the financial standing to pay its service providers, the obligor provides an undertaking to pay fees and expenses due to them and a general indemnity to keep them 'whole' in discharge of the services that they provide. The governing law for the cost undertaking is usually English law.

8. *Sharia* transaction documents

The extent and nature of the *Sharia* transaction documents depend on the structure of the *sukuk* used. For a *sukuk al-ijara* structure, for instance, the *sukuk* proceeds will be passed on to the obligor as consideration for the sale of assets by the obligor under a sale and purchase agreement. *Sukuk* return or periodic distribution amounts will be paid from rental under an *ijara* or lease agreement and redemption will be pursuant to a put under a purchase undertaking. For a structure which does not involve a sale, the *sukuk* proceeds will typically be applied or invested in an enterprise or transactions which must fit in with the commercial objective of the obligor, and redemption will typically be pursuant to a put under a purchase undertaking. Whatever structure is used, the *Sharia* transaction documents will need to be reviewed by the *Sharia* scholars providing the *fatwa* for the *sukuk* because those documents form the essence of the *sukuk* for *Sharia* compliance.

9. Global *sukuk* issuances

The AAOIFI ruling has had the effect of limiting *sukuk* issuances which are not *ijara* based. The global financial crisis and the resulting stagnation in lending predictably served to stifle structural innovation. The *sukuk* market also experienced its first defaults. These included Kuwait's Investment Dar, East Cameron Gas Company (the first *sukuk* issued by a US-based company) and Saudi's Saad Trading. The media coverage surrounding those defaults paled into insignificance to the furore over the Nakheel $3.52 billion *sukuk*, with a Dubai World guarantee. This has led to much commentary as to how *sukuk* holders would fare as compared to creditors generally, bearing in mind their *pro rata* ownership of *sukuk* assets. However, much of this commentary overlooks the commercial intent: that *sukuk* asset ownership is intended to achieve a *Sharia*-compliant return and redemption of the *sukuk* investment, and not necessarily a preferred creditor position.

There have been some developments of note since the advent of the financial crisis. The unique economic conditions of 2009 also enabled the *sukuk* world to experience its first 'buy-back' – if *sukuk* are traded on the secondary market at a significant discount to their issuance amount, an opportunity exists for obligors to take commercial benefit. Although buy-back bonds feature regularly in the conventional capital markets, the Dubai Islamic Bank (DIB) *sukuk* buy-back was the first transaction of this kind in the *sukuk* market, demonstrating that the *sukuk* market can accommodate liability management considerations in a *Sharia*-compliant manner. In 2009 DIB invited *sukuk* holders to tender up to $200 million of *sukuk* for purchase by DIB for cash, pursuant to a modified Dutch auction procedure. The *sukuk* were tendered on the basis that DIB was allowed to determine the aggregate face amount of *sukuk* that it was willing to accept for purchase and a single purchase price that it was willing to pay for the *sukuk*, taking into account the aggregate face amount of *sukuk* validly tendered and the prices at which such *sukuk* were tendered. The total *sukuk* accepted by DIB for purchase was approximately $50 million.

Geographically, however, the dominance of the Malaysian *sukuk* market is to be applauded (see Table 5). Paradoxically, it could also be considered as a hindrance to the development of a truly global *sukuk* market, due to Malaysian *Sharia* scholars sanctioning *sukuk* structures that are purely backed by receivables. Along with Malaysia, the next Southeast Asian *sukuk* market to watch is Indonesia, which

Table 5: Global *sukuk* issuance in 2009

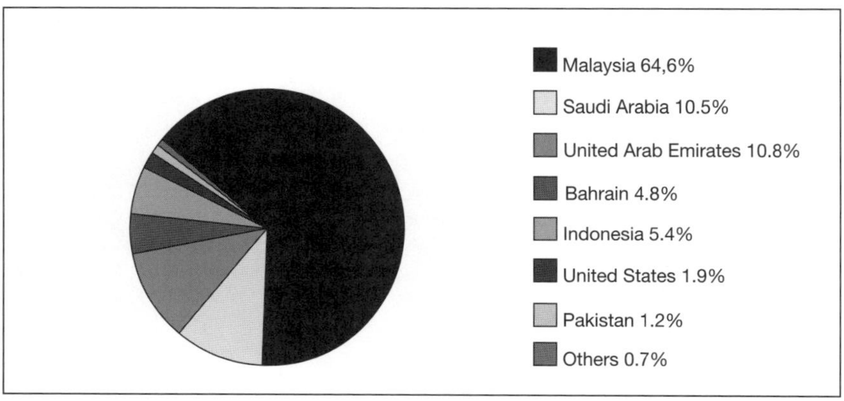

together with Saudi Arabia and Malaysia tops local currency issuances and benefits from a sizeable economy and liquidity of its local currency. Singapore's regional financial centre credentials cannot be overlooked if it backs up its interest in Islamic finance with rigour.

As for the Gulf Cooperation Council (GCC) region, the demise of the regional real estate markets resulted in the shelving of numerous *sukuk* plans. Some of the largest issuers of *sukuk* in the GCC before 2008 were large real estate companies. Nevertheless, the GCC remains a key *sukuk* market due to investor appetite for *Sharia*-compliant products and the need to finance the billions of dollars in infrastructure projects that are planned over the next decade. The *sukuk* market has not even begun to tap its potential as an infrastructure capital development instrument.

Saudi Arabia remains a sleeping giant, although there are signs that its markets are stirring. The Saudi Arabian Capital Markets Authority continues to take a keen interest in the development of the Saudi *sukuk* market, which has the potential to rival the depth of the Malaysian market. Elsewhere, governments in Hong Kong, South Korea, the United Kingdom and France have indicated an interest in developing the *sukuk* market to enable a level playing field for Islamic finance. The 2010 *sukuk* issuance for Kuveyt Türk signalled Turkey's interest in the *sukuk* market. Those initiatives are praiseworthy, but the more profound issue is whether a truly level playing field can really be achieved in debt-driven global financial markets. The ethical investment movement has sharpened its focus on conventional regulation of financial markets. *Sukuk* are, above all, ethically driven. So perhaps the biggest driver for *sukuk* in years to come will be ethically driven constituencies, of which the Islamic finance industry is very much a member.

The Islamic money market and its relevance to the Islamic capital markets

Mark Morris
Latham & Watkins LLP

1. Introduction

Islamic financial institutions (IFIs) differ from conventional banks in many respects. However, like their conventional counterparts, IFIs run long-term asset and short-term liability portfolios, creating a cash-flow mismatch which exposes them to the same short-term liquidity risks as faced by any bank operating in the fractional reserve banking system. Due to the prohibition on *riba* (interest), IFIs cannot raise short-term funding in the conventional money markets; thus, a separate Islamic money market has had to develop in jurisdictions where Islamic banks exist. With the exception of Malaysia, the Islamic money markets in most countries are not yet sufficiently developed to provide suitable short-term funding for IFIs. In particular, the lack of an Islamic repurchase agreement (known as 'repo') is seen as a major hurdle to liquidity in both the Islamic money markets and the Islamic capital markets.

The shortage of suitable Islamic money market instruments has resulted in the treasury functions of IFIs assuming central importance. The lack of short-term money market products into which IFIs can invest excess liquidity and earn a return reduces the competitiveness and profitability of IFIs. Unlike conventional banks, IFIs cannot leverage their balance sheets by trading in debt.

This chapter explores:

- the current state of play of the Islamic money market;
- the relationship between the Islamic money market and the Islamic capital markets; and
- current initiatives designed to address certain deficiencies in the Islamic money market.

This chapter is divided into three sections. The first section provides an overview of the Islamic money market and an explanation of the liquidity shortfall/liquidity surplus dilemma faced by IFIs. The second discusses deficiencies in the current Islamic money market model, as well as the relationship between the Islamic money market and the Islamic capital markets. The final section describes the latest proposals by the International Islamic Financial Market (IIFM)-International Capital Market Association (ICMA) working group on the development of an Islamic repo and 'collateralised *murabaha*' product.

2. Overview of Islamic money market

2.1 What is the Islamic money market?

The 'Islamic money market'[1] is generally understood to refer to the market in which creditworthy, *Sharia*-compliant instruments with maturities of not more than one year are issued or traded.[2] In this context, 'creditworthy' means instruments issued by entities (including sovereigns) which are typically investment grade and do not pose significant counterparty risk. This status reduces the borrowing costs for an Islamic issuer and helps to keep the overall market liquid. Unlike conventional money market instruments, which usually do not differ greatly across jurisdictions, Islamic money market products are "highly varied among countries... and different interpretations of *Sharia* ruling on financial matters across jurisdictions have led to differing methods of structuring [these] financial instruments".[3] A country's Islamic money market is typically characterised by domestic supply and demand, and Islamic money market instruments are not traded internationally to the same extent as conventional money market securities.

Geographically, there is a marked difference between the Malaysian Islamic money market and the Islamic money market in the Gulf Cooperation Council (GCC). Unlike the GCC, Malaysia's acceptance of *'bai al dayn'* (ie, the sale of debt at a discount or premium) and *'bai al inah'* (ie, the sale and buy-back of an asset), as well as the support of its central bank, has meant that "the government, Bank Negara Malaysia and [IFIs] have successfully developed an array of *Sharia* compliant financial instruments that are comparable with the conventional money market".[4]

Participants in the Islamic money market fall into two categories:

- entities such as IFIs, *takaful* firms and Islamic investment firms which run mismatched asset and liability portfolios and therefore, depending on their balance sheet on any given day, need access either to short-term funds to plug liquidity shortfalls or to low-risk investment products to invest liquidity surpluses; and
- central banks which use the money markets to 'mop up' excess liquidity (eg, the Central Bank of Bahrain's *sukuk-al-salam* and *sukuk-al-ijara* programmes), conduct monetary policy operations and, in a limited number of countries, act as lender of last resort.

In countries that operate a dual banking model, where Islamic money markets are integrated into the conventional banking system (eg, Malaysia and Sudan), a third category of participant exists: conventional banks that enter into Islamic

---

1 Technically, the Islamic money market also includes Islamic rate protection products, such as hedging, foreign exchange and derivatives tools designed to be *Sharia* compliant. A discussion of these instruments is outside the scope of this chapter, but this is a topical area in Islamic finance.

2 In certain jurisdictions trading of Islamic money market instruments is limited due to the *Sharia* prohibition on the trading of debt. This is discussed further in section 3 of this chapter.

3 *Technical note on issues in strengthening liquidity management of institutions offering Islamic financial services: the development of Islamic money markets*, Islamic Financial Services Board, published in 2008. Technically, this results in each country having its own Islamic money market, but for ease of reference the term 'the Islamic money market' refers generically to this market.

4 *Ibid.*

interbank facilities with their Islamic counterparts.

Within the wider Islamic money market is the Islamic 'interbank' market. The Islamic interbank market is similar to the Islamic money market, except that only IFIs participate in this market to the exclusion of central banks, *takaful* companies and other non-deposit-taking entities. In the conventional money market, interbank funding between conventional banks is (by volume) the largest sector of activity within the overall conventional money market. By contrast, the Islamic interbank market is much smaller in relative terms compared with the conventional money markets.

From a regulatory perspective, in most jurisdictions financial regulation does not differentiate between conventional and Islamic banks. This has resulted in some Islamic banks resorting to 'financial engineering' in order to mimic conventional treasury products, including – in the eyes of certain scholars – an over-reliance on *tawarruq* (ie, an unsecured, interbank loan).[5]

The Islamic money market continues to be dominated by commodity *murabaha* (on both the asset and liability sides of the balance sheet). In October 2008 the IIFM launched the Master Agreement for Treasury Placement, a standardised form of *murabaha* contract approved by many of the world's most prominent scholars and intended to increase cross-border interbank liquidity by reducing transaction costs and standardising documentation. Other than Malaysia's sale and buy-back agreement, these instruments are generally not collateralised and thus represent unsecured debt.

The Koranic ban on *riba* means that IFIs cannot participate in the conventional interbank market; nor can they avail of 'lender of last resort' facilities from central banks, most of which are interest bearing. Therefore, the explosion of Islamic banking over the past 40 years[6] has necessitated the evolution of an Islamic money market to enable IFIs both to mitigate liquidity risk and to invest excess liquidity.

2.2 What is liquidity risk and what is its relationship to the Islamic money markets?

'Liquidity risk' for any bank refers to the potential difficulty in obtaining cash (on a short-term basis) at a reasonable cost either by borrowing in the Islamic money market (funding liquidity risk) or by selling its assets (asset liquidity risk).[7] IFIs face liquidity risk because, like conventional banks, they operate a fractional reserve banking model. This means that IFIs are required by law[8] to keep only a fraction of their *mudaraba* deposits in cash or cash-equivalent reserves (usually with the central bank), but are free to on-lend or invest the balance (and in practice do so in order to maximise profitability). The upshot of this is that the typical balance sheet of an IFI will comprise short-term liabilities[9] (ie, customer deposits repayable by the bank on demand) and long-term assets (ie, receivables owed to the bank from investment in *sukuk*, project finance *ijara* loans and other long-term assets whose repayment

5 In April 2009 the OIC Fiqh Academy declared that organised *tawarruq* (which is one of the common liquidity tools used by banks in the Islamic interbank market) is not *Sharia* compliant.

6 Since the first Islamic banking experiment in Mit Ghamr, Egypt in 1963, the number of IFIs (whether operating the window, subsidiary or fully fledged model) as at January 1 2010 is estimated to be in excess of 300.

7 Kabir Hassan and Mervyn Lewis, *Handbook of Islamic Banking*, (2008).

8 The cash reserve ratio is set by a country's central bank, but in some countries there is no cash reserve requirement.

profiles can range up to 20 years).[10] Thus, IFIs are said to run mismatched asset and liability portfolios.

Although, for reasons explained below, IFIs tend to suffer more from excess liquidity than from deficit liquidity, and have arguably been more stable than their conventional counterparts (see below), history has shown that IFIs are not immune to bank runs and liquidity crises (see "Spotlight" below). Without an ability to obtain cash at short notice in order to fund the mismatch gap on their balance sheets, IFIs would incur significant costs in meeting their short-term liabilities and in times of financial stress would expose themselves to the possibility of a bank run by depositors. Therefore, one of the principal purposes of the Islamic money market is to enable an IFI to borrow funds on a short-term basis in order to ensure its ability to meet its short-term payment liabilities.

Spotlight: What happens when an IFI suffers a liquidity crisis?

During the Turkish financial crisis of 2000-2001, there was a run by depositors on Ihlas Finans, a wholly Islamic bank, and the bank was subsequently liquidated. The bank could not access sufficient interim liquidity and stem the flow of deposit withdrawals, leaving it insolvent. In 1984, against the backdrop of the Kuwait stock market crash (the 'Al-Manakh crises') and subsequent credit illiquidity, Kuwait Finance House unexpectedly announced that it would make no dividend distribution to shareholders for the 1984 financial year. Following the announcement, panicked depositors attempted to withdraw their deposits from all the bank's branches and a full-blown run on the bank was averted only by reassurances from the Ministry of Finance.[11]

It is important to distinguish between a liquidity crisis at a deposit-taking Islamic bank and a liquidity crisis at a non-deposit-taking Islamic institution (eg, an investment house). The former is normally due to a freeze in the interbank money market and/or a run on the bank by its depositors, whereas the latter may occur due to a severe depreciation in the value of a firm's investment portfolio, resultant decreased cash flow and impaired funding lines. A writedown of an investment portfolio in this way is not strictly the same as a liquidity shortfall at a deposit-taking bank, although such asset impairment will adversely affect the ability of an investment house to obtain bank lending following a book writedown. For example, in May 2009 Kuwait's Investment Dar became the first Islamic gulf entity to default on its debt when it failed to make a coupon payment on its $100 million *sukuk*. Investment Dar is a wholly Islamic investment firm, but is not a deposit-taking institution.

9 In theory, an IFI's withdrawal risk is different from that of a conventional bank because the deposits held by IFIs are on a *mudaraba* basis (ie, depositors (as *rab al maal*) technically agree to share in losses made by the IFI). However, in practice this mitigant is insignificant, due to what the Accounting and Auditing Organisation for Islamic Financial Institutions describes as 'displaced commercial risk' (ie, the inability of an IFI to pay as competitive a rate of return as its IFI competitors and ask shareholders to forgo profits in order to pay a competitive *mudaraba* profit rate to depositors).

10 For example, the tenor of the Islamic tranche of the Shuwaihat project financing is 20 years.

11 "Financial status of Kuwait Finance House", *Islamic World Review* (May 1985).

2.3 Why do IFIs suffer from excess liquidity?

The other main purpose of the Islamic money market is to enable IFIs to park excess liquidity in safe, liquid investments. A key feature of IFIs which differentiates them from conventional banks is that historically, IFIs have retained cash and cash equivalents on their books in excess of the statutory reserve requirements set by the relevant central bank. In other words, they have not deployed the maximum amount of capital available to them in their lending and investment operations. A recent survey by the Islamic International Rating Agency[12] of eight wholly Islamic banks in the GCC and Pakistan showed that in 2007 liquid assets (ie, cash, receivables owed to the banks under interbank facilities and investments in government *sukuk* and quoted stock) constituted almost 47% of the total short-term liabilities (ie, customer deposits and borrowings) on those banks' balance sheets, while in 2008 that figure was around 32%. This is significantly higher than the equivalent ratio at conventional banks.

The excess liquidity position of most IFIs is the polar opposite of conventional banks, which can "squeeze every cent of value from the variety of their deposits since their spectrum of investment options allows this".[13] The Islamic Financial Services Board (IFSB) cites two main reasons for the excess cash position on IFIs' balance sheets, as outlined below.

(a) Shortage of suitable money market instruments

The IFSB Technical Note states that: "[in] most countries, efficient money and interbank markets for *Sharia* compliant instruments have not yet developed... because of weaknesses in the available instruments, and the small number and size of [IFIs]. In general, the way [IFIs] have most commonly solved this problem is to maintain a larger amount of cash – excess reserve balances with the central bank – than would be the case with their conventional counterparts."

(b) No lender of last resort

As demonstrated by the multitude of government bail-outs around the world during the recent credit crisis, conventional financial institutions could not operate successfully without the active support of central banks and governments, particularly during times of financial turmoil. The position of a central bank as lender of last resort:

- protects depositors;
- prevents widespread panic withdrawal; and
- avoids disruption in the supply of productive credit to an economy.

However, in most countries bail-out money and other central bank credit support take the form of interest-bearing loans, which makes them out of bounds for IFIs. The exceptions include:

---

12 *Liquidity assessment of Islamic banks*, IIRA (June 2009).

13 "Islamic liquidity management and treasury", IIFM, published in *Islamic Investment Banking* (Yasaar Media, 2009).

- Malaysia, where Bank Negara Malaysia provides *Sharia*-compliant credit facilities to IFIs based on *wadia, mudaraba* and *rahn* principles;
- Indonesia, where collateral-backed funds can be borrowed from Bank Indonesia in return for a profit linked to the realised rate of return on *mudaraba* deposits of the borrowing bank; and
- Iran, where the Central Bank of Iran provides interest-free overdrafts (effectively a form of '*qard hassan*').

From an IFI's perspective, this has meant that "reliance on the central bank for liquidity management is low, as most short-term borrowing facilities from central banks have not been adapted to accommodate the *Sharia*", which in turn has led IFIs to mitigate liquidity risk by overcompensation in the form of retention of excess cash. In March 2010 the Union of Arab Banks announced that, in conjunction with the Islamic Development Bank, a plan was being finalised to allow *Sharia*-compliant banks to approach central banks for *riba*-free liquidity support.

2.4 What are the consequences of excess liquidity? Is it necessarily a bad thing?

Much of the writing about the issue of excess liquidity at Islamic banks ends by concluding that this is a serious impediment to the competitiveness and profitability of Islamic banks. The rationale behind these conclusions is that the aim of any bank is to maximise profitability by lending out as much of its capital base as possible, subject only to the reserve requirements set by central banks. Put another way, the higher a bank's excess reserves, the lower the amount of cash which is 'at work' earning a return for the bank, resulting in lower profitability. In good times, when there is little or no withdrawal risk from depositors and the creditworthiness of banks has not been called into question, the profitability point is well made. Regarding competitiveness, this assumes that Islamic banks are necessarily competing with conventional banks, which is debatable. From a retail perspective, Muslims whose belief system requires them to bank in a *Sharia*-compliant manner are not choosing between conventional and Islamic banks. From a commercial deposit and investment banking perspective, there are similar counterarguments as companies (particularly in the GCC and Malaysia) are increasingly opting to run their businesses in a *Sharia*-compliant manner.

In what circumstances is excess liquidity advantageous? In the wake of the credit crisis, industry commentators and regulators have pointed out that "Islamic banks often rely on their excessive liquidity base, largely in the form of surplus liquid assets, which has to some extent sheltered them from the global financial meltdown".[14] Ironically, in times of financial upheaval, the inability of IFIs to invest in conventional money market instruments and related treasury products (eg, derivatives, credit default swaps, options and forwards) actually preserves the capital base of IFIs and makes them less likely to fail. In a paper presented at the 2009 Davos Summit, Justice Mufti Taqi Usmani wrote: "it is incorrect to claim that [IFIs] were not

14 *The liquidity/leverage trade-off for Islamic banks and its impact on their ratings*, Moody's Investors Service (2009).

affected at all [by the credit crisis], but it is correct to say that they remained pretty safe from the horrors faced by conventional financial institutions. The reason is obvious. In order to be compliant with *Sharia* (Islamic law), [IFIs] are bound to remain at a distance from interest, derivatives, short sales and sale of debts."[15]

Therefore, Islamic banks are faced with a constant trade-off between liquidity and profitability (in the sense of return on risk-adjusted capital). History has shown that the periods of financial stability are much longer than the periods of economic turmoil. So, while the Islamic money markets must evolve in order to increase profitability during the good times, treasury desks at IFIs would do well to remind themselves occasionally of the virtue of excess liquidity in difficult times.

3. Deficiencies in the Islamic money market and the relationship between the Islamic money market and the Islamic capital markets

3.1 What are the principal drawbacks of the Islamic money market?

(a) *Higher relative borrowing cost*

A distinguishing feature of Islamic money market instruments when compared with their conventional equivalents is that they are unsecured (ie, not backed by collateral). Although many conventional money market instruments (eg, T-bills, gilts and interbank loans) are also unsecured, one of the most commonly used conventional money market instruments is the repo. Although not technically a secured loan, a repo has the same commercial effect as a secured loan, which means that repos are less expensive for the borrower than unsecured borrowing. Therefore, the overnight repo rate lies slightly below the US federal funds rate on the yield curve.[16] Other than a few exceptions, there is currently no Islamic equivalent of a repo. Section 4 below discusses this subject more fully and also describes the initiatives being undertaken by the IIFM in this area.

(b) *Lack of tradable instruments*

Excluding those jurisdictions (eg, Malaysia) which permit *bai al dayn*, as illustrated above, most Islamic money market instruments are based on debt-like instruments such as *murabaha* and *salam* (eg, Central Bank of Bahrain's *Al Salam Sukuk* programme). Outside Malaysia, there is general consensus among scholars that these instruments cannot be traded on the secondary market at a premium or discount, because that would attribute a time value to money and therefore be *haram*. The inability of an IFI to trade money market instruments exacerbates the issue (in good times) of excess liquidity, reduces price transparency and perpetuates the buy-and-hold culture prevalent in the GCC.[17]

---

15 *Post-crisis reforms: some points to consider*, Justice Mufti Taqi Usmani (2009).

16 *Stigum's money market*, Marcia Stigum (2006).

17 *Overcoming barriers to liquidity: commoditisation, sukuk, promoting issuance and a secondary market*, a paper presented by the IIRA at the Islamic Finance and Investment World Europe Conference 2007.

(c) ***Limited number of instruments***

Whereas the conventional money markets have had over 200 years to develop money market products,[18] Islamic finance is a nascent industry representing only a tiny fraction of global finance. The growth of innovative products has been hampered by:

- the low level of market participants;
- the lack of a central clearing system; and
- the time it takes to undertake the *Sharia* process and bring new products to market.

(d) ***Impediments to securitisation***

In Organisation for Economic Cooperation and Development countries and certain emerging markets such as Malaysia and Singapore, conventional financial institutions actively securitise their long-term assets (ie, the cash flows from credit card loans, vehicle loans, mortgages and other commercial loans) in order to reduce asset/liability mismatch. As already noted, the balance sheets of most IFIs are underleveraged because IFIs typically have a low ratio of disposable risk assets to capital, which disincentivises IFIs from securitisation.

In addition to these drawbacks, industry commentators cite the following factors as problem areas:

- the lack of *Sharia* standardisation;
- a limited range of tenors for existing products (few Islamic money market instruments are available for overnight or one-week borrowing); and
- the failure to achieve a separate, Islamic interbank rate to give products credibility (most interbank *murabahas* are pegged to the London Interbank Offered Rate).

3.2 The relationship between the Islamic money markets and the Islamic capital market

The 'Islamic capital market' refers to the market where *Sharia*-compliant securities with a tenor in excess of one year are issued and traded. The Islamic capital market is typified by *sukuk*. From a risk perspective, Islamic money market instruments are generally considered low risk due to their short-term nature and low counterparty risk (particularly in respect of government-issued paper), and are therefore inexpensive. By contrast, the longer tenor of *sukuk*, its structural complexity and relative illiquidity make it more expensive to issue, resulting in the traditional upward-sloping yield curve.

Although at different ends of the yield curve, a well-functioning Islamic money market is key to successful growth in the Islamic capital markets.

---

18 A standard definition of 'excess reserves' is the amount of balances held with central banks (whether in two accounts or one account) over and above the statutory requirements. Excess reserves as defined above can never be zero, regardless of investment opportunities available, as banks will always need some balances to settle interbank payments on the books of the central bank. The more efficient and liquid the money market is, the less the level of working balances needed at the central bank. Banks with access to a well-developed lender of last resort and active money markets will keep less cash in their current account held at the central bank.

(a) ***Collateralisation: reducing borrowing costs and 'funding'* sukuk *positions***

The development of an Islamic equivalent to repo in the Islamic money market would enable holders of Islamic capital market instruments with long maturities to liquidate their positions, resulting in a more efficient distribution of capital and increased trading of *sukuk*: "The Islamic bond market will struggle to regain its position for a long time if an alternative for creating short-term cash flow is not developed...a 'repo alternative' offers holders of [*sukuk*] the opportunity to create cash flow by selling their bond to the bank for short period and then buying it back at a slightly increased rate".[19]

As described above, developing *Sharia*-compliant money market instruments which can be backed by collateral will reduce short-term borrowing costs for issuers and improve profitability.

(b) ***Increased secondary market liquidity in* sukuk**

The ability to use *sukuk* as collateral for either an Islamic repo or collateralised *murabaha* would lead to an increase in secondary market trading of *sukuk*. This in itself would give more depth to the *sukuk* market, potentially increasing the listing of *sukuk* and creating pricing transparency, as well as encouraging investment grade issuers to access the Islamic capital markets.[20] In the GCC, the launch in January 2010 of the Gulf Bond and *Sukuk* Association is expected to enhance development of the regional *sukuk* market and confidence in the secondary market.

(c) ***Encouraging government issuances***

An efficient, well-functioning money market relies on debt instruments with low counterparty risk. Government-issued paper typically carries a lower default risk than corporate bonds due to the fact that governments have means available to them to meet their debt obligations (eg, raising taxes) which are not available to corporate issuers. Many of the GCC governments have very high credit ratings, and thus compliant paper issued by these governments are prime candidates for collateral in a repo or secured *murabaha* transaction: "As the Government is a major issuer, it can in principle generate a programme of regular [*sukuk*] issues of different maturities in sufficient volume, and in standard maturities, thereby providing a basis for a liquid market in instruments suitable for both monetary policy and public financing operations, and which can be used as convenient benchmarks for the pricing of other Islamic financial instruments."[21]

(d) ***Central bank monetary policy***

The issuance of short-term government securities can be used both to facilitate cash-raising by governments and as a form of open-market operation to decrease the money supply in an overheating economy and thus increase interest rates.[22] Given

---

19 "Cashflow a must says Islamic finance chief", *Zawya Dow Jones*, March 23 2010.

20 See footnote 15 above.

21 See footnote 3 above.

22 When governments issue securities, the money supply decreases because buyers pay the government cash consideration for those securities. Interest rates (at least, interbank interest rates) rise due to decreased supply of cash reserves in the banking system.

that conventional bonds (and *sukuk*) are generally fixed income instruments, any interest rate fluctuation will affect the yield curve, which is why *sukuk* prices move inversely to interest rates. This change in the money markets translates into pricing transparency for new issuances and secondary trading in the capital markets. In practice, especially in the GCC, there has not been a huge incentive to issue *sukuk* (or even conventional bonds) as a result of budget surpluses due to high oil prices.

(e) ***Parking excess liquidity and the role of central banks***

In addition to capital raising and monetary policy implementation, central banks are beginning to take a more active role in providing liquidity to IFIs in the domestic and regional economy. In 2002 the Central Bank of Bahrain introduced short-term *sukuk* based on *salam* and *ijara* principles; since then, including during the recent credit crisis, this paper has been oversubscribed. In 2006 Brunei also introduced short-term *sukuk* and its inaugural issuance was oversubscribed in a matter of hours. In 2008 the State Bank of Pakistan introduced *ijara*-based *sukuk*, which are eligible for reserve requirement thresholds. Finally, in early 2009 the Singapore Monetary Authority launched a short-term *sukuk* product.

Despite this progress, according to data from Zawya Dow Jones, sovereign issuances of *sukuk* represented only 7% and 23% of total *sukuk* issued worldwide in 2008 and 2009, respectively.[23] As already described, sovereign *sukuk* issuances are vital to the Islamic money market because they are instruments with low counterparty and credit risk.

4. Current initiatives: collateralised money market instruments

4.1 IIFM and ICMA joint initiative

As already noted, one of the biggest deficiencies in the Islamic money markets is the lack of collateralised products. Under the *I'aadat Al Shira'a* project, the IIFM and ICMA are exploring ways to create a *Sharia*-compliant repo and a secured (ie, collateral-backed) *murabaha*. The initiative is aimed at the GCC market, as Malaysia already has its own form of repo based on a structure which is currently unacceptable to most Middle Eastern scholars.

4.2 Islamic repo: challenges and considerations

A *Sharia*-compliant repo would be a major commercial milestone for the Islamic money markets as it would give IFIs access to a tradable money market instrument and would also be a boon for the secondary market in *sukuk*. The product could be structured to suit tenors ranging from overnight to six months.

In order to replicate a bilateral, conventional repo (see "Spotlight" below), a bilateral, Islamic repo would need to involve two distinct sales. Under the first sale, the 'borrower' would sell *Sharia*-compliant securities (eg, investment grade *sukuk* certificates) to the 'lender' in return for cash consideration, thereby funding its liquidity shortfall. At the same time as it entered into this first sale, the borrower

---

23 This data excludes so-called 'quasi-sovereign' *sukuk*.

would give a *wa'ad* undertaking to the lender, pursuant to which it would agree to buy back from the lender the original securities on a fixed date for a fixed price. At maturity, the second sale would take place, pursuant to which the lender would sell back to the borrower the same, original securities in return for payment of a sale price equal to cost plus mark-up (ie, an Islamic 'repo rate'). (A variation on this theme would be the so-called 'open repo' where the price, but not the maturity, for the second sale would be fixed and the lender would be permitted to exercise the wa'ad undertaking at any time within a specified period).

From a *Sharia* perspective, while the first sale is compliant, for the majority of scholars the second sale constitutes *bai al inah,* as sale and buy-back of the same commodities between the same parties is not permissible (in addition to *riba* issues regarding the fixed price). Possible solutions to these issues include structuring the repo such that only unilateral (ie, non-binding) *wa'ad* are issued, or using the structure described above but with the sale price for the second transaction being determined by reference to the market price of the underlying securities as at the maturity date of the repo. However, the former solution is likely to pose insurmountable legal risk, while the latter would ask participants to take equity risk on the underlying securities which defeats the purpose of the repo.

Spotlight: conventional repos

In conventional terms, a 'repo' is shorthand for a repurchase agreement or a sale and repurchase agreement which allows a borrower to use a financial security (typically government bonds) as collateral for a cash loan at a fixed rate of interest.

In a repo arrangement, the 'borrower' agrees to sell a security to a 'lender' for cash consideration and at the same time undertakes to buy back the same security from the lender at a fixed price at some later date (typically, repo tenors range from overnight to six months). A repo is thus a bilateral arrangement, equivalent to a cash transaction combined with a forward contract. The cash transaction results in transfer of money to the borrower in exchange for legal transfer of the security to the lender, while the forward contract ensures repayment of the loan to the lender and return of the collateral of the borrower. The difference between the forward price and the spot price is the interest on the loan, while the settlement date of the forward contract is the maturity date of the loan.

Although repos result in the legal transfer of the security from borrower to lender, the economic benefit of the security (in the case of an investment grade stock, this would be dividend entitlement) typically remains with the borrower.

An alternative to a bilateral repo being considered by the IIFM/ICMA project team is a tripartite repo. A form of this structure has been proposed by the Central Bank of Bahrain and is set out in diagrammatic form opposite.

This structure comprises the following three steps:

- Step 1 – Party A uses its *sukuk* position as collateral for the first sale to Party B (an independent, third-party buyer) and receives cash consideration to fund its liquidity needs. At the same time as this sale take place, Party A gives a *wa'ad* undertaking to the Central Bank of Bahrain to purchase back the original *sukuk* certificates for an agreed (marked-up) price at a future date. (This is not *bai al inah* as the *sukuk* certificates which are subject to the *wa'ad* are the same *sukuk* certificates sold to Party B, but the seller (ie, the Central Bank of Bahrain) is different.)

- Step 2 – Party B then sells the *sukuk* certificates to the Central Bank of Bahrain for spot payment and delivery.
- Step 3 – On the agreed future date, the Central Bank of Bahrain sells the 'original' *sukuk* certificates to Party A for consideration equal to cost price plus mark-up, thus completing the repo.

This structure is a viable option only because of the role of the central bank. However, borrowers would have to take insolvency risk on Party B, although arguably this would be a 'daylight' risk only where the securities are on-sold to the central bank within a short timeframe from the original first sale. Other issues being considered by the IIFM/ICMA working group are:

- accounting treatment;
- profit (ie, coupon) treatment (as technically profit payment on a *sukuk* is justified because the owner owns a share in the underlying asset); and
- the terms of any margin call should the value of the *sukuk* deteriorate before maturity.

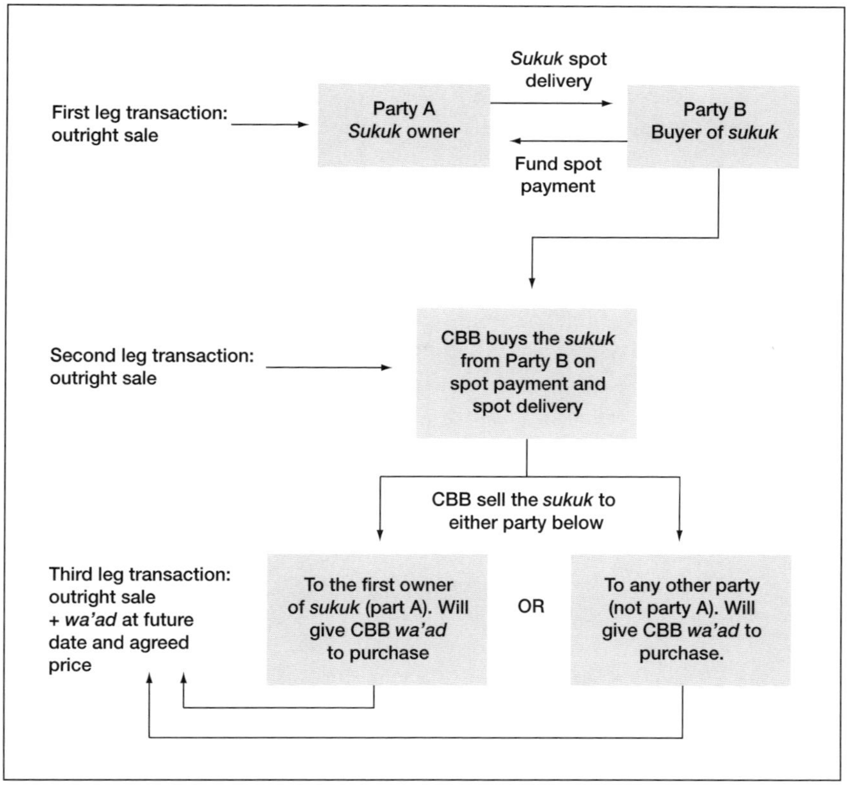

4.3 Collateralised *murabaha*: challenges and considerations

'Collateralised *murabaha*' is a term used to describe a secured interbank loan (ie, a structure whereby a commodity *murabaha* (which is already a prevalent interbank funding tool) is secured by collateral posted by the borrower). As with a conventional repo, the advantage of using this structure is that it would enable 'secured lenders' in the interbank market to provide funds at a lower margin than under an unsecured arrangement. The collateral would need to comprise *Sharia*-compliant assets capable of being secured quickly and cost effectively, given the short-term nature of Islamic interbank lending (ie, overnight to one-year tenors).

The obvious candidate for such collateral is *sukuk*; more precisely, *sukuk* which are highly rated, as the higher the quality of the collateral, the lower the funding cost for the borrower. The effectiveness of this tool would be heavily dependent on the ability of borrowers to perfect security over the *sukuk* over a very short timespan (eg, in a day or so) – if the market value of the *sukuk* were to fall below a certain percentage of the *murabaha* deferred sale price, a lender would require a borrower to maintain the security cover ratio by posting additional *sukuk* (and *vice versa* if a lender were to become over-collateralised). The counterparties to such a transaction would most likely be either a central bank (as lender) and an IFI (as borrower), or two IFIs.

5. Conclusion

The Islamic money market has come a long way since the birth of Islamic finance almost 40 years ago. Malaysia, in particular, has a thriving and well-diversified money market in which conventional and Islamic banks operate side by side and in respect of which an appropriate regulatory framework has been put in place. It is only a matter of time before the GCC catches up with product innovations which allow IFIs to earn a return on their excess liquidity and create a robust and vibrant Islamic money market.

Comparisons and differences between *sukuk* and conventional products

Yavar Moini
Morgan Stanley

1. Introduction

'*Sukuk*' are often referred to as 'Islamic bonds', which explicitly equates them with conventional fixed income instruments. While this is inaccurate from a *Sharia* perspective, many contemporary *sukuk* structures have attempted to simulate the characteristics of conventional bonds that typically relate to senior, unsecured debt. This has caused confusion among investors and considerable debate among *Sharia* scholars.

This chapter discusses the key structural characteristics of *sukuk* and compares them with conventional bonds. In addition to these core structural underpinnings, there is a comparison of critical execution requirements for *sukuk* and bonds, especially in terms of their implied preparatory and 'go to market' timelines, marketing, investor base and secondary markets. The chapter also discusses the additional documentation and principal agents involved in *sukuk* execution. PETRONAS's two-tranche *sukuk* and bond offering in August 2009 is then presented as a case study to illustrate the similarities and differences between *sukuk* and bonds. The chapter concludes with a discussion on the current state of the market and what needs to be done to promote *sukuk* issuance.

2. *Sukuk* explained

Sukuk represent the undivided, *pro rata* ownership rights to the underlying asset and do not represent a debt-based receivable. The *sukuk* holder has the right to receive a proportionate share of the profits or rental flows emanating from the underlying asset.

Typically, the ownership rights relate to a beneficial interest in the underlying asset which does not necessitate a 'true sale' of the asset. *Sharia* compliance can be achieved by transferring the productive use of the asset or usufruct to the *sukuk* holders without necessitating a legal transfer of title. Consequently, *sukuk* have not necessarily entailed any asset transfer in a formal or 'off-balance sheet' sense, but have been asset based rather than asset backed. In the event of a default by the obligor or on maturity, the only recourse available to *sukuk* holders is to 'put' the assets (or, specifically, the beneficial interest that has been purchased) back to the obligor, which creates a payment obligation in favour of *sukuk* holders. In this respect, *sukuk* holders' claims on the obligor are equivalent to those of other unsecured creditors on the basis that *sukuk* holders have no retention of title to the assets underpinning the *sukuk*.

3. Credit risk versus asset risk

Despite the necessity to base *sukuk* around present or future assets, *sukuk* holders are not typically exposed to any asset or price risk. The initial value of the *sukuk* assets should be founded on a reasonable basis, but this is really a number that needs to be justified to *Sharia* scholars as a good-faith transaction. It is not usually disclosed in any public document, since *sukuk* holders as unsecured creditors have no recourse to the underlying assets and are therefore disinterested in any asset or price risk. Therefore, *sukuk* holders are exposed only to the credit risk of the obligor. Typical investor protections such as covenants, negative pledges, cross-default provisions, indemnities, warranties and representations are included in the *sukuk* documentation in a manner that equates the inherent risk and associated return of a *sukuk* with a conventional unsecured bond.

4. Comparison with conventional unsecured bonds

While *sukuk* have typically been structured to represent unsecured credit that is akin to a conventional unsecured bond, it is important to be cognisant of the key structural differences between the two instruments.

Sukuk represent ownership rights to the underlying asset and do not represent debt in the conventional sense. This is due to the *Sharia* prohibition on debt trading, and the fact that money is not considered a commodity under *Sharia* and therefore has no intrinsic value. Consequently, all *sukuk* tend to be either asset based or constructed around the future development of assets. Bonds, on the other hand, represent a contractual obligation to pay interest and principal on a specified date – that is, a claim or a right to money. Thus, while the end result is similar in terms of achieving instruments that essentially focus on unsecured credit risk, the underlying structure is diametrically different, as *sukuk* represent an asset-based interest while bonds create a claim to cash. The former is a *halal* return on investment, but the latter is *haram*.

In addition, the underlying assets and contracts in a *sukuk* should be *Sharia* compliant. Therefore, it is not possible to structure *sukuk* if the underlying contracts are conventional, interest-bearing leases or on a portfolio of zero coupon bonds. However, the pricing of *sukuk* can be benchmarked to the London Interbank Offered Rate (LIBOR) or any other conventional reference, provided that they are structured in the manner described above. Given that the instruments are structured to replicate the credit risk that investors would incur should they buy a bond from the same or a similar rated obligor, prices for *sukuk* are usually very close to those for bonds, while issuance costs are also virtually identical to such issuance.[1]

5. Comparison with conventional secured or asset-backed securities

The discussion thus far has focused on a comparison of *sukuk* with conventional unsecured bonds. Due to the asset-based nature of the instrument, *sukuk* are also compared with conventional asset-backed securities (ABS), and this section identifies the key differences between the two.

---

1 See section 11.3 below on execution.

There is no *Sharia* prohibition on structuring *sukuk* as asset backed. Instead of a beneficial interest being provided, a 'true sale' of assets can be effected to the *sukuk* special purpose vehicle (SPV), which will transfer title and move the assets off the books of the obligor. In addition to the beneficial ownership, *sukuk* holders would then also hold title to the assets evidencing absolute ownership of the assets under *Sharia*. Such an arrangement would also enable *sukuk* to reflect the two key features of ABS in relation to the cash flows and credit risk related to the underlying asset pool.

Conventional ABS are structured as pass-through securities that capture the cash flows emanating from the underlying asset pool and transfer these to the holders of the instruments. Often, multiple tranching on the same asset pool is effected to offer different rates of return to various classes of investor, depending on their respective risk appetites. While creating such pass-through securities and offering either fixed or floating rates of return using the *sukuk* structures discussed above is easily achieved, tranching or offering different returns on the same asset pool presents *Sharia* issues.[2] Although structures have been developed that attempt to address these concerns, or at least capture the economic effects of tranching in a *Sharia*-compliant manner, this increases the complexity of the transaction.

Credit risk in conventional ABS reflects the quality of the underlying asset pool and can commonly be enhanced either for the complete pool or for individual tranches by offering third-party guarantees, overcollateralisation or monoline insurance against defaults. Often reserve cash funds are also created to mitigate default risk. Except for obtaining insurance against default risk, all other means of credit enhancement are possible under *Sharia* and can therefore be used in *sukuk* structures.

The fact that *sukuk* are inherently compatible with the nature of ABS but have not been structured as such is due to issuer preferences rather than any inherent *Sharia* impediment. The potential creation of new *Sharia*-compliant asset-backed *sukuk* involving securitisations, ABS and covered bonds will therefore present Islamic finance with new products and serve to deepen its nascent capital markets.

6. Creditors' considerations in issuing *sukuk*

Why do potential issuers choose *sukuk* over the wide range of financing alternatives that are available? Fundamentally, *sukuk* offer the following advantages.

6.1 Access to largest liquidity pool

Both conventional and Islamic investors can invest in *sukuk*, thus enabling the issuer to tap the full spectrum of investors. This is especially relevant for regional credits that may be relatively unknown internationally. Strong anchor investors closer to home enable a robust order book to be built and more competitive pricing to occur. This is especially relevant in markets such as Saudi Arabia, where investors exhibit a strong bias for *sukuk* over bonds and where domestic liquidity is abundant. In these

2 Tamweel's 2007 securitisation involved tranching based on consent as investors agreed to subordination in respect of the cash waterfall. This has not met with universal acceptance among scholars.

circumstances, issuers can arbitrage on cost and capitalise on their name and reputation. However, such opportunities are currently available only to domestic issuers as the investor base remains largely averse to non-local or regional credits.

6.2 Diversify funding sources

Sukuk allow issuers to access a new pool of investors which have not previously had access to credits that have not issued *sukuk*. *Sukuk* issues by International Finance Corporation and General Electric Credit Corporation illustrate this concept and the growing global significance of this market. In addition to the diversification benefits, *sukuk* issuance enables companies to align their investor base with their strategic business interests in the region.

6.3 Promotion of domestic Islamic finance industry

Often, issuance at sovereign level or by public sector institutions has been motivated by a desire to promote a nascent domestic Islamic finance industry. *Sukuk* issuance is often preceded by legislation being enacted that creates a level playing field in terms of a regulatory, accounting and tax perspective. The issuance then creates an effective benchmark that is designed to encourage further issuance from the private sector. Bahrain and Malaysia present typical examples of such an approach, and recently countries such as the United Kingdom, France and Indonesia have begun to reform their regulatory regimes or invited discussion from interested parties.

7. Market

Any potential benefits of *sukuk* issuance must also be weighed against the inherent characteristics of the product. The typical tenor of the market remains five years and longer tenors are difficult to accommodate. The requirement for *Sharia* compliance does introduce greater structuring and documentation, and consequently higher (but by no means prohibitive) transaction costs. *Sukuk* issuers are subjected to additional requirements for 'tangible assets' to ensure tradability and greater documentation.

The *sukuk* market is also relatively new, with total issuances of $100 billion; the United Arab Emirates – particularly Dubai – and Malaysia are the largest issuers.

Historically, the market developed on the back of bank syndications and typical deal sizes were below benchmark (less than $500 million). Unrated *sukuk* were placed with a 'club' of investors which generally took a 'buy and hold' approach. Consequently, liquidity was adversely affected. As the market evolved and *sukuk* sizes increased, rated products have been placed among a much larger investor base spread across multiple jurisdictions. However, given the overall size of the market, *sukuk* are perceived to be a more illiquid instrument in relation to bonds, although for the benchmark-sized issues this is less of a concern. Consequently, prospective issuers should consider *sukuk* issuance on the basis of the above-mentioned benefits and should not expect any pricing arbitrage to occur in relation to a bond issuance.

8. Identifying *sukuk* investors

The *sukuk* investor base tends to be primarily bank driven and in any benchmark-sized issue, banks would typically comprise three-quarters of investors. The balance is made up by family offices, government investment funds, pension funds and *takaful* companies. In the Gulf Cooperation Council (GCC), Saudi Arabia represents the most diversified investor base and, in combination with the United Arab Emirates, represents the deepest pool of liquidity. Malaysia represents the other large base of *sukuk* investors, with its sovereign wealth fund, central bank, state-owned provident fund and banks being significant investors of *sukuk* issued by both domestic and GCC issuers.

The above-mentioned investor base is obviously very different from typical bond investors that comprise real money asset managers, hedge funds, banks, insurance companies and pension funds. The real money fund managers represent significant pools of capital that are greatly in excess of the total size of the *sukuk* market and are often located in the United States. It is therefore imperative that more *sukuk* be issued in 144A format to meet the requirements of this market, which will serve to deepen the pool of available capital and increase tenors from the current five years to 10 years and beyond.

Traditionally, *sukuk* investors have been yield hungry rather than risk averse and have therefore not 'paid up' for stronger credits. This has obviously been reflected in the recent occurrence of *sukuk* defaults, especially in unrated *sukuk* which have been issued by weaker credits. International *sukuk* investors comprise traditional bond investors, as mentioned above, although there is an obvious need to increase product awareness within this group further.

Since 2008, *sukuk* investors have become very parochial in nature, with large local currency issues, especially in Saudi Arabia and Malaysia, dominating the market. There is currently not much appetite for non-regional credits – a trend that needs to be reversed in order to grow the market. Just as it is critical to educate to 144A investors about the product, it is also important for *sukuk* investors in the GCC and Malaysia to be more accepting of potential issuers from Europe and the United States in order to diversify their portfolios. In combination, this two-way movement of capital will serve to deepen and widen considerably the current *sukuk* market.

Sukuk investor segmentation for benchmark GCC issues

9. Executing a *sukuk*

Sukuk issuance does not extend the execution time in relation to a bond. For a first-time issuer, the process typically takes around 13 weeks and is divided into four main stages, as follows:

- Structuring/*Sharia* board review process – commencing with obtaining 'in-principle' approval from the *Sharia* board.
- Documentation/legal preparation – focusing on the issuer's due diligence conducted by the lead bank(s), preparation of offering circular, obtaining requisite comfort letters from auditors and final legal opinions.
- *Sukuk* offering process – involving roadshowing the trade, contacting potential investors to build up the order book (book-building) and pricing the issue.
- Closing – finalising and signing of documentation and cash settlement of the trade when investors' funds are received by the issuer. The *fatwa* (an approval) is typically signed during the *sukuk* offering process on the basis of draft documentation, but can also be issued on the basis of signed documentation.

Should a credit rating be required, a parallel process is followed that commences with providing the agencies with all available public information on the issuer and then working with the latter to prepare a detailed presentation. This process, which typically takes 12 weeks, concludes with the issuance of the rating, which is released publicly once it has been discussed and agreed with the issuer.

Sukuk investors, comprising primarily banks in the GCC, have normally required a longer book-building period of up to two weeks, as their investment decisions are based on a credit approval-type process. However, recent benchmark issues have sought to shorten this period through pre-marketing, whereby a club of significant investors are sounded out before the public launch of the transaction.

The timeline mentioned on the previous page is identical for a bond issuance, except for the workstream related to the *sukuk* structuring, which does not impede any of the other phases. Consequently, the process of *sukuk* execution is similar to that of a public bond issue, with the additional requirement to obtain *Sharia* approval being easily managed within the issuance timetable.

10. *Sukuk* documentation

While issuance costs and execution timelines for *sukuk* are equivalent to those for bonds, the product entails greater documentation. This section summarises the key documentation of an asset-based *sukuk* structured as an *ijara*, which involves the sale of a beneficial interest in income generative assets to the issuer SPV and a leaseback of such assets by the obligor.

10.1 Purchase agreement

The obligor, as seller, sells a beneficial interest in the assets to the issuer SPV. The proceeds received by the issuer from the issuance and sale of the *sukuk* certificates are used to pay the purchase price of the assets, consisting of the usufruct rights for the term of the *sukuk*. The 'purchase agreement' also defines the exact assets that have been purchased and is typically governed by the laws of the jurisdiction where the assets are physically located.

Indicative timetable

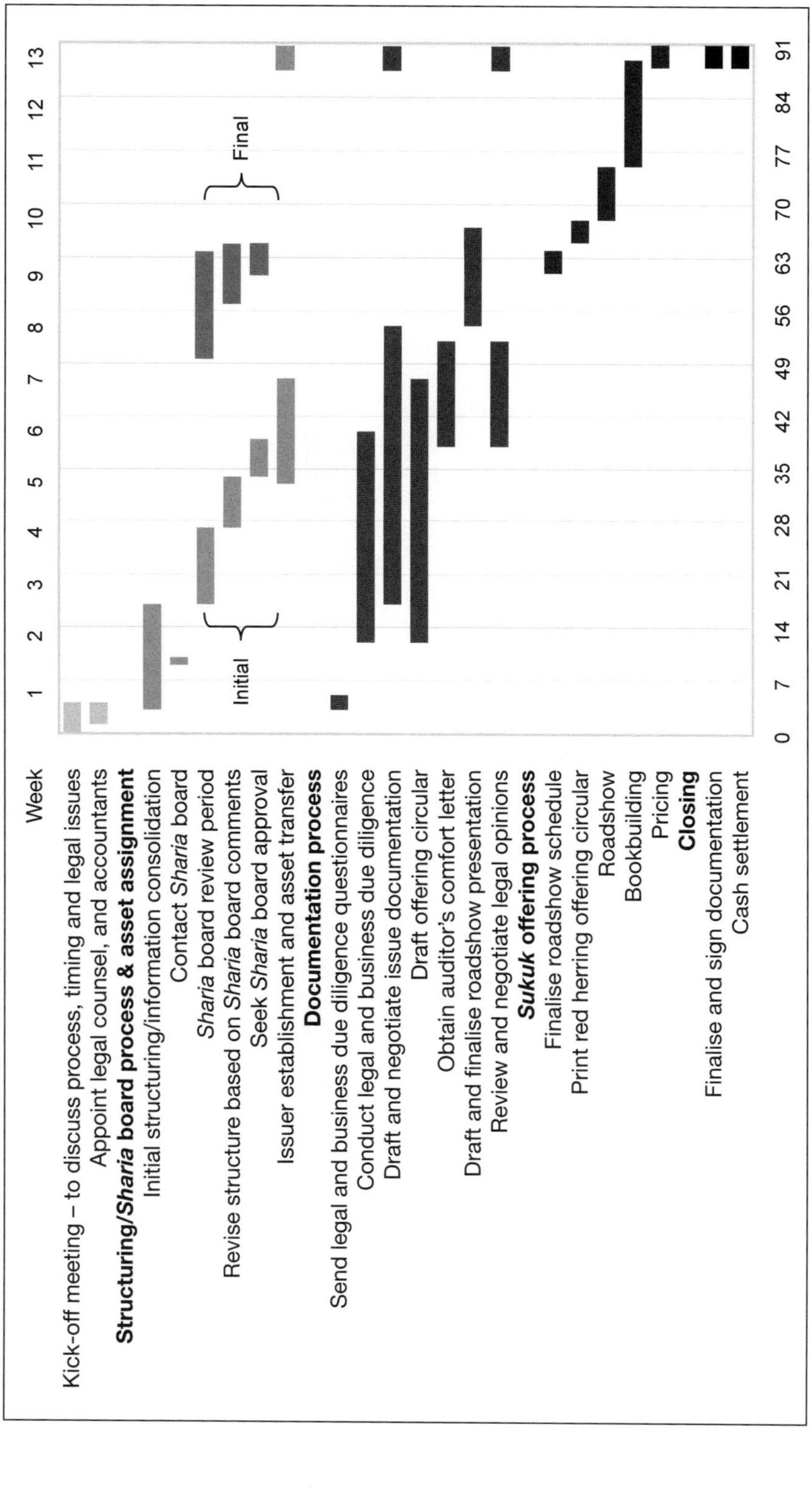

10.2 Lease agreement

The 'lease agreement' captures the relationship between the lessor and the obligor as lessee. The lease will commence on the closing date of the transaction and defines the rental (coupon) periods and amounts. The lessee remains responsible for all ordinary maintenance of the assets, while major maintenance remains the lessor's obligation. The agreement also defines termination events in relation to the lease which are default events for the *sukuk*. A total loss of the asset is also required to be a termination event for *Sharia* purposes, as a loss of the underlying asset makes it impossible for the lease to continue. Typical covenants in relation to financial ratio, cross-default and change of control provisions can be included in the lease agreement. The agreement is usually governed by the law of the jurisdiction in which the assets are located.

10.3 Servicing agency agreement

Typically, the issuer SPV also appoints the obligor or lessee to act as its 'servicing agent' for the assets. In this capacity, the obligor becomes responsible for all major maintenance on the assets, in addition to maintaining all necessary insurance. Should there be a total loss, the servicing agent is responsible for collecting all necessary insurance proceeds within 30 days, failing which the agent becomes directly liable to pay the necessary amount. In effect, commercially, this transfers the responsibility for making good on any total loss event back to the obligor. The agreement is governed by the laws of the jurisdiction in which the assets are physically located.

10.4 Purchase undertaking

The purchase undertaking is the operative document that transfers the credit risk to the obligor, as it provides an irrevocable undertaking to buy the assets on the trustee's exercise of the put that has been granted under the agreement. The exercise price payable by the obligor is equivalent to the redemption amount of the *sukuk* inclusive of any outstanding periodic distribution and principal. The exercise of the purchase undertaking transfers all rights and interests of the trustee to the obligor and creates a payment obligation for the obligor. Therefore, having exercised the put, *sukuk* holders' claims are regarded as *pari passu* or equivalent to those of other unsecured creditors of the obligor. The purchase undertaking is usually governed by English law on account of its creditor friendliness.

10.5 Sale undertaking

The sale undertaking is granted by the issuer SPV/trustee in favour of the obligor and represents a call option for the latter. This defines the events under which the *sukuk* may be called; however, for non-callable *sukuk*, this is confined to tax events which will require the obligor to pay more than the initial amount of the *sukuk*. Asset substitutability can also be built into the sale undertaking, which enables the obligor to substitute the initial assets with new assets of equivalent value. The undertaking is typically governed by English law.

10.6 Declaration of trust

The declaration of trust constitutes the *sukuk* by designating the issuer SPV as trustee on behalf of the *sukuk* holders in relation to the trust assets. The declaration defines the powers and responsibilities of the trustee and typically also enables these to be delegated these to a third party. The document also defines the terms and conditions governing the *sukuk* and is invariably governed by English law.

10.7 Other documents

The above-mentioned documents encompass the *Sharia*-related documentation. Additional agreements include:

- an agency agreement, which requires the issuer to appoint paying and calculation agents and a registrar;
- a costs undertaking, which requires the obligor to pay for all transaction costs; and
- a subscription agreement, which defines the terms and conditions under which investors subscribe to the certificates.

The *Sharia*-related documentation has become relatively standardised through usage, which enables execution within the stated timeframe and legal costs to remain within limits. The offshore *sukuk* SPV can usually be incorporated in around one day and is managed by a firm that provides trust administrative services. The annual fees for such firms are relatively small and identical to fees that would be charged should a bond be issued by a SPV fully guaranteed by the obligor.

11. Agents involved in *sukuk* issuance

The agents involved in a *sukuk* issuance are similar to those found in a bond issuance and are as follows:

- The principal paying agent is responsible for all payment services in relation to the *sukuk*, much as a fiscal agent would be for a bond. The paying agent acts on behalf of the issuer and ensures that the latter pays the stipulated payments.
- The calculation agent determines benchmark rates applicable to each coupon period.
- The reference agent calculates payment amounts and, if relevant benchmarks such as LIBOR are not available, can use a fallback reference rate.
- The replacement agent replaces old certificates with new ones should there (however unlikely) be any update or amendment to the terms and conditions of the *sukuk*.
- The transfer agent transfers individual certificates (however unlikely) in favour of holders and informs the registrar to enable the appropriate certificates to be issued.
- The registrar maintains the register which records the ownership details of individual certificates in addition to all physical details of the certificates (eg, date of issue, serial number) and any cancellations or replacements.
- The delegate is given the powers and responsibilities of the trustee in relation to exercising the purchase undertaking on maturity or an event of default. In addition, the delegate may agree, with or without the consent of the *sukuk* holders, to waivers or modifications proposed in the terms and conditions of

the *sukuk*, provided that such amendments are within defined parameters.
- The common depository holds the global *sukuk* as nominee for the clearing system and enables trading to occur in a paperless, electronic environment.
- The listing agent may be required for listing on certain exchanges.

The agent that is particular to *sukuk* is the delegate, as all the other agency roles also occur in bond issuance. In most cases the trust services of major banks can take on all the above-mentioned roles, allowing for maximum efficiency in execution and keeping issuance costs equivalent to those of bonds.

12. PETRONAS *sukuk*: case study

In August 2009 Malaysia's state-owned oil and gas company, Petroliam Nasional Berhad (PETRONAS), issued a $1.5 billion five-year *sukuk* and a $3 billion 10-year bond through separate Labuan-based SPVs. The transaction, led by Morgan Stanley, represented one of the two largest global *sukuk* ever and the first-ever combined offering of a *sukuk* and a bond by an Asian corporate. The trade illustrates many of the issues discussed above in terms of the rationale, investors and execution of a *sukuk* in comparison with a bond.

12.1 Key considerations for *sukuk* issuance

The rationale for *sukuk* issuance was based on tapping the largest possible liquidity pool, including both Islamic and conventional investors. PETRONAS benefited by tapping a new investor base that had previously been unable to get exposure to its credit. The *sukuk* also helped to align PETRONAS's growing business in the Middle East with a new investor base. In addition, as the first global corporate *sukuk* from Asia in 2009, it provided impetus to the Malaysian government's initiative to establish the country as a global centre for Islamic finance.

Sukuk structure

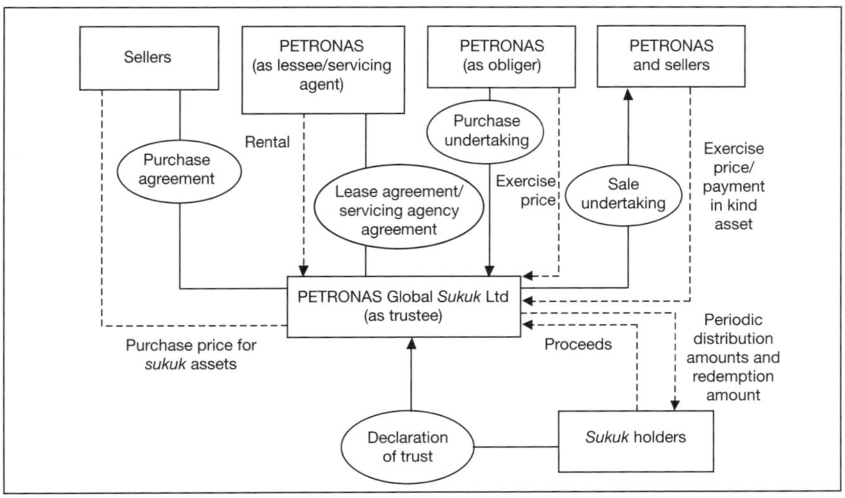

The *sukuk* was based on an *ijara* (Islamic lease) structure where a beneficial interest in a refinery and plants owned by PETRONAS's wholly owned subsidiaries was sold to an issuer SPV incorporated in Labuan. There was no legal transfer of registered title. The issuer then leased these 'assets' to PETRONAS, with rentals on the lease equivalent to the coupon payable on the *sukuk*. PETRONAS also granted the issuer/trustee a purchase undertaking whereby PETRONAS, as the obligor, undertook irrevocably to purchase from the issuer the assets at a specified price. Investors have no other recourse to the assets, except to exercise the purchase undertaking and to require PETRONAS to purchase the assets at a specified price on maturity or a dissolution event. The trustee also granted a sale undertaking to PETRONAS and certain of its subsidiaries that allowed for redemption of the *sukuk* on the occurrence of a tax event. On maturity or a dissolution event, the trustee will exercise the purchase undertaking, pursuant to which PETRONAS will purchase the assets and the trustee will distribute the sale proceeds to the investors to redeem the *sukuk*.

The structure enabled identical covenants to be included in the documentation, achieving equivalent investor protection in comparison to the bond. The purchase undertaking ensured that the credit risk was solely based on PETRONAS, while the non-recourse to the assets in terms of only being able to put them back to PETRONAS

PETRONAS $1.5 billion *sukuk* certificates allocation breakdown

By geography

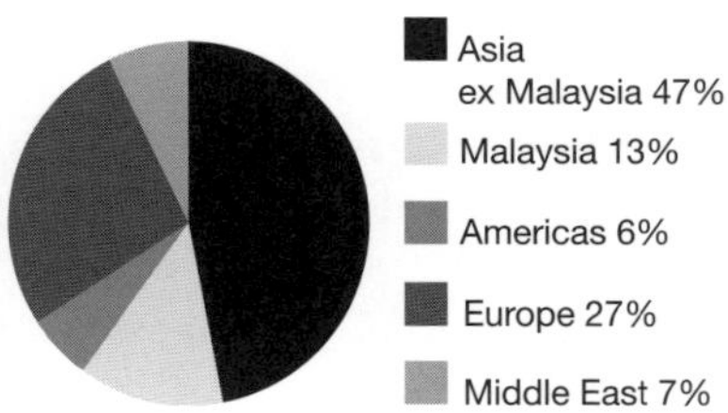

By investor type

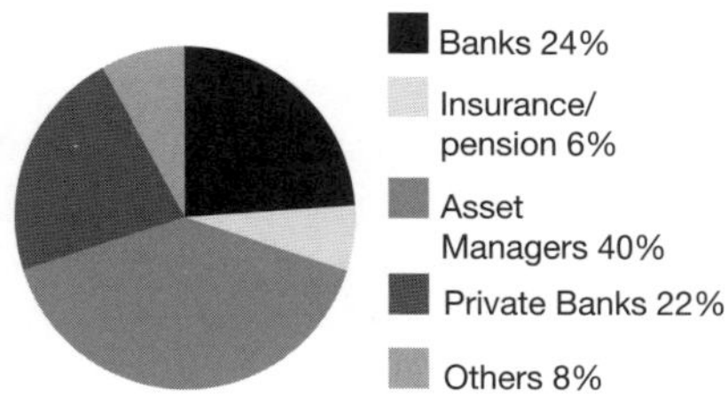

PETRONAS $3 billion conventional notes allocation breakdown

By geography

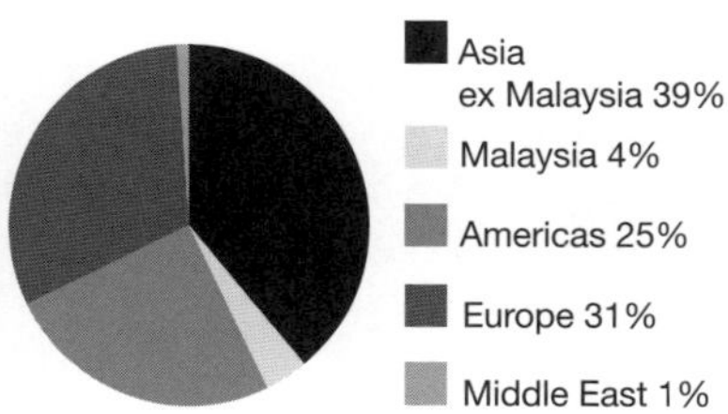

By investor type

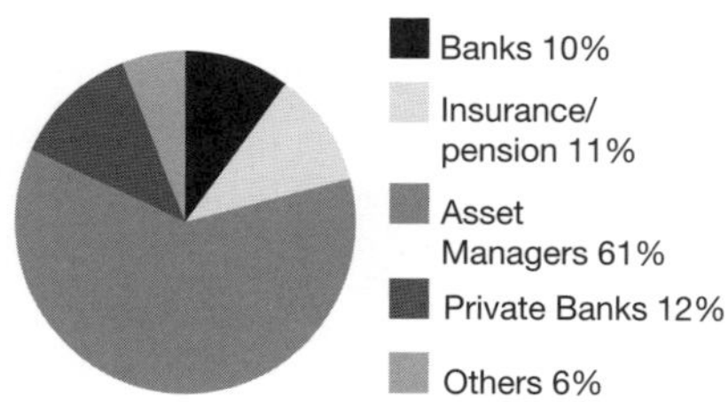

created an unsecured instrument. Therefore, the *sukuk* achieved the same credit rating as the bond and was treated equivalently from a regulatory, legal, tax and accounting perspective.

12.2 Main differences between the bond and *sukuk*

Although the bond was also issued through an SPV, *Sharia* compliance required different issuance vehicles to be used. The bond issuer was fully guaranteed by PETRONAS, while the *sukuk* issuer had a purchase undertaking from PETRONAS.

The *sukuk* was structured as a sale of a beneficial interest in specific fixed assets of PETRONAS which were sold by its wholly owned subsidiaries. This did not represent a 'true sale' or collateralisation of the assets. Therefore, while the *sukuk* was based on rental payments by PETRONAS, the bond was based on interest payments by the company.

The issuer is also a trustee for the *sukuk* holders and is responsible for protecting their interests under a declaration of trust. PETRONAS performed the additional roles of lessee (the issuer is the lessor) and servicing agent for the lessor, in addition to the obligor. In order to achieve *Sharia* compliance, the *sukuk* also required a *fatwa* from the *Sharia* advisory board of all the *sukuk* bookrunners.

12.3 Execution

The final order book was $19 billion, representing $6 billion of demand on the *sukuk* and $13 billion on the bond across 500 investors. The strength of the order book enabled both tranches to be priced at the same credit spread (162.5 basis points) to benchmark US treasuries, which refuted claims that *sukuk* need to be priced wider than bonds due to their inherent illiquidity or smaller market size. In essence, benchmark *sukuk* issues generate sufficient liquidity and final pricing is typically based on the strength of the credit and the resultant order book rather than any inherent bias to the instrument.

Sixty percent of the *sukuk* was supported by anchor demand out of Asia, while 27% was placed in Europe. Investor appetite was considerably less in the Middle East, reflecting the region's strong preference for GCC credits, while US investors preferred the longer tenor of the bond and were comfortable with the latter instrument's structure. The *sukuk*'s investor base comprised real money asset managers as the largest base, with both commercial and private banks accounting for just under half the allocation.

The bond's geographic allocation was led by Asia, but also experienced heavier take-up from Europe and the United States, which together contributed more than half the allocation. The Middle East contributed only 1% to the final allocation, which reflects the preference for regional credits and shorter tenors in the region. Real money asset managers also contributed a much heavier component of the investor base at 61%, reflecting their preference for the 10-year tenor.

12.4 *Sukuk* and bonds commercially compared

The final size of the *sukuk* and its final distribution proved that the GCC need not be a major investor in order for a *sukuk* to be successful. Clearly, the market for the product is expanding, but greater investor education and awareness are needed, especially among US investors.

The *sukuk* was also executed according to a typical bond timeline, with no pre-marketing or extended bookbuilding period, which would have impacted on pricing for the bond. In addition, the trade was made in August, which is traditionally a slow period for Middle Eastern investors. Despite these factors, the eventual size of the issue is a testament to the growing maturity of the market and its allocation across over 142 investors is indicative of an increasingly diverse investor base that is less reliant on banks.

13. Where are *sukuk* in comparison to bonds?

In comparison to the global market, the *sukuk* market is minuscule but nascent. The *sukuk* market grew exponentially from 2005 to 2007 on the back of significant transactions (in excess of $1 billion) for both straight and convertible *sukuk*. However, post-2007 the momentum has been lost, despite 2009 being a record year for bond issuance globally, with dollar issuance aggregating $986 billion and GCC activity totalling $32 billion. The instruments of choice for issuers in the GCC during this period have been bonds, as *sukuk* represented only 3% of total issuance (a reversal of the situation pre-2007). This section examines the current dynamics of the *sukuk* market and identifies the key factors that must be addressed in order to move forward.

13.1 New markets and structures

Recent issuance from the GCC has been dominated by sovereigns and sovereign wealth funds, and has been global in nature. Driven by a desire to reach a new investor base and to term out maturities, the issuances have been in bond rather than *sukuk* format. In addition, the sovereign wealth funds are typically holding companies with shares of public sector entities as their principal asset, which does not lend itself easily to creating structures with 51% tangible assets.[3] Therefore, in order to provide a viable alternative to such issuers, *sukuk* must have tenors of greater than five years and devise more structures that meet the requirements of issuers that may not have ready asset availability.

The first part of this equation can be solved through greater investor education, as has been discussed above. However, this process must also explain that recent *sukuk* defaults have had everything to do with the inherent credit risks and nothing to do with the intrinsic nature of the instrument. In addition, the perceived lack of liquidity in the *sukuk* market must be answered through a comparison of the secondary market trading occurring in benchmark-sized *sukuk* issues. Investors must be aware that managing *sukuk* default risk is possible through the creation of *Sharia*-compliant credit default swaps through a purchase undertaking or conventionally for non-Islamic investors.

---

3 The shares would need to be in compliance with *Sharia* requirements from both a business and financial ratio perspective throughout the tenor of the *sukuk*. *Sharia* scholars on the whole now disapprove of asset light structures that are fundamentally equity based.

The second part of the equation is trickier, as it requires all stakeholders – especially scholars, bankers and lawyers – to devise a greater range of instruments. Failing this, *sukuk* will be confined to issuers with tangible or fixed asset availability. Bonds are merely 'IOUs' and there is no limit on them.

13.2 New issuers and investors

Until 2008, the largest issuers of *sukuk* were real estate companies (mostly based in Dubai) that have since become sub-investment grade credits. Given the predominantly bank-driven investor base in the GCC that has had its own liquidity issues and excess exposure to this sector, both supply and demand sides have been affected. The market needs greater depth, which will emerge from the development of indigenous debt capital markets; this should also create greater pools of institutionalised capital.

Typically, these would come from *sukuk* funds, insurance companies, pension funds and sovereign wealth funds. Vibrant domestic capital markets will stimulate increased *sukuk* issuance, as it will tap the full capital pool and an investor base that best comprehends the credit risk and instrument. In addition to these demand-side factors, a greater array of corporate issuers will be encouraged to come to market and reduce their reliance on bank funding. Greater depth in domestic debt markets will also promote more issuance from outside the region and a greater acceptance of non-regional credits. Malaysia is the global leader in terms of *sukuk* issuance, based largely on its domestic market, and the development of such active markets in the GCC will add considerable depth to the industry.

13.3 New products

Sukuk are extremely flexible products that can be used to create a variety of instruments, ranging from straight unsecured debt to subordinated issues that can count towards the lower tier two capital of Islamic banks. In addition, *sukuk* naturally lend themselves to securitisations, which may well be the first step in bringing real estate-based issuers back into domestic markets. Consequently, much development can be done to create new products that facilitate financial sector recapitalisations and renew capital market access for others. It is also only a matter of time before a market for high-yield *sukuk* emerges, while short-term commercial paper such as *sukuk* that offer liquid money market products to Islamic investors and banks will offer viable alternatives to commodity *murabaha*.

14. Conclusion

This chapter has attempted to demonstrate that *sukuk* present a viable and competitive product to bonds in terms of structure, pricing and issuance costs. In addition, *sukuk* provide access to an incremental investor base that cannot participate in conventional bond issues. In order to sustain issuance momentum, a greater diversity of structures, issuers and investors must be found while increasing awareness among traditional bond investors. Robust domestic capital markets will make *sukuk* the product of choice as an all-inclusive capital-raising instrument. In challenging times, when bond investors may be less eager to invest in anything unfamiliar or require pricing discounts, indigenous investors that best understand the product will form a critical mass of anchor investors.

It is also important to realise that the need is to create regional rather than parochial domestic capital markets, where local currency issues are placed with a club of bank-dominated local investors that adopt a 'buy and hold' approach. While this may be the legacy of the *sukuk* market, there is a distinct need to move away from such antecedents.

More benchmark-sized issuances in domestic and foreign currencies will also increase the competitiveness of the product and deepen swap markets. Fundamentally, *sukuk* issuance must be driven on the basis of a grassroots demand for the product, which has defined the growth of the Islamic finance industry to date. The next generation of products and future issuance activity will need such support, combined with hospitable regulatory regimes, in order to ensure that the gains of the last few years are maximised to the benefit of the Islamic finance industry.

Legal and structural anatomy of a *sukuk*

Rahail Ali
Imran Mufti
Hogan Lovells (Middle East) LLP

1. Legal risk and commercial return

Legal risk concerns conventional and Islamic investors alike. Accordingly, legal certainty, predictability and stability are variants on the same basic investor need: investors want to be sure that legal risks (for these purposes, the risk that a person's rights or obligations are or will become invalid or unenforceable) do not detract from the commercial enterprise or deal. Removing legal risks in their entirety is not a legitimate expectation, but an informed assessment of the probability of an adverse legal outcome is a basic investment consideration. This chapter explores key legal and regulatory challenges for the *sukuk* market.

Calling *sukuk* Islamic bonds is a misnomer, if not a contradiction in terms, because *sukuk* are not IOUs. But the loose terminology serves to highlight that in the vast majority of cases, *sukuk* have been issued without the creation of a special or tailored legal regime. The reasons for the absence of specific *sukuk* facilitative regimes are simple: the *sukuk* market is new and it needs critical mass – supply and demand ultimately dictate the pace of development of any bespoke or tailored legal regime, even if to create a level playing field with commercial counterparts (ie, bonds). With any structured product, understanding its structural and documentary components is key to getting a comprehensive grasp on it – and *sukuk* are no different.

While *sukuk* are structured instruments, in their most basic cash-flow analysis they involve the following transactions:

- typically, issuance of the *sukuk* by a special purpose vehicle (SPV) and payment of the *sukuk* proceeds in a *Sharia*-compliant investment or transaction to or for the account of the corporate, bank or sovereign 'originator,' whose creditworthiness is the economic rationale for investing in the *sukuk* (commonly called the obligor), resulting in *pro rata* and undivided ownership of assets held on trust for *sukuk* holders – no *sukuk* holder can claim a specific part of the assets as its own, as they are co-owned with other *sukuk* holders *pro rata* as beneficiaries of a trust;
- return on the *sukuk* deriving from ownership of those assets; and
- redemption on maturity or following default resulting from an obligation to purchase those assets by the obligor.

2. Legal considerations on the role of the SPV

2.1 Independence

To help to market the *sukuk*, the SPV's name is usually similar to or includes part of the name of the obligor. However, the SPV must be independent from the obligor, including its tax status and liabilities. The SPV is a separate legal entity from the obligor and typically has segregated ownership from the obligor. The SPV usually has only nominal share capital, which is owned by an offshore service provider and held on trust for a charitable purpose (ie, an orphan SPV). This separation ensures that the SPV is not treated as a subsidiary of the obligor and that its balance sheet is kept separate from that of the obligor.

Use of an orphan SPV is preferred, but not compulsory. Instances where orphan SPV issuers have not been used include sovereign issuances, where sovereigns are sensitive to any view that the sovereign has divested or alienated sovereign assets to a company where it has no interest, and cases where use of an orphan SPV is problematic because the relevant jurisdiction mandates the compulsory use of local companies.

Management of the SPV is usually provided by an offshore services provider. To prove the SPV's independence of the obligor and minimise the risk that the obligor is considered to be a shadow director or partner of the SPV, the SPV should always hold itself out as carrying on its business independent of the obligor.

2.2 Purpose and insolvency remote

Part and parcel of having an SPV is that it will have no liabilities outside its specific purpose. Therefore, the articles of the SPV, as well as the provisions of the trust deed, will limit the power of the SPV to dealing with the *sukuk* assets in accordance with the transaction documentation. Typically, an SPV has no offices, employees or expenses other than its pre-agreed management fee payable to the service provider. To minimise the risk that the SPV will be declared insolvent, parties which contract with the SPV are prevented by 'limited recourse' or 'non-petition' clauses in the transaction documents from commencing insolvency proceedings against it or taking enforcement action against the SPV or any of its assets.

SPVs are usually incorporated in a tax-free jurisdiction (typically the Cayman Islands or one of the Channel Islands) in order to ensure that no tax liability arises on the *sukuk* issuer. As few Gulf Cooperation Council (GCC) states impose corporation tax capital gains or sales tax, it is not common for GCC issues to use local SPVs.

Some GCC states impose legal limits on the ownership of real property and shares in local companies. Ownership restrictions must be discussed with local lawyers during the due diligence. The solution may lie in the SPV, or its ultimate shareholders, being nationals of the state. In this case, it will be necessary to check whether a variant on the charitable trust ownership structure remains possible. Otherwise, suitable shareholders willing to take the responsibility and any liabilities must be found. Finding such shareholders is difficult.

2.3 The role of the trust

A declaration of trust is required because the *sukuk* must create an undivided *pro rata* interest in the assets that the *sukuk* represents for the holders of the *sukuk*. 'Undivided' means that no *sukuk* holder can point to any part of the *sukuk* assets and claim them as exclusively its own – the interest of each *sukuk* holder is indivisible and *pro rata* according to the face amount that it holds. The declaration of trust achieves this through the issuer declaring a trust over the *sukuk* assets in favour of the trust beneficiaries (ie, the *sukuk* holders). It sets out the relationship between the *sukuk* holders with regard to those assets. Pursuant to the declaration of trust, the issuer, as trustee, will hold the *sukuk* assets for the *sukuk* holders *pro rata* according to the face amount of *sukuk* held by each *sukuk* holder. The issuer also agrees to distribute all income from the trust assets in accordance with the terms and conditions of the *sukuk*. This document is entered into by the obligor, the issuer (as issuer and trustee) and a service provider typically acting as a delegate of the trustee. The governing law for the declaration of trust is usually English law. The unique feature of a *sukuk*, as compared to a conventional bond or conventional structured note, is that the issuer of the *sukuk* is also the trustee, but the issuer has no obligation independent of the *sukuk* assets to pay because the *sukuk* is not an IOU – payment comes from the obligor under the *Sharia*-compliant contracts it signs with the issuer as trustee. The declaration of trust will set out its duties and responsibilities and will seek to exclude general, non-applicable provisions of English law generally relating to trustees.

If a *sukuk* must be structured in circumstances where the use of an English law declaration of trust is not valid to confer the undivided, *pro rata* interest in the *sukuk* assets of the *sukuk* holders (eg, the *sukuk* is based in a civil law jurisdiction in which the SPV issuer must be incorporated locally), an agency declaration can be considered to create a relationship of principal and agent, as opposed to trustee and beneficiaries, between the SPV and the *sukuk* holders.

2.4 Choosing the governing law

Within the *sukuk* structure, each document must be considered in turn when choosing the applicable governing law. The governing law for the document transferring the title to the *sukuk* asset to the SPV may be prescribed by mandatory rules of law. For example, transfers of land are usually effective and enforceable only if carried out under the law of the country in which the land is located (*lex situs*).

2.5 Transferring ownership

Various methods of transfer of the *sukuk* assets to the SPV are available, as follows:

- Sale – the outright sale of the asset is most preferable from a *Sharia*-compliance perspective.
- Lease – a long lease may be an alternative to an outright sale, on the basis that *Sharia* scholars may take the view that long lease may be akin to outright ownership.
- Assignment – if the assets in question are contractual interests, they may be transferred via an assignment. Under English law (Section 136 of the Law of Property Act), an assignment is valid if it is:

  - an absolute transfer of the whole contractual interest or debt (this may include current as well as future assets, including choses in action);
  - in writing and signed by the assignor; and
  - notified in writing to the counterparty under the contract that is being assigned.
- Under English law, in principle, contracts are assignable and assignment does not depend on the consent of the other party to the contract, unless the contract is expressed to be personal or non-assignable.
- The assignment perfection mechanism in other jurisdictions may be different and substantially more onerous. Conflict of law questions may arise where assignments need to be governed by a jurisdiction different from that which governs the original contract to which the assignment relates.
- Novation – a novation is a contractual agreement to end an existing contract and to replace it with a new contract substantially in the terms of the old contract, but with a new party stepping into the role of one of the original parties. Therefore, the novation effects a full transfer of contractual rights and obligations, but does not transfer an asset in itself.
- Declaration of trust – under a declaration of trust, no transfer of legal title takes place. Only the equitable interest in the asset is transferred to the beneficiary.

In all of these scenarios, *Sharia* requires that the risks connected with ownership of the asset be transferred from the transferor to the transferee (ie, the SPV issuer of the *sukuk* as trustee of the *sukuk* holders). As the *sukuk* holders are the equitable owners of the assets underlying the *sukuk* issue, the *sukuk* holders bear the ongoing ownership risks. These include real risks in relation to property and liability to third parties, such as occupier's liability. Consequently, the drafting must consider and protect the *sukuk* holders against ownership risks in a manner that is *Sharia* compliant.

If the asset transfer is revisited by, for example, an insolvency practitioner appointed over the obligor, the *sukuk* investors need protection from a prospective clawback in the event that the initial transfer is set aside, not recognised as a true sale or recharacterised as a loan. In many jurisdictions an insolvency practitioner can claw back assets or recharacterise the transfer as a loan if the documentation fails to display certain characteristics. It is helpful if the legal system in question is clear on the circumstances in which this could occur.

The jurisdiction(s) of the obligor's main activities determine which laws govern a potential insolvency of the obligor. The risk of any clawback or recharacterisation of the *sukuk* structure as a loan in this jurisdiction (or in each of these jurisdictions) will need to be considered and local lawyers will need to advise on methods to minimise this risk. Under English law, for example, a transaction can be set aside if the transfer was a "transaction at an undervalue" or a "preference".

2.6 Due diligence

Whatever method of asset transfer is used, rudimentary due diligence is needed to determine deal viability at the outset. Unlike a conventional bond, *sukuk* are structured instruments and as such need the involvement of skilled and experienced legal and any other relevant advisers to ensure, in simple terms, that the *sukuk* ceases to be a *Sharia*-compliant means for the obligor to receive financing and for the *sukuk* holders to get a *Sharia*-compliant investment.

Interposing asset ownership into any financing structure, including *sukuk*, requires early due diligence considerations for deal viability. Considerations to be addressed include whether there are any security interests on other third-party rights over assets. What regulatory consents, approvals and so on are required for any sale? Are the assets *halal*? If not, can they be effectively excluded from any sale? Must documents be registered, recorded or filed at any public office or registry? Are any notarial or other fees payable? Registration fees will be payable in most jurisdictions when the asset being conveyed is land. What taxes could be charged on the sale in principle? Are there any capital gains, value added tax, sales or other local taxes such as stamp or other documentary taxes that could be charged by a sale of the assets or even a disposal of the *sukuk*? If significant taxes or fees are chargeable (eg, because they are linked to the value of the assets), what can be done to mitigate them?

3. Conclusion

Sukuk are still at an early stage of development relative to conventional capital markets. *Sukuk* often share the same pool of investors as conventional bonds – that is, conventional investors subscribe to *sukuk*, not necessarily because of *Sharia* compliance or ethical aspects, but for commercial considerations. To accommodate these investors and to create critical mass for liquidity in the *sukuk* market, there is a need to articulate to investors in general the nature of *sukuk* and how they are distinguishable from bonds, but at the same time – and this is critical – not to detract from the commercial intent. A legal understanding of *sukuk* is the easiest way to comprehend those differences and the commercial similarities.

The role of the SPV issuer

Manuela Belmontes
Tahir Jawed
Maples and Calder

---

1. Introduction

Many international financial centres, such as the Cayman Islands, the British Virgin Islands and Jersey, have been quick to lend assistance to the structuring of Islamic finance products (particularly in respect of the issuer of such products) and have proven very useful to the development of the Islamic finance industry.

This chapter discusses the origin of the special purpose vehicle (SPV), the general uses of SPVs and their growing popularity in the world of Islamic finance. It also examines the structure and role of the SPV issuer in *sukuk* transactions and the benefits of domiciling the SPV issuer in certain jurisdictions.

2. What is an SPV?

An SPV (also known as a special purpose entity) is a legal entity typically formed as a limited company to carry out a specific, narrow business purpose. As such, the constitutional documents of the SPV and/or the agreements and documents into which it enters will often restrict its powers and activities to fulfilling such purpose, and the SPV is typically wound up or dissolved once its purpose has been achieved.

SPVs are primarily used to finance acquisitions and to hold a variety of properties and assets. SPVs are often created by large companies to segregate and ringfence certain assets from their other assets and operating businesses. While providing additional protection from liability, this structure also facilitates an easier transfer or disposition of the assets held. When used in this manner, the SPV is often formed as a wholly owned subsidiary, and is managed by the employees and officers of the entity establishing the SPV (the 'sponsor').

In the world of finance, another common SPV structure is one that is independent (from an ownership and management perspective) from the sponsor; this is discussed in more detail in this chapter. This form of SPV (often referred to as an 'orphan SPV') has been widely used in the financial services industry for off-balance sheet transactions, which basically involve the sale of certain income-generating assets by the sponsor to an SPV. The SPV issues securities to investors and utilises the proceeds to acquire the assets from the sponsor, and payments are made on the securities from the cash flow derived from the assets acquired. By transferring the underlying assets to an orphan SPV, the assets are safeguarded from the financial (or bankruptcy) risk of the sponsor, which is an important consideration for investors. Whichever SPV structure is used, it is important that the SPV carefully comply with all relevant generally accepted accounting principles and other accounting rules and standards.

The independent form of SPV has been used for several decades in a variety of international capital markets and structured finance transactions. The 1970s witnessed the first issuance of mortgage-backed securities by an SPV (securities that are backed by residential or commercial mortgages), which stemmed from the US secondary mortgage market. The use of the SPV expanded in the 1980s to securitise further classes of cash-generating asset (eg, car loans, home equity loans and credit card receivables). Further innovative financial products were developed throughout this period. The creation of collateralised debt obligations (including collateralised mortgage obligations and collateralised loan obligations) allowed the SPV to issue different classes of securities with varying risk profiles, reaching a wider base of investors. In the 1980s SPVs were also largely used in 'synthetic' lease transactions to finance the acquisition of large equipment, aircraft and commercial real estate, with the SPV buying and leasing back to the sponsor the asset being financed. Synthetic leasing arrangements are still popular today and are also used in a *Sharia*-compliant format for Islamic finance transactions in the Middle East and Asian markets.

The use of the SPV has evolved over the years to include many types of asset-backed and asset-based transaction and other complex capital markets and structured financing products, such as asset-backed commercial paper conduits and other forms of synthetic securitisation and securities repackaging. The listing of SPV shares, bonds and other securities is common on all major stock exchanges.

SPVs are also now commonly used in Islamic finance transactions, most popularly as the issuing vehicles for *sukuk*, which can be based on a number of underlying *Sharia*-compliant structures, including *ijara* (sale and leaseback), *musharaka* (partnership/joint venture) and *mudaraba* or *wakala* (both principal/agency) arrangements.

3. Use of SPVs

SPVs are typically formed in international financial centres that offer, among other things, a relatively inexpensive, easy and quick formation process, low or zero taxation, and a reliable and creditor-friendly legal regime. The benefits of using SPVs formed in such jurisdictions are discussed in detail later in this chapter.

The jurisdiction of choice for the formation of SPVs depends to a large extent on the proposed use of the SPV, investor preferences and where the securities to be issued by the SPV will be marketed and sold. The most popular jurisdictions for the formation of SPVs are generally the Cayman Islands (particularly for securitisations, *sukuk* and investment funds), the British Virgin Islands (which domiciles the largest number of offshore companies), Ireland (for undertakings for collective investments in transferable securities and other investment funds), Jersey (for European securitisations and real estate investment funds) and Luxembourg (for the Eurobond market).

As indicated above, in addition to their dominant use as capital markets and structured finance vehicles, SPVs are used for a variety of other transactions, including to:

- raise capital as investment funds;

- reinsure and transfer risks as captive insurance companies; and
- acquire and hold assets as holding and/or leasing companies.

3.1 Funds

The Cayman Islands is a market leader in the formation of collective investment vehicles, particularly hedge funds and private equity funds, for which several international financial centres are prominently used to domicile such vehicles. In the fund context, the specific benefits of using a jurisdiction such as the Cayman Islands or the British Virgin Islands relate to regulation and taxation. Both jurisdictions offer streamlined registration processes (and thus lighter but effective regulation) for funds which target high-net-worth or sophisticated investors and tend to impose fewer restrictions on investment strategies pursued by funds. They and similar offshore jurisdictions impose low or no taxation on funds, thus avoiding double taxation (ie, tax on income at both company/fund level and investor level when income is distributed by way of dividends, return of capital or otherwise). However, investors do still need to consider their own personal tax and regulatory positions in their home jurisdictions.

These benefits have attracted Islamic asset managers and private equity houses in the Middle East to turn to the same international financial centres for the formation of *Sharia*-compliant funds. The traditional fund structures available in such jurisdictions have been revised and moulded to meet the specific requirements of the *Sharia*. *Sharia*-compliant private equity funds are typically structured as limited partnerships to give flexibility in relation to investments and the arrangements between investors. Funds structured as companies must comply with the relevant companies law, which often dictates how investors must be treated; partnership law tends to allow more flexibility. This can be particularly useful when incorporating *Sharia*-compliant provisions into a fund structure. The *Sharia* board of the investment manager or sponsor of the fund often acts as an adviser to approve investments as being *Sharia*-compliant. The challenges for *Sharia*-compliant funds remain identifying investments that qualify as being *Sharia*-compliant and arranging appropriate financing to leverage funds.

4. Islamic finance and international financial centres

Although Islamic finance is now practised globally, the focus has historically and predominantly been in the Middle East and Asia, which host the majority of the global Muslim population. Historically, offshore jurisdictions were used by Middle Eastern investors to organise investments and structure personal wealth, thus addressing concerns about local inheritance laws and political instability. When practitioners, particularly lawyers, were presented with the challenges of structuring *Sharia*-compliant transactions, most were already familiar with the uses of offshore jurisdictions and utilised the efficiency of such international financial centres to structure the new wave of Islamic finance products.

The Cayman Islands has the largest share of the global capital and securitisation markets, being the jurisdiction of choice for the formation of SPVs for use in such transactions. In recent years it has also become a popular jurisdiction (and arguably the jurisdiction of choice for Middle Eastern clients) for the formation of SPVs for use in Islamic finance transactions. Malaysia and the South Asian markets have historically favoured Labuan (which was declared an international offshore financial centre in 1990) as the preferred jurisdiction for raising *Sharia*-compliant funds. The Middle East historically favoured Bahrain (which is stated to host the largest global concentration of Islamic financial institutions) as the SPV jurisdiction of choice for Islamic finance transactions. However, this is changing as certain international financial centres, such as the British Virgin Islands, Jersey and most particularly the Cayman Islands, become more commonplace in Islamic finance.

A relatively new jurisdiction which is entering the Islamic finance market is the Dubai International Financial Centre (DIFC). Originally established to act as a primary international financial centre to compete with centres such as London, New York and Hong Kong, the DIFC has recognised the benefits of offering more flexible vehicles similar to offshore SPVs. To facilitate the growing Islamic finance industry, the DIFC has recently introduced regulations to permit the formation of 'special purpose companies' (SPCs). SPCs created pursuant to the DIFC Special Purpose Companies Regulations can be utilised for the same Islamic and conventional finance transactions, such as *sukuk*, securitisation and asset finance transactions, for which the traditional SPVs have become renowned. These SPCs can be incorporated quickly and inexpensively, and have minimal annual reporting requirements.

It will be interesting to see how successful the DIFC SPCs become. Other Middle Eastern jurisdictions, such as Dubai's free zones and Bahrain, have had limited success in establishing themselves as primary domiciles for SPVs. There are a variety of reasons for this, including the lack of legal stability required by structured finance transactions (especially for those transactions seeking listings on stock exchanges or ratings by international rating agencies), and the fact that these jurisdictions operate in Arabic, while structured finance transactions are documented in English. However, the DIFC may prove to be an exception, as its SPCs may become an attractive alternative to using SPVs of the traditional offshore centres.

5. Structure of SPV issuer

The most common form of SPV used to issue *sukuk* or debt instruments in capital markets transactions is a company (as opposed to a partnership or trust).

5.1 Orphaned status/bankruptcy remoteness

Originally, the issuer in *sukuk* transactions was usually structured as a subsidiary of the sponsor (or obligor) and was managed by the sponsor. Recently, however, this was viewed as being too synthetic, as effectively the sponsor was selling assets to itself (or at least a wholly owned subsidiary), and most *Sharia* scholars now require some distance between the sponsor and the issuer.

The issuer in *sukuk* transactions is now typically structured as an orphan entity, which means that its ownership and management are independent from the sponsor of the transaction. This is desirable because an orphan SPV as issuer can transact on an arm's-length basis with the sponsor. Also, if structured and operated properly, the orphaned SPV issuer will be bankruptcy remote from the sponsor – that is, creditors of the sponsor will not have a claim against the SPV and/or the SPV's assets in the event that the sponsor becomes bankrupt or insolvent. This is most relevant in securitisation transactions where there is a true sale of the assets of the sponsor to the SPV.

Under the laws of several international financial centres, including the Cayman Islands and the British Virgin Islands, an SPV issuer can be orphaned if it is structured as a company with its ordinary shares held by a trustee (the 'share trustee') on trust either for charitable purposes (through the use of a charitable trust) or for the purpose of the transaction itself (through the use of a special purpose trust).

The charitable trust is the most common trust structure currently used to orphan SPVs in *sukuk* transactions. When using such a structure, it is important to ensure that proper mechanics are in place to flow all funds and profits arising from the transaction to the *sukuk* holders and relevant transaction parties, as any residual profits that remain in the SPV issuer at the end of the transaction will be paid out to charity pursuant to the terms of the charitable trust. A small profit should be retained by the SPV issuer to ensure that it accrues some corporate benefit for entering into the transaction. This will ultimately be paid out to charity pursuant to the terms of the charitable trust.

Regardless of which trust structure is used, the result is that the ordinary voting shares of the SPV issuer will not appear on the balance sheet of the sponsor and the accounts of the SPV should not be consolidated into the accounts of the sponsor – therefore, the SPV will not be regarded as a subsidiary of the sponsor.

5.2 Management and administration of SPV issuer

Where an orphan SPV issuer is used in a *sukuk* transaction, the trust company establishing the charitable or special purpose trust will also usually act as administrator to the issuer, providing the SPV with a registered and business office and providing members of its staff to act as directors of the company. The administrator's services may also extend to preparing accounts, arranging an audit and/or providing a secretary to the issuer, if required. The provision of an independent board of directors and independent officers ensures that the SPV issuer functions as a wholly independent entity and is not viewed as the alter ego or instrument of the sponsor (which further enhances the bankruptcy remoteness of the issuer).

5.3 Directors' duties and liability

The directors of the SPV will need to ensure that they fulfil their fiduciary duties (eg, those of loyalty, honesty and good faith) and the duties of care, diligence and skill imposed by applicable law when acting in such capacity. A breach of these duties and failure to act in the best interests of the SPV may, in certain circumstances, result in personal liability on the part of the director(s).

The directors of an SPV issuer will usually be required to accept responsibility expressly for the contents of the offering document pursuant to which the *sukuk* are offered, particularly where the *sukuk* are to be listed on a stock exchange. The SPV issuer (and arguably the directors of the SPV) have a duty to ensure that the offering document contains no misstatements. Where an investor has relied on a statement in the offering document which turns out to have been untrue or inaccurate, and suffers some loss as a result, the directors of the SPV may, in certain circumstances, become personally liable to such investor for negligent or fraudulent misstatement. If misrepresentations are made by an SPV issuer (and/or its directors) to investors (whether orally or written) and have resulted in a loss on the part of the investor, the directors of the SPV may become personally liable where such misrepresentations are found to have been fraudulently made and/or have induced an investor to invest in the SPV.

In a typical *sukuk* transaction, the SPV issuer will delegate most of its duties to other service providers. The directors of the SPV must take due care in the selection of the service providers, ensuring that they are appropriately suited and experienced for the applicable roles they are to fulfil. Once this has been done, the SPV itself (and its directors) will typically be absolved in most circumstances (and in the absence of fraud, wilful default and, if the relevant contract so provides, gross negligence) from any liabilities arising from the performance of the SPV's duties by the retained service providers.

As mentioned above, where an orphan SPV is used as the issuer of *sukuk*, the directors of the SPV will usually be employees of the local trust company acting as administrator or corporate services provider to the SPV. As they delegate most of their functions and the duties of the SPV issuer to other service providers, such directors do not typically take an active role in the operations of the SPV. Accordingly, in order to provide additional protection to the SPV issuer and to the directors themselves (and to absolve them from personal liability), the directors of the SPV will usually require that the transaction documents contain provisions which limit the recourse of the *sukuk* holders and other transaction parties against the SPV to the assets held under trust, and which expressly acknowledge that the obligations of the SPV under the transaction documents are corporate obligations and that no recourse in respect of any breaches of any duty or obligations of the SPV arising under the transaction documents shall be had against any directors, officers or shareholders of the SPV in their capacity as such.

6. *Sukuk* transactions

In recent years, *sukuk* issuances have grown to become a mainstream product for raising funds in the Islamic world for both Islamic and non-Islamic institutions. The basic use and role of SPVs in *sukuk* transactions are discussed below.

6.1 Common form of *sukuk* transaction – *mudaraba* and *ijara* structures

In a typical *sukuk* transaction, the SPV issuer is structured as an orphan company. The SPV enters into a corporate services agreement, usually with the local trust company that holds its ordinary shares, for the provision of corporate administration services (including independent directors) to the SPV.

The SPV issues *sukuk* to investors. When acting in such capacity, the SPV is known as the 'issuer'. *Sukuk* are usually structured as trust instruments under English law and constituted pursuant to a declaration of trust made by the issuer and entered into between the SPV, the sponsor and one or more other transaction parties.

The proceeds from the issuance of the *sukuk* certificates are used by the SPV to acquire the beneficial ownership of certain assets from the sponsor, whose purpose for undertaking the transaction is to raise financing. In this capacity, the sponsor is known as the seller. The acquisition is carried out by way of a purchase agreement entered into between the issuer and the seller.

The SPV issuer declares a trust over the assets pursuant to the declaration of trust and undertakes to hold the assets as trustee on behalf and for the benefit of the *sukuk* holders. In this capacity, the SPV issuer is known as the 'trustee'. Each trust certificate issued by the SPV entitles the holder thereof to an undivided beneficial interest in the assets held under trust.

Where a *mudaraba* or *wakala* structure underlies the *sukuk* transaction, the SPV contracts with the sponsor (through a management or investment agency agreement) to manage or invest the assets to generate profit. In this capacity, the sponsor is known as the 'manager' (or, in some structures, as the 'investment agent'). Profits generated by the assets are used to pay to investors periodic profit amounts due under the trust certificates during the financing term. Where an *ijara*

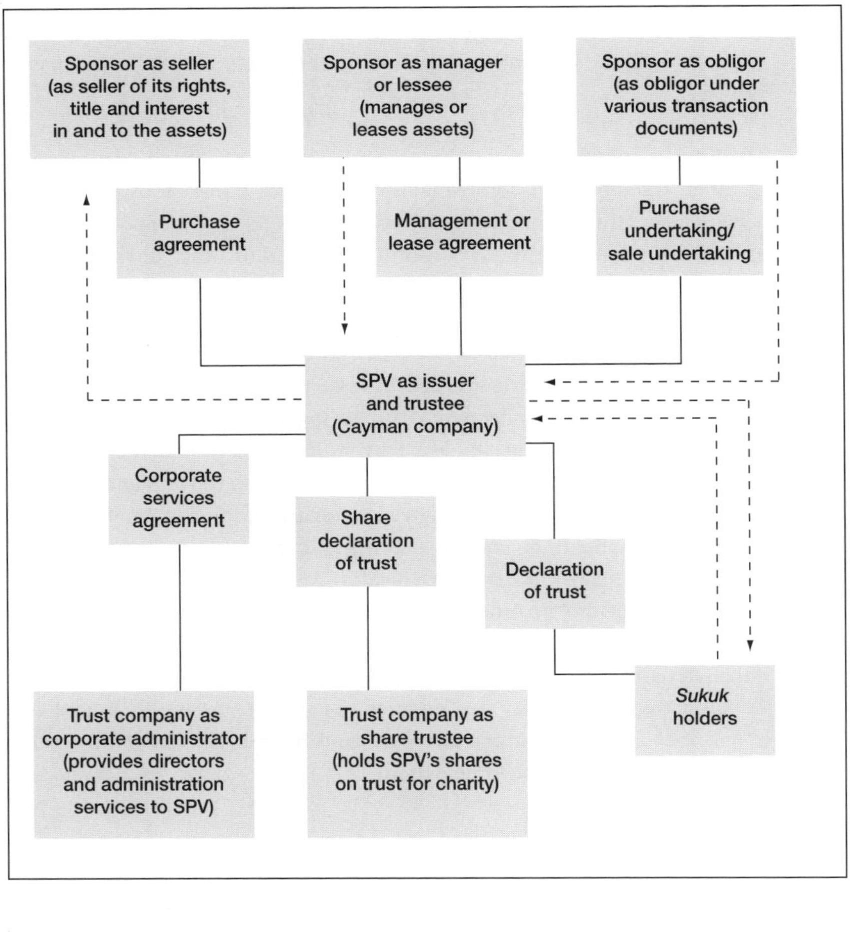

arrangement underlies the *sukuk*, the assets are leased back to the sponsor in return for periodic rental payments. In this capacity, the sponsor is known as the 'lessee' and the SPV as the 'lessor'. The rental payments received from the lessee are then used by the SPV to pay the periodic profit amounts due under the trust certificates.

The sponsor separately undertakes with the SPV to re-purchase all the assets at the end of the financing term in order to facilitate the redemption by the SPV issuer of all of the *sukuk*. These undertakings are given by way of a purchase undertaking made by the sponsor for the benefit of the SPV. In this capacity, the sponsor is known as the 'obligor'. The purchase undertaking will also contain provisions requiring the obligor to repurchase all of the assets from the SPV at any time during the course of the transaction if certain events of default occur.

The SPV will also provide undertakings pursuant to a sale undertaking made by the SPV for the benefit of the obligor. In the sale undertaking the SPV typically undertakes to sell all of the assets to the obligor on the occurrence of certain tax events.

The diagram on the previous page illustrates the example discussed above, which is a very basic description of a *sukuk* transaction where the underlying structure used is either a *mudaraba* or *ijara* structure (there are various differences between these two structures which are not detailed above, such as how profits are shared between the sponsor and the SPV and at what value the assets may be repurchased by the sponsor).

6.2 *Musharaka sukuk*

Another structure which sometimes underlies *sukuk* transactions is the *musharaka*. In a *musharaka* structure, the sponsor and the SPV form a joint venture/partnership arrangement, with the sponsor contributing land or other physical assets and the SPV contributing cash (ie, the proceeds from the sale of the *sukuk*) to the *musharaka*. In return, the SPV receives *musharaka* shares or units which entitle it to substantially all the profits from the *musharaka*. The sponsor is appointed by the *musharaka* as agent to develop the assets and sell or lease the developed assets on behalf of the *musharaka*. The profits generated by the *musharaka* assets are used to make periodic distributions to the *sukuk* holders and to pay agency and incentive fees to the sponsor as agent. The sponsor undertakes to purchase the *musharaka* shares or units that are held by the SPV at pre-agreed intervals during the life of the transaction, with the remainder to be purchased at the end of the transaction, thus enabling the SPV issuer to redeem all trust certificates. An orphaned SPV is utilised with the *musharaka* structure in order to ensure that there is independence between the partners of the *musharaka* and that the SPV can transact with the sponsor on an unbiased basis.

Sukuk transactions may be structured in a variety of ways (including, in addition to the above, through *istisna*, *murabaha* and hybrid structures); however, the cash flows generally follow the same pattern.

6.3 Islamic securitisation

While in most *sukuk* transactions only the beneficial (and not the legal) ownership of assets is transferred to the SPV, *sukuk* transactions are also used for Islamic securitisations, where it is intended that a 'true sale' of the underlying assets be made by the sponsor to the SPV. This is preferred where investors do not wish to be exposed to the credit risk of the sponsor – that is, they do not wish the *sukuk* to constitute (from an economic perspective) unsecured obligations of the sponsor.

In a typical Islamic securitisation transaction, the SPV issuer plays the same basic roles and the structure of the transaction is very similar to that described above. Basically, the SPV issuer is incorporated in an international financial centre, most commonly the Cayman Islands, and structured as an orphaned entity that is bankruptcy remote from the sponsor. The SPV acquires legal title to the underlying assets, which are then leased back to the sponsor or invested/managed by the sponsor (depending on the underlying structure of the *sukuk*). The profits generated from the assets are used to make periodic payments on the *sukuk*. In order to secure its obligations, the SPV grants security over the assets for the benefit of the *sukuk* holders. At the end of the transaction, once all payments on the *sukuk* have been made and they have been redeemed in full, the assets are repurchased by the sponsor pursuant to a purchase undertaking. In the event of default under the terms and conditions of the *sukuk*, the *sukuk* holders would have recourse to the underlying assets, legal title to which would be retained by the SPV. This differs significantly from the case where the *sukuk* transaction involves the transfer of the mere beneficial ownership of the assets, as in that case, on default, the SPV's only usual recourse is to give up beneficial ownership of the underlying assets in return for an unsecured claim against the sponsor through the purchase undertaking. If the Islamic securitisation is properly structured, the sponsor will lose all rights to the use and benefit of the underlying assets and such assets will not be open to attack by creditors of the sponsor.

6.4 Restricted activities of SPVs

Sukuk transactions are typically structured in a manner that limits the activities of the SPV. The transaction documents will include provisions to restrict the activities of the SPV to those related to the financing. The documents will usually contain provisions which limit recourse of the *sukuk* holders and other transaction parties against the SPV to the assets held under trust and include covenants of the *sukuk* holders and transaction parties not to bring any actions or steps to petition the SPV into bankruptcy during the financing term. Such structuring enhances the independence of the SPV and further reduces any bankruptcy risk to the SPV in the event that the sponsor becomes insolvent. This is of course critical where the transaction is structured to involve a true sale of the underlying assets to the SPV.

7. Benefits of using an SPV

The overall structure for *sukuk* transactions is similar to that used for conventional securitisation transactions, although the documentation and detail vary. All the benefits that attracted the conventional securitisation industry to establish bond issuers in certain international financial centres also apply to *sukuk* issuers; these are discussed below.

7.1 Taxation benefits

If efficiency of an Islamic finance transaction is to be maximised, the SPV should be formed in a jurisdiction that will introduce no additional tax costs to the transaction. Certain international financial centres impose no corporation, income or capital gains taxation on SPVs that are formed as exempted (or non-resident) companies, partnerships or trusts, or on shareholders or other equity holders of such SPVs. Generally, payments of income or principal made by SPVs formed in such jurisdictions are not subject to withholding tax.

This is the case in the Cayman Islands, the British Virgin Islands and the DIFC. However, a Jersey-incorporated SPV must apply for exempt company status (which is renewable annually) in order to receive tax-neutral treatment (in respect of its non-Jersey source income). Exempt company status will typically be granted where no beneficial interest in the SPV is held by a resident of Jersey and the business or trading activities of the SPV do not take place in Jersey.

An SPV incorporated as an exempted company in the Cayman Islands may obtain a 20-year exemption undertaking from the Cayman Islands government guaranteeing that the company will be exempt from tax for that period should current taxation laws be changed. The exemption may be extended for an additional 10 years. A similar undertaking is also available for exempted trusts and exempted limited partnerships formed in the Cayman Islands. No such assurance or guarantee is currently available to SPVs formed in the British Virgin Islands. In the DIFC, the tax legislation specifically provides a 50-year 0% tax rate guarantee to businesses and employees in the DIFC from the date of implementation of the law (in 2004), which may be extended further by the ruler of Dubai. In Jersey, an application for a tax clearance letter may be made to the Jersey tax authority confirming the Jersey tax treatment of a proposed capital markets or securitisation structure.

When structuring an Islamic finance transaction, it is critical that the sponsor and arrangers of the transaction obtain tax advice in all relevant jurisdictions in order to ensure that the SPV is compliant with all tax laws applicable to it and its proposed business.

7.2 Familiar and creditor-friendly legal regime

The sponsor of an Islamic finance transaction will often seek a domicile for the SPV that has a creditor-friendly regime and one that is familiar to its investors. The laws of many traditional offshore jurisdictions have their roots in English common law (as a result of being former British colonies or remaining dependencies of the British crown), and therefore many of the legal concepts of importance in Islamic finance and other capital markets transactions (eg, corporate personality, corporate power and corporate benefit) are recognised under such laws. Furthermore, final appeals from the courts of these jurisdictions are often still made to the Privy Council and the interpretation of statutes is guided by English and local case law. This provides a degree of familiarity and certainty to sponsors and investors in terms of understanding their legal rights and how to enforce them. Even the DIFC has an international legal system based on the common law of England and Wales. This is the only common law jurisdiction in the Middle East.

Although based on English common law, the legislation of several international financial centres, including Cayman, the British Virgin Islands and Jersey, is much more flexible than that in England. For example, English law prohibits financial assistance, whereas this is not the case under the Cayman Islands or BVI law, provided that there is some material benefit accruing to the company (financial assistance is still prohibited under the laws of Jersey). Also, under English law, there remains some uncertainty regarding the effectiveness of contractual subordination, while under Cayman Islands law contractual subordination is expressly recognised by statute. This means that contractual arrangements as to priority of payments (or other distribution waterfalls) will be given effect by, and will be enforceable against, a Cayman Islands SPV without the need to provide its creditors with a security interest.

The Cayman Islands insolvency laws provide one of the most creditor-friendly regimes in the world, making the Cayman Islands well suited to Islamic finance and conventional capital markets and securitisation transactions. Benefits that creditors of Cayman Islands SPVs may enjoy include the following:

- Secured creditors may enforce their security in liquidation of a Cayman Islands SPV (outside the liquidation process).
- Cayman insolvency law focuses on the rights of creditors, all of which are treated equally, whether foreign or domestic. Therefore, there are no formal 'corporate rescue' provisions that mirror the US Chapter 11 or English administration proceedings that would allow a debtor effectively to suspend the rights of creditors including, in certain cases, secured creditors.
- Onerous contracts cannot usually be disclaimed by liquidators of a Cayman Islands SPV; creditors' contractual rights survive liquidation.
- Contractual netting and set-off arrangements are expressly recognised by Cayman law and can be enforced before and after insolvency, assuming that they are effective as a contractual matter under the governing law of the agreement in which they are contained.
- The enforceability of non-petition covenants by creditors or shareholders is expressly recognised by statute in the Cayman Islands.

Similar provisions to some of those detailed above are also available under the laws of the British Virgin Islands and Jersey.

7.3 Light but effective regulation

As discussed above, several offshore jurisdictions have introduced flexible legislation in order to accommodate the needs of international financial markets, as well as those of the rating agencies. This flexibility facilitates the structuring of various types of Islamic finance, as well as conventional capital markets and securitisation transactions.

Recognising the growing importance of the Islamic finance market, the Cayman legislature has pioneered legislation to create further legal certainty and efficiency for those seeking to issue *sukuk* through a Cayman Islands SPV. In 2008 the Cayman Islands introduced amendments to the Mutual Funds Law and the Banks and Trust Companies Law specifically to deal with the regulatory status of *sukuk*. The amendments clarify that *sukuk* instruments are alternative financial investments falling outside of the scope of such laws, an approach that is consistent with international stock exchanges and the accounting rules generally applied to *sukuk* instruments.

Furthermore, regulation in certain international financial centres, such as the Cayman Islands, the British Virgin Islands and also the DIFC (in regards to its SPCs), is effective yet light and non-intrusive. The finance industry in these jurisdictions is closely regulated, yet the regulatory framework and policies accommodate the demands of the various structures used in such transactions.

In the Cayman Islands and the British Virgin Islands, there is no specific regulation of debt issues unless (for Cayman Islands SPVs) such issues are listed on the Cayman Islands Stock Exchange. There are no foreign exchange controls in the Cayman Islands, the British Virgin Islands or the DIFC. There are no restrictions under Cayman law on a Cayman Islands SPV lending, borrowing or issuing debt securities or entering into derivatives transactions, except that no offer of securities may be made to the public in the Cayman Islands unless the SPV is listed on the Cayman Islands Stock Exchange. Such is the case in several other offshore jurisdictions, although in some jurisdictions, such as Jersey, the consent of the local regulatory authority must be obtained in connection with the issue of securities, and there may also be ongoing regulation in Jersey by means of conditions imposed on the consents granted.

Due to the light but effective approach adopted by several international financial centres, SPVs formed in such jurisdictions are attractive to businesses that operate across several countries, eliminating red tape at the SPV level. Many offshore jurisdictions allow directors and shareholders to be situated anywhere in the world, which increases flexibility in operations. Most offshore jurisdictions now comply with the Financial Action Task Force guidelines on money-laundering checks and the jurisdictions most prominently used in Islamic finance and conventional capital markets and securitisation transactions, including the Cayman Islands, the British Virgin Islands and Jersey, are on the Organisation for Economic Cooperation and Development's White List. Regulated institutions in such jurisdictions are required to satisfy 'know your client' checks and to determine the sources of funds before receipt. This adds a level of protection and offers additional confidence in an environment which already offers advantages to business.

7.4 Professional infrastructure

As noted above, in Islamic finance and conventional capital markets transactions it is often essential that the SPV be seen to be separate from and outside the control of the sponsor, and that it operate and be centrally managed and controlled in an offshore jurisdiction. This would not be possible without an infrastructure of true professionals – trust companies and company management firms – that can supply the necessary experienced and qualified trustees and boards of directors to manage and operate the SPVs.

Many international financial centres used to domicile SPVs, particularly the Cayman Islands, the British Virgin Islands and the DIFC, have a depth of professional expertise in Islamic finance and/or conventional capital markets and securitisation transactions. There are a number of highly able and experienced trust companies and administrators in these jurisdictions which provide trustee, management and director services to SPVs. The major accounting firms are also well represented in these jurisdictions, offering full auditing services, and a large number of law firms are available to provide competent advice on such transactions.

7.5 Formation costs and timing

Another key consideration in selecting a jurisdiction for the issuer in an Islamic finance transaction is the speed, ease and cost of establishing the SPV. In the Cayman Islands, for example, an exempted company can be incorporated and registered within 24 hours. The British Virgin Islands do not offer express incorporation services, but companies are incorporated on the date of application to the BVI registrar, with incorporation documents being returned in most cases within one week of filing. In Jersey, local regulatory consents must be obtained before the SPV can be formed.

Below is a sample timeline for the formation and maintenance of a Cayman Islands SPV to act as issuer in a *sukuk* transaction.

Day 1	Days 2 to 7	Prior to signing date	Signing date	By January of each subsequent year
• Sponsor selects name of SPV. • Incorporation documents filed with registrar. • Initial directors appointed. • Initial share of SPV transferred to local trust company.	• SPV's incorporation documents returned from registrar. • Initial board resolutions passed by SPV's directors to approve organisational matters. • SPV's directors review transaction documents.	• All necessary resolutions passed by board to approve transaction and appoint service providers.	• SPV's directors and other authorised signatories sign all transaction documents on behalf of SPV.	• SPV pays annual Cayman government registration fee and admin fees to corporate services provider (unless paid through priority of payments or waterfall).

The cost of setting up an SPV in many offshore jurisdictions, including the Cayman Islands and the British Virgin Islands, is competitive and relatively inexpensive. In the Cayman Islands, the British Virgin Islands and the DIFC (in respect of the formation of SPCs), there are no minimal capital requirements and the issued share capital can be relatively minimal.

8. Conclusion

Offshore jurisdictions play an important part in the structuring of SPV issuers for *sukuk* and other capital markets transactions, offering sponsors, investors and (where applicable) the rating agencies the key elements they require. Several international financial centres have shown their commitment to the Islamic finance market by, in the case of the Cayman Islands, implementing legislative provisions to deal with the regulatory status of *sukuk*, and generally through the initiatives taken by service providers from various of these centres establishing a presence in the Middle East and Asia. As the Islamic finance industry continues to grow and new innovative Islamic products are introduced, these international financial centres will be ready and well positioned to assist with the offshore structuring needs.

The role of the delegate and paying agent in *sukuk* transactions

Sema Kandemir
Hogan Lovells International LLP
Daniel Rankin
Hogan Lovells (Middle East) LLP

1. Introduction

The roles of a delegate trustee and the agents in a *sukuk* transaction are vital, not only from a functional perspective, but also for fundamental legal reasons. A *sukuk* issuer will inevitably be a special purpose vehicle (SPV) and, more often than not, an orphan offshore entity. This is for both legal and tax liability reasons, stemming from the fact that a *sukuk* transaction must be based on income-producing assets. In contrast, a bond can be simplified as an 'IOU'. The English law concept of a trust has been adopted to provide a legal framework for the rights of *sukuk* holders in relation to the underlying *sukuk* assets. Accordingly, *sukuk* investors participate in *sukuk* assets by investing in trust certificates because the *sukuk* represents, in essence, their ownership of the *sukuk* assets – it is not a debt from the issuer. Unsurprisingly, almost all *sukuk* transactions are governed, at least in part, by English law.

This chapter explores the mechanics of the appointment of the delegate trustee and these agents, and the role that such entities play in the greater *sukuk* transaction.

2. The incorporation of trust

The ultimate credit in a *sukuk* transaction, which in a bond issuance would be the issuer itself, is referred to as the 'obligor' – the entity whose name is attached to the issuance which supplies the underlying assets to the issuer, much as in a securitisation, where the originator sells the relevant receivables to the SPV issuer. The phrase 'ultimate credit' is appropriate in this scenario, as for the majority of *sukuk*, the obligor will supply the funds for redemption of the *sukuk*.

The standard *sukuk* structure involves the transfer of the asset that is the focus of the *sukuk* to an SPV which will act as issuer of the certificates to investors. The SPV issuer will declare a trust over the assets earmarked for the *sukuk* transaction (whatever form they may take) and its rights under the *sukuk* transaction documents in favour of the *sukuk* holders. The issuer will act as trustee for the *sukuk* holders and the *sukuk* assets that are the subject of the trust become 'trust assets'.

The incorporation of the trust structure means that the trustee is the only route through which *sukuk* holders can acquire their ownership in the trust assets, and communicate with the issuer and obligor. A trustee's duties are to the beneficiaries of the trust (in this case the *sukuk* holders). This contrasts with a bond issuance, where a trustee may or may not be appointed, depending on the credit standing of the issuer; it may take the view that investors will be sufficiently happy with merely a fiscal agent, which is appointed by and whose duties are owed to the issuer.

However, since a *sukuk* issuer will almost universally be an orphan SPV which is managed by a corporate services company, the *sukuk* holders' legal rights, which are housed in the trust, must be passed onto a party which can effectively perform its duties and exercise its rights. Much as a conventional bond issuance will make use of a corporate trustee to undertake any trustee functions, the trustee in a *sukuk* transaction (ie, the SPV issuer) will unconditionally and irrevocably delegate certain of its powers, duties and authorities to a designated entity – typically, the corporate trustee arm of a financial institution. Importantly, this delegation will include the power to enforce against the obligor and the assets on which the *sukuk* is based in the event of a default.

The role of delegate trustee can thus be understood as the fulcrum between *sukuk* holders on the one hand, and the issuer and the obligor on the other. It is the only meaningful entity interposed between the *sukuk* holders and the obligor; without the delegate trustee, the *sukuk* holders would be unable to enforce their rights. In a conventional bond transaction the appointment of a trustee will mean that if enforcement action ever needs to be taken by bondholders to enforce their right to payment, they cannot take individual actions against the issuer and are forced to act through the trustee, partly since they have no direct contractual relationship with the issuer. This means that the issuer is protected against multiple actions and the bondholders can rely on the trustee to take action on their behalf (after due consultation, if necessary).

In a *sukuk* transaction a declaration of trust is made whereby the SPV issuer or trustee appoints a delegate trustee to act on its (and therefore the *sukuk* holders') behalf. The delegate trustee will take action on behalf of *sukuk* holders, but only in the circumstances prescribed by the documentation. These circumstances must be given careful consideration, as the documentation will also ensure that individual *sukuk* holders cannot act against the issuer or obligor unless and until the delegate trustee has failed to take action.

The nature of the SPV issuer and the restrictive nature of the trustee delegate's mandate necessitate the appointment of agents to undertake the set payment and administrative functions which the issuer is obliged to carry out so that investors receive profit and principal payments under the *sukuk* when due. The entities appointed for these functions are usually related entities of the corporate trustee company which acts as the delegate trustee so, in effect, the review of the legal documentation is undertaken by the 'agency and trusts' section of the relevant entity for both the delegate trustee and the agents.

3. Appointment and role of delegate trustee

The delegate trustee is the independent arbiter for the stakeholders in a *sukuk* transaction, unrelated to the obligor group and not merely an SPV. Through the trust mechanism, the delegate trustee's role is to represent the *sukuk* holders and not the issuer or the obligor (although it is appointed by the issuer – in its role as trustee –

and its fees and expenses will be paid by the issuer or obligor). The role of delegate trustee is invariably carried out by a corporate trustee company which specialises in performing trustee duties in capital markets (and other) transactions.

An alternative structure might have the corporate trustee company acting as 'transaction administrator', as an agent of the trustee. The duties of a transaction administrator will be broadly similar and the documentation will go as far as possible to replicate this. In addition, where a particular jurisdiction does not recognise the concept of trust, often the provisions of the declaration of trust document may be replicated in an 'agency declaration', whereby the issuer is appointed as agent for the *sukuk* holders and the delegate trustee is appointed as a delegate for the *sukuk* holders, so that the roles are recognised under the laws of agency in the relevant jurisdiction. This is particularly pertinent if the *sukuk* is issued in a civil law jurisdiction which does not recognise the trust concept in its English law sense.

3.1 Declaration of trust

The creation of the trust, and the delegation of all duties of the SPV trustee to the delegate trustee, will take place within a single document, typically named the 'declaration of trust' or 'trust deed'. The delegate trustee is involved in the formulation of the transaction documents at an early stage of a *sukuk* structuring and typically will instruct its own lawyers to advise on and negotiate its position under the documentation. The corporate trustee company will seek to define its duties narrowly in the declaration of trust. The declaration of trust document thus fulfils separate functions:

- It is the operative document through which the trust is created, allowing investors to gain an interest in the *sukuk* assets;
- The delegation of trustee functions by the SPV issuer or trustee to the delegate trustee will take place within this document; and
- The scope of such functions and the liability of the delegate trustee will be contained in the declaration of trust.

The declaration of trust will set out two types of duty for the delegate trustee: a monitoring function, with the power to check the issuer's and the obligor's compliance with their respective obligations, and a duty to take enforcement action on behalf of *sukuk* holders. The delegate trustee is tasked with ensuring that the obligations of the obligor are observed in relation to the *sukuk* holders. Owing its duty of care exclusively to the *sukuk* holders, the delegate trustee is the person through whom the rights of the *sukuk* holders can be enforced, particularly in the event of a default.

The delegate trustee is the only active entity in a *sukuk* structure and as such is tasked with ensuring that the *sukuk* operates as the parties intend. The delegate trustee has the discretion to make amendments to the *sukuk* documentation and the terms and conditions of the *sukuk*, acting either on the instructions of *sukuk* holders or without consulting *sukuk* holders in certain circumstances, predominantly where the changes are of a minor or technical nature and do not adversely affect the interests of the *sukuk* holders. In contrast, certain changes may be 'reserved' as matters that must be agreed by a certain majority of, or unanimously by, the *sukuk* holders (eg, a change in the maturity date of the certificates or a change in the periodic distribution dates).

The delegate trustee must typically be consulted by the obligor and/or issuer before taking certain actions, which may be restricted in the covenants given by both the obligor and the issuer.

As further discussed below, pursuant to the declaration of trust, the delegate trustee will have the power and duty to convene and hold certificate holder meetings, and will represent *sukuk* holders in any major discussions with the issuer. On default by the issuer, the delegate trustee will take enforcement action on behalf of the *sukuk* holders as instructed by them and will manage any enforcement action on their behalf. In addition, it will supervise the distribution of proceeds to the *sukuk* holders after such action is taken.

3.2 Choice of governing law and delegate protections

As the appointment of a delegate trustee necessitates the creation of a trust, the governing law of the relevant documentation must recognise the trust concept. Therefore, typically the governing law chosen will be that of a common law jurisdiction and, in the vast majority of *sukuk*, English law is chosen. Under English law, the duties and powers of trustees are laid down in a combination of common law (through judgments and precedent) and statutes, such as the Trustee Acts 1925 and 2000.

The trustee, and thus also the delegate trustee in a *sukuk* transaction, must comply with the standards set out by law as well as the particular provisions of the declaration of trust. The delegate trustee may seek to limit the application of certain statutory provisions in the declaration of trust – particularly that it will seek to rely on the advice of professional third parties such as lawyers, valuers, bankers and accountants, and will appoint such parties as its agents; potentially also to exclude its liability for any misconduct by such parties, provided that it has acted diligently in appointing them. Commonly, it may also seek to disapply the statutory duty of care set out in Section 1 of the Trustee Act 2000 for the trustee to "exercise such care and skill as is reasonable in the circumstances, having regard in particular – (a) to any special knowledge or experience that he has or holds himself out as having, and (b) if he acts as trustee in the course of a business or profession, to any special knowledge or experience that it is reasonable to expect of a person acting in the course of that kind of business or profession".

As a commercial point, it is also commonly required that the delegate trustee have no obligation to act unless and until it is satisfied that it has been indemnified, secured or funded for any expenses it may occur in doing so. Although the exact threshold for liability is debated on each transaction, the best way for delegate trustees to protect themselves is to ensure that they have done what a reasonable person ought to have done to discharge their fiduciary duties. Despite the protections put in place when the declaration of trust was initially negotiated, wherever possible delegate trustees will seek to minimise their exposure to liability further by obtaining approval from the *sukuk* holders before taking any action which could be contentious. In a *sukuk* structure this will typically require a meeting of the *sukuk* holders.

3.3 Meetings of *sukuk* holders

The stakeholders for meetings of *sukuk* holders are the obligor on the one hand, with or without the SPV issuer, and the delegate trustee and the *sukuk* holders on the other. The agents, as is discussed below, may also be involved in such meetings. Depending on the structure of the transaction, there may be a multitude of agents, including a registrar, a principal paying agent and an investment agent. In some instances, a security agent is appointed to take security over the trust assets backing the *sukuk* offering. The main agents involved in restructuring obligations or a default situation are a transaction administrator and, potentially, a calculation agent (which may need to be appointed subsequent to the delegate trustee determining to take action).

At the meeting, the *sukuk* holders will be invited to vote on options presented to them in relation to the event which made the meeting necessary. A meeting of *sukuk* holders can commonly be convened by the delegate trustee at any time or following the request in writing of *sukuk* holders holding a specified amount of the certificates outstanding at such time. Generally, at least seven days' notice of a meeting must be given and such notice must specify the place, day and hour of the meeting, as well as stating the nature of the business to be transacted and, in the case of 'extraordinary resolutions', the particular language of each such extraordinary resolution proposed to be passed at such meeting.

If their interests are represented by a global certificate, *sukuk* holders, on receiving notice of a meeting through the 'clearing systems' (ie, international systems through which investors hold their interests – the usual way in which *sukuk* are held and traded) may:

- abstain from responding;
- notify (through the clearing systems) that they wish to appoint a specified person as their proxy (usually the delegate trustee), indicating how they wish to vote on the resolutions at such meeting; or
- respond that they wish to attend the meeting in person and, in the case of a corporate entity, nominate the individual who shall attend the meeting on their behalf. Accordingly, a voting certificate is prepared for such individual entitling him or her to attend the meeting.

These are the only ways in which a certificate holder is entitled to vote or attend the meeting.

Once a certificate holder has made an indication through the clearing systems, its certificates are blocked, preventing any ability to trade or deal in its certificates until the meeting has been completed, whereupon the certificates are released. The provisions for quorum and voting at meetings (including whether votes are taken by a show of hands or poll, and the provisions for adjournment of meetings) are set forth in the declaration of trust. Common benchmarks for voting are majority approval for ordinary resolutions and two-thirds approval for extraordinary resolutions. Depending on the declaration of trust, there may also be the ability for the *sukuk* holders at a meeting to approve, by extraordinary resolution, the formation of a committee that is empowered to act on all *sukuk* holders' behalf and has the power to undertake actions which the *sukuk* holders could otherwise approve by extraordinary resolution. This can be a very powerful option and, accordingly, can be far reaching in its scope. Before empowering a committee with such powers, careful thought must be given to, among other things, the composition of the committee, the extent of its powers and what the *sukuk* holders wish to achieve.

The purpose of certificate holder meetings is to act as a procedural step to carry out a defined task. It is convened to approve particular actions and, therefore, it is imperative that there is a pre-defined purpose for the meeting. Such purpose, or restructuring proposal, will likely be driven by one or more *sukuk* holders in private meetings before the *sukuk* holders' meeting. The calling of a formal certificate holder meeting is required to:

- ascertain the identity of fellow *sukuk* holders; and
- call a vote which will be binding on the other *sukuk* holders and the delegate trustee.

If an obligor defaults in the performance of its obligations under the transaction documents, or if an attempt has been made but *sukuk* holders in a certificate holder meeting have been unable to agree on a satisfactory method to revise or restructure an obligor's obligations, the probable next step is that a vote will be taken to dissolve the trust. Following such a vote, the delegate trustee should give notice to the *sukuk* holders that the certificates are to be redeemed and the trust dissolved.

Although the *sukuk* holders are requested to indicate whether they wish the trust to be dissolved, the trust should not be dissolved until rights under the transaction documents have been exercised to the fullest extent possible to attempt to obtain the funds necessary to redeem the certificates. Therefore, any request to dissolve the trust should be made subject to the carrying out of certain preliminary actions by the delegate trustee to ensure recovery of the *sukuk* holders' investment, if possible.

4. The appointment and role of agents

As mentioned above, in a *sukuk* transaction a variety of agents are appointed by the issuer to undertake administrative functions on its behalf. As such, the agents owe their duty of care to the issuer as their principal, in contrast to the delegate trustee, whose duties are owed to *sukuk* holders. Although performing related tasks, each agent will be separately appointed by the issuer (although usually within the same agency agreement). Their liabilities to perform their duties will be several and not joint, and so no agent will be liable for default or breaches of contract by another agent. In most cases all agents will be part of the same corporate group – usually the agency arms of the corporate trustee company which is acting as the delegate trustee.

While a contrast is drawn between the person(s) to whom duties are owed by the delegate trustee on the one hand and the agents on the other, it is important to recognise that they both fulfil the function of acting as intermediary between the *sukuk* holders (as a class), and the obligor and the issuer.

4.1 Roles and duties

Unless there are jurisdiction-specific requirements, the various agency roles will usually be undertaken by the same corporate group, albeit in different capacities and perhaps in different countries. The agents will also normally be entities related to the delegate trustee. As such, at the initial documentation stage, the review and negotiation will be undertaken by the same team within the relevant service provider.

There are many administrative functions that the SPV issuer (and even a bond issuer) will wish to delegate to agents. This is partly for administrative ease, but the presence of a well-known corporate services provider will also provide some comfort to potential investors. Typical tasks which issuers and obligors will prefer an agent to carry out (and *sukuk* holders will prefer to rely on a professional agent to perform) include:

- making payments in relation to the *sukuk*, including fees and expenses (to illustrate the importance of their functions, in accordance with the 'waterfall', the delegate trustee and agents' expenses are always paid first);
- keeping a register of *sukuk* holders; and
- calculating the payments due to *sukuk* holders, particularly in the case of a floating rate issuance.

These functions are not all undertaken by one agent (as would be the case in a bond where a fiscal agent was appointed). Various agents will typically perform, separately, the roles of paying agent(s), registrar, transfer agent, conversion agent (in the case of an equity-linked or convertible *sukuk*) and calculation agent. The separate roles and the tasks allocated to such agents are described further below.

(a) Paying agent(s)

At least one paying agent will be appointed in every *sukuk* transaction. Its role is to process and make periodic and final payments to *sukuk* holders on the issuer's behalf, usually through the clearing systems. In some cases more than one paying agent will be appointed (usually due to regulatory or listing requirements providing that a paying agent must be appointed within a certain jurisdiction), in which case one of the paying agents will be designated the 'principal paying agent' and will undertake a coordinating role. There may be an obligation on the issuer to maintain a paying agent in a certain jurisdiction (ie, other than its home jurisdiction) to avoid having to pay withholding tax. The EU Taxation of Savings Income Directive (2003/48/EC) requires EU member states to provide to the tax authorities of other EU member states details of payments of interest or similar income paid by a person within its jurisdiction to an individual who is resident in the second member state. As such, it is generally recommended that there be an obligation to maintain a paying agent in an EU member state that does not require a withholding to be made.

The principal paying agent will apply the moneys it receives from the issuer in accordance with a pre-agreed waterfall, usually allowing the fees, costs and expenses of the delegate trustee and agents to be paid out before payment of the balance to *sukuk* holders, which is distributed to the paying agents for onward payments. Any surplus after final payment of the redemption amount to *sukuk* holders can be paid back to the issuer.

(b) *Registrar, transfer agent and replacement agent*

A registrar's first duty will come immediately at the close of the transaction, when it authenticates the global *sukuk* certificate. Most *sukuk* issuances use 'registered' rather than 'bearer' form. Bearer securities are appearing less in both conventional bonds and *sukuk* issuances for various reasons, partly due to central bank anti-money laundering regulations or tax authority restrictions in various jurisdictions, and also due to the difficulty in tracing investors at a later point in time if necessary. For these reasons a global certificate, in which investors hold their interests in the certificates through the clearing systems (predominantly Euroclear and Clearstream in Europe, and the Depository Trust Company in the United States) is now standard. In addition, most *sukuk* transactions are now signed remotely, possibly with the relevant parties spread across the world; in order to ensure that all conditions to issuance are met, the documentation, including the global certificate, will be signed a few days before issuance. To avoid a live certificate being in circulation before the rest of the documentation coming into force, the registrar will authenticate the certificate on the closing date (by counter-signature) – this is the point at which the certificate becomes 'live'.

During the life of the *sukuk*, the registrar will be required to maintain the register at a specified office (usually in or outside a specific jurisdiction for tax reasons). While the global certificate is held through the clearing systems, which will record the ultimate ownership of the certificates, the register will indicate the name of the registered holder and will show the outstanding face amount of certificates represented by the global certificate. The register will also show the payments made in respect of certificates and any cancellations.

In case, for any reason, individual certificates (as opposed to a single global form) must be issued and the certificates must be held outside the clearing systems, the registrar function will increase in importance. The registrar must carry out exchanges of interests in the global certificate for individual certificates, keep a record of all exchanges and ensure that the principal paying agent, the issuer and the delegate are notified immediately of such an exchange. The register will then show:

- the outstanding face amounts and serial numbers of any individual certificates;
- their date of issue;
- all subsequent transfers and changes of ownership; and
- the names and addresses and account details of *sukuk* holders.

Similarly, if individual certificates are issued and need to be replaced for any reason, the replacement agent will be responsible for undertaking this task.

(c) *Conversion/exchange agent*

In the case of convertible or exchangeable *sukuk*, a conversion/exchange agent will be appointed to carry out and assist with the conversion or exchange, acting as a conduit between the issuer and *sukuk* holders.

(d) Calculation agent

Particularly in the case of a floating-rate rather than a fixed-rate *sukuk* issuance, the calculation agent will be required to calculate the periodic payments due to *sukuk* holders and may also be responsible for ascertaining the relevant floating rate itself (eg, the London Interbank Offered Rate).

(e) Other agents

Listing agent: Certain stock exchanges and listing authorities (eg, the Luxembourg and Irish Stock Exchanges) stipulate the appointment of a local listing agent, whose duties are primarily carried out before the listing of the *sukuk* on the exchange at the listing application stage, acting for the issuer or obligor as a listing adviser and a liaison with the exchange and listing authority. Unlike the other agency roles, this role is usually undertaken by advisers such as a law firm or consultancy service.

Security agent: Although the vast majority of *sukuk* are unsecured, if security were to be granted over certain assets for the *sukuk*, this would necessitate the appointment of a security agent to oversee the security and enforce if necessary. The identity of the security agent will typically depend on the jurisdiction in which the relevant assets are located – for example, in the United Arab Emirates, only a UAE-licensed financial institution can take mortgage security.

4.2 Agency agreement

The SPV issuer will appoint the relevant agents in an agency agreement in which the duties are allocated to each agent separately. As such, the obligations of the agents are several rather than joint under the agency agreement, so that no agent is liable for the default of another agent. Since the agents' fees and expenses will be payable by the obligor (as the ultimate credit), the obligor will also usually be a party to the agency agreement.

The trustee and the delegate trustee will be party to the agency agreement in order to enable the delegate trustee to require the agents to act on its behalf rather than the issuer's behalf (particularly following an event of default), and to create direct legal obligations between the delegate trustee and the agents in case the delegate trustee needs to take action on behalf of the *sukuk* holders. The agents will confirm in the agency agreement that they are aware of the trustee's delegation to the delegate trustee of its rights to enforce and realise the trust assets in the event of a default.

At the documentation stage of the *sukuk*, the principal paying agent tends to take the lead on behalf of the other agents in reviewing the documentation to ensure that it is functional from their perspective. Much of the agency agreement provides specific mechanics for payments to be made to and by the agents, for notification of non-payments and duties of the other entities. Common commercial issues which arise in the negotiation of the agency agreement between the obligor and the agents include the following:

- The timing of payment from issuer to paying agents – depending on the agents' perception of the credit quality of the obligor and the currency in which payment is to be made, the agents may require that any moneys to be paid on to the *sukuk* holders be received from the issuer either on the same day as the onward payment (if the agents are satisfied that they are sufficiently comfortable with the likelihood of payment), or one or more days in advance of such payment, to minimise the risk that the paying agents are forced to make payment to *sukuk* holders when they may not yet have been placed in funds by the issuer.

- Counter-indemnity – some agent functionaries have a policy against counter-indemnifying the obligor or the issuer against any loss caused by the agents' negligence, gross negligence or bad faith (or some combination of the above). The obligor and issuer might strongly argue to the contrary, given that a professional agent should be comfortable to give such an indemnity. As such, this is often a commercially negotiated point.

5. Conclusion

The modern financial instrument which we refer to as a *sukuk* is facilitated by the English law concept of trust law. The result of this combination is a highly flexible financial instrument, but one that depends on third-party service providers to ensure its proper functionality. While the forms and structures of *sukuk* are constantly evolving, today's *sukuk* are very much dependent on the use of a delegate trustee to monitor the transaction and enforce the rights of *sukuk* holders. Similarly, as the issuers of *sukuk* are SPVs, they must rely on agents to facilitate the payment, administration and custody of the *sukuk*. Accordingly, for the foreseeable future the role of the delegate trustee and the paying agent in *sukuk* transactions is that of a key facilitator – controlling the flow of information and funds and thereby the economic operation of the *sukuk* itself.

Sukuk: standardisation and regulation

Rahail Ali
Hogan Lovells (Middle East) LLP
Mustafa Kamal
Al Yaqoub Attorneys & Legal Advisers in association with Hogan Lovells

1. Introduction

As the Islamic capital markets develop and mature, two interrelated issues have become the subject of repeated discussion and debate: standardisation and regulation. While regulation generally takes the form of legislation and standardisation is often market driven, there are several points where the two intersect – the aim of both standardisation and regulation is to bring some form of stability and certainty to the Islamic capital markets.

When considering an Islamic capital markets transaction or product, a *Sharia* scholar or board will take into consideration several factors, including any relevant points from the vast treasures of 14 centuries of Islamic jurisprudential tradition. In the absence of such direct precedent, the *Sharia* scholar may deduct a conclusion on the basis of established authority such as the *Qur'an, Hadeeth* (the sayings of the Prophet) or past legal rulings that are not directly on point. Alternatively, or in conjunction with the above, the *Sharia* scholar may confer with other eminent contemporary *Sharia* scholars in order to establish some form of consensus on a novel issue. It is important to appreciate that as the contemporary application of Islamic finance is not straightforward, prominent scholars may have different views on the same issue. While overcoming differences of opinion between *Sharia* scholars is the most important task facing supporters of the standardisation of Islamic capital markets transactions, given the dynamic nature of the *Sharia*, it is also the most difficult. Indeed, standardisation and statutory codification of *Sharia* have not been the norm in Islamic legal history.

Before delving into Islamic legal history and the issue of standardisation and regulation, we must consider the place of Islamic finance within the Islamic legal tradition. 'Islamic law' is a modern term used generally to describe the *Sharia* and *fiqh*. The '*Sharia*' refers to the general corpus of laws and ethics contained in the four principal sources – the *Qur'an* (the holy book of Islam); the *Sunnah* (the sayings and practices of the prophet); *Ijma* (consensus); and *Qiyas* (analogy)) – as well as the detailed rules derived by *Sharia* scholars from the four principal sources over the past 1,400 years. The *Sharia* (literally meaning 'the clear, well-trodden path to water' in Arabic) is the general corpus of laws and ethics; *fiqh* (literally meaning 'deep understanding' in Arabic) refers to the body of detailed legal rulings derived by *Sharia* scholars over the last 14 centuries, from the detailed sources of the *Sharia*. Although there is only one general corpus of laws and ethics (ie, the *Sharia*), historically there have been different schools of thought in *fiqh* (*madhahib* in Arabic) based on the interpretive tools used by different *Sharia* scholars. Today there are only four remaining main schools of thought (*Hanafi*, *Shafi'*, *Maliki* and *Hanbali*), while historically there were up to 14 different schools of *fiqh* (including the *Tabari*, *Awzai* and *Zahiri* schools of *fiqh*), which evidences the potential for diversity of opinions in Islamic law. This diversity in legal opinions arises from a diversity in interpretive tools; all schools of *fiqh* agree on the four principal sources of Islamic law mentioned above, but beyond these there is diversity and complexity on the issue of which interpretive tools are to be used in the process of *ijtihad* (independent judicial reasoning to deduce rules for new legal issues). The resultant diversity of opinion in the Islamic legal tradition extends across all areas of Islamic jurisprudence, from the rules associated with prayer and fasting to the rules governing financial transactions. The question arises as to what can or should be the extent of standardisation in relation to Islamic finance where the underlying legal tradition is hardwired for multiplicity of opinions and is composed of multiple schools of *fiqh*, each with different interpretive tools for *ijtihad*.

There have been several attempts by political authorities to codify or standardise *fiqh*. The Abbasids, caliphs of their age, were famously rebuffed by Imam Malik (one of the founders of the four traditional schools of *fiqh*) when they expressed their desire to disseminate Imam Malik's masterpiece of Islamic jurisprudence, the *Muwatta*, in the four corners of the Islamic empire – it was argued then, as it often is now, that a single code would contradict the nature of interpretation in the Islamic legal tradition which leans towards diversity in jurisprudential interpretations. The Mughal emperor of India Aurangzeb Alamgir commissioned hundreds of *Sharia* scholars in a monumental effort to compile the *Fatawa Alamgiriyyah* (also known as *Fatawa Hindiyyah* in the Arab world) to aid him in his plan to establish *Sharia* as the principal law of the land at the height of the Mughal empire's expansion. While Aurungzeb's efforts were swept away by the tides of the British Raj in India, the *Hanafi fiqh* of financial transactions was codified and distributed within the Ottoman empire as *Al-Majallah Al-Ahkam Al-Adaliyyah* during its final decades. The codification of the *Majallah* is by far the most significant and influential contemporary attempt to codify traditional Islamic law in relation to financial transactions and later influenced the development of civil codes in many Arab countries. The contemporary call for standardisation and regulation of *Sharia* rules in relation to finance is, of course, driven not by caliphs and emperors, but by the need to regulate and develop the Islamic finance industry that has gained momentum in the last few decades.

2. Standardisation of *sukuk*

Supporters of standardisation and templates assert that to maintain the extraordinary growth of the Islamic capital markets, the standardisation of Islamic finance principles into market-standard documentation for Islamic capital markets transactions is essential. Proponents of standardisation argue that the introduction of standards to Islamic financings would lead to more certainty in transaction methods. Consequently, transaction costs would be reduced. The clear enshrining of Islamic finance principles into documentary form would be established in order to assist not only the practitioners of Islamic financings, but also the investors. This would further streamline the transaction process and ease any concerns of investors that may be unfamiliar with *Sharia* principles. It could also save valuable time by making the process of obtaining *Sharia* approval from *Sharia* supervisory boards more efficient and 'documenting out' legal risk. These are laudable objectives, but the dynamic nature of *Sharia* application in contemporary capital markets makes standardisation problematic and, more fundamentally, questions whether it is in fact desirable.

The counterargument is that standardisation is a hankering for conventional or interest-based financing which requires homogeneity to churn out 'renting money' transactions – 'commoditising' documents is undesirable in the context of the Islamic finance industry, which is developing the implementation of its principles in the contemporary debt capital financial markets and in the face of banking regulation that is geared towards conventional or 'IOU' banking. Put differently, opponents of standardisation point to the fact that Islamic finance is not a subject which should be condensed into standard documents because that detracts from the development of its principles.

3. Standardisation of *Sharia* principles

Over the past few decades, the Accounting and Auditing Organisation for Islamic Financial Institutions (AAOIFI) has led the way in developing *Sharia* standards for major Islamic financing techniques. Since 1991, the AAOIFI's guiding principle has been to nurture cooperation between Islamic financial institutions around the world with the aim of harmonising the Islamic finance industry. The AAOIFI's influence has grown dramatically since it was established and it now has more than 180 members from more than 46 countries. The AAOIFI's ability to bring together the world's top *Sharia* scholars specialising in financial transactions has meant that its committees have been able to develop more than 20 *Sharia* standards which specifically document the general (but not absolute) contemporary *Sharia* consensus on Islamic financings. The AAOIFI's undertakings are held in high regard by Islamic finance practitioners and, although they are not always adhered to, these standards are one of the first points of reference in the industry.

Indeed, without the AAOIFI's *Sharia* standards, standardisation of the more complex aspects of Islamic capital markets, such as documentation, processes and indexing, would be impossible. As such, the AAOIFI represents the top of the standardisation pyramid and continues to lead the way in the development of *Sharia* standards by issuing new standards for *gharar* (uncertainty) in financial transactions, *rahan* (pledge), *takaful* (*Sharia*-compliant insurance), Islamic reinsurance, *waqf* (religious endowments) and *zakat* (*Sharia*-mandated alms tax). For some, the expectation is that the standards prepared by entities such as the AAOIFI will help to develop the standardisation of *Sharia* market practices and legal documentation further, and act as a catalyst for the standardisation of other areas, such as *Sharia*-compliant rating and indexing.

The leading example of the influence of the AAOIFI's *Sharia* rulings is the recent AAOIFI ruling in relation to *sukuk* (*Sharia*-compliant debt instruments). In November

2007 Sheikh Taqi Usmani, one of the world's leading *Sharia* scholars and chairman of the AAOIFI Board of *Sharia* Scholars, stated that 80% of *sukuk* were not *Sharia* compliant, mainly because their method for redemption incorporates a repurchase undertaking (a promise that the borrower will redeem the *sukuk* by repurchasing the underlying assets at a price representing the face amount of the *sukuk* at maturity or following an event of default, thereby effectively mirroring the features of a conventional bond). According to Sheikh Taqi Usmani, a promise to pay back capital violates the principle of risk and profit sharing on which such *sukuk* should be based. In an attempt to clarify this position, the AAOIFI brought together its Board of *Sharia* Scholars to lay out a common position. After much discussion, the AAOIFI Board of *Sharia* Scholars published a paper outlining its position on *sukuk*, which included a ruling that purchase undertakings at face value on maturity under a *musharaka* or *mudaraba sukuk* structure are no longer permitted. It is significant that following publication of this paper, financial institutions and industry practitioners which have structured recent *sukuk* issuances have made a concerted effort to try to adhere to this ruling.

While the AAOIFI's *Sharia* standards are the most significant development in relation to the standardisation of Islamic rulings, there is no unanimity. For example, there is the much unresolved disagreement between scholars over the controversial *tawarruq* financial instrument. While the AAOIFI developed a *Sharia* standard in relation to *tawarruq* in April 2009, the International Islamic *Fiqh* Academy of the Organisation of The Islamic Conference, a body of prominent *Sharia* scholars, ruled that the "organised use" of *tawarruq* was prohibited.

The Islamic finance industry is also faced with regional differences in interpretation. *Sharia* interpretations predominant in Malaysia have a basis in the legal rulings of the *Shafi'* school of *fiqh*, and the view on what is *Sharia* compliant differs drastically between Malaysia and the rest of the Muslim world; the Gulf Cooperation Council (GCC) countries, particularly Saudi Arabia and Pakistan, are considered to be the most conservative Islamic countries concerning *Sharia* rulings. Furthermore, country-specific considerations such as regulatory and legal issues and tax must be addressed before standardisation can be attempted.

Although there are no final authorities for the Islamic finance industry on an international level, standardisation of *Sharia* rules has started on a national level in Malaysia. The National *Sharia* Advisory Council of the Malaysian Central Bank is the final national authority on *Sharia* matters pertaining to Islamic banking within Malaysia. The development of this council reflects increasing awareness of the importance of national supervision of *Sharia* issues within various governments. The council acts as a reference point for courts and arbitrators in disputes involving *Sharia* issues in Islamic banking cases. The council's decisions are binding on arbitrators and are to be "taken into consideration" by the court. The Malaysian Central Bank periodically releases compilations of *Sharia* resolutions passed by the council with a stated aim of "greater cross-border harmonisation in the interpretation and application" of *Sharia*. All Islamic financial products offered by Islamic financial institutions in Malaysia must comply with the rulings published in the *Sharia* resolutions.

Significantly, in 2010 the Securities Commission of Malaysia appointed a new *Sharia* advisory council, comprising 11 members serving two-year terms. This council is the central authority responsible for determining *Sharia* principles pertaining to the Islamic capital markets in Malaysia.

In order for the standardisation of *Sharia* rules to become a global phenomenon, other governments must see the importance of cooperation with Islamic financial institutions and encourage the development of similar national-level authorities on *Sharia* issues based on the Malaysian model. To this end, the *Sharia* board of the State Bank of Pakistan and the *fatwa* board of the Kuwait Ministry of *Awqaf* have been set up in recent years; however, these boards do not have the same level of national supervision as in Malaysia. One might even argue that Malaysia has taken standardisation to its logical conclusion – that is, where standardisation paves the way to regulation.

4. Standardisation of market practice

The Malaysia-based Islamic Financial Services Board (IFSB) has become an important entity concerned with the standardisation of market practices in the Islamic finance industry. Inaugurated in 2002, and with more than 190 members (from the International Monetary Fund and the Islamic Development Bank to 135 market players and professional firms), its stated aim is to ensure the soundness and stability of the Islamic financial services industry. To date, the IFSB has issued more than 10 standards and guiding principles, including standards on capital adequacy requirements for *sukuk* and securitisations and guiding principles on governance for Islamic collective investment schemes.

Central banks from various Muslim countries are also endeavouring to standardise market practice. The establishment of the International Islamic Financial Market (IIFM) in Bahrain was a direct consequence of a collective effort of various central banks to achieve uniformity in documentation, products, best practices, infrastructure and systems. The IIFM liaises with stakeholders such as national regulators and supranational Islamic institutions, as well as other market participants. The International Capital Markets Association has been working with the IIFM to develop guidelines on market practice, as well as introducing standard documentation and standard language for *sukuk* issuances in primary markets and assisting with the development of rules and recommendations for secondary market transactions involving *sukuk*.

The IIFM and the International Swaps and Derivatives Association (ISDA) launched the ISDA-type *Tahawwut* Master Agreement in March 2010, giving the Islamic capital markets model documentation for hedging transactions such as profit-rate and currency swaps that are purportedly *Sharia* compliant. While this is a significant development, there still is no immediate consistency in the market, as many banks have their own preferred forms of document, many of which they have prepared themselves. The challenge will be to adapt the *Tahawwut* Master Agreement to the legal peculiarities of each jurisdiction, as it is unlikely that the longstanding local Islamic hedging techniques such as those used in Malaysia will quickly or easily be displaced by the *Tahawwut* Master Agreement. Of course, there is also disquiet as to whether providing a standard form for *Sharia*-compliant rate and currency protection products is a slippery slope to derivatives and the turmoil that they have created.

5. Standardising legal documentation

Law firms have generally played a leading role in helping to standardise documentation in the conventional capital markets. However, transaction methods in Islamic capital markets transactions vary in complexity. As such, overcoming the *Sharia* issues for the different financial instruments in Islamic financings will be potentially easy for some transaction methods, but almost impossible for others, due to their fluid and structured nature. While it might be possible to standardise the legal documentation relevant to a *sukuk al-ijara* structure, all *sukuk* structures must be tailored to the legal, regulatory, tax and commercial context, as well as to evolving standards illustrated by the recent AAOIFI ruling on *sukuk*.

6. Regulation of *sukuk*

While standardisation aims to bring stability to the Islamic capital markets through initiatives that are largely market driven, regulation is enshrined in law and is largely driven by the regulatory authorities. Across the various jurisdictions, the process of implementing regulations related to *sukuk* is often preceded by wide-ranging consultations with industry players, Islamic finance experts, legal experts and other key stakeholders.

7. United Kingdom

In the West, some of the most important regulatory developments in Islamic capital markets are taking place in the United Kingdom, which has positioned itself as a leader in Islamic finance. The UK government has expressed its desire to establish London as a global centre for Islamic finance by introducing tax and regulatory changes, and has made significant progress towards its goal of facilitating *sukuk* transactions – for example, tax changes provide relief from stamp duty land tax where transactions are a part of an alternative finance investment bond issue. As alternative finance investment bonds include *sukuk*, the changes will mean that alternative finance investment bonds will now be treated as specified investments on the same basis as instruments creating or acknowledging indebtedness. Alternative finance investment bonds will now also be excluded from the definition of 'collective investment schemes'.

The developments in the United Kingdom are important because of London's pre-eminence as a global financial centre. In addition, as the premier common law jurisdiction on the European side of the Atlantic, regulatory developments in the United Kingdom create a well-trodden path for other common law jurisdictions to follow. While sleeping giants such as India risk missing out on the potential of becoming an Islamic finance hub, other Asian common law jurisdictions, such as Singapore and Hong Kong, have taken great strides to develop Islamic capital markets, and even Australia is poised to amend its tax regulations to provide a level playing field for *sukuk*. Keen to take advantage of the growth in trade between Asia and the Middle East, Singapore has begun to position itself as a hub for Islamic finance in Asia. Like the UK regulators, the Monetary Authority of Singapore is seeking to accommodate Islamic finance within the existing conventional regulatory framework and to level the playing field by ensuring the neutrality of regulations where Islamic financing is similar to conventional financing in economic substance and risks. Among other amendments to facilitate Islamic finance, Singapore has also removed the imposition of double stamp duties in Islamic transactions involving real estate, and accorded the same concessionary tax treatment on income from Islamic bonds. Exemptions from income tax were also granted on amounts payable to investors from Islamic bonds which are qualifying debt securities. Following these regulatory developments, Singapore is now expected to take the lead in making the requisite regulatory amendments to facilitate the further development of the Islamic capital markets.

8. Malaysia – setting the bar for regulating Islamic capital markets

Of those countries with a Muslim majority, Malaysia has emerged as a leader in *sukuk* regulation. While its robust regulatory infrastructure for the capital markets contains the elements of what would be expected in an advanced capital markets jurisdiction, it has supplemented this with regulations which specifically facilitate the development of Islamic capital markets. Since its establishment in 1993, the Securities Commission of Malaysia has tailored capital markets regulations to facilitate the development of the Islamic capital markets. In addition to the general capital markets regulations, the Guidelines on the Offering of Islamic Securities consist of a series of practice notes for parties intending to issue Islamic securities – these are distinct from the Guidelines on the Offering of Private Debt Securities, which apply to conventional bonds. The Malaysian government recently introduced further incentives to promote *sukuk* issuances and listing on Malaysia's bourse by providing cost-efficient issuance infrastructure. As the development of the Islamic capital markets has been on the government's agenda for several decades, further harmonisation of the Malaysian legal system to facilitate *sukuk* is expected.

Another key Muslim jurisdiction for *sukuk* is Saudi Arabia, where the capital markets have developed fairly recently. The Saudi case is unique – as it is historically a traditional *Sharia* system located in a country that was never colonised, it never applied a common law or civil law system. Recently it has been developing its own *Sharia*-based legislation to suit the Saudi legal environment. As Saudi Arabia develops its capital markets, the Capital Markets Authority will have the benefit of the combined experience of regulators from across the globe, including western jurisdictions and Malaysia.

9. *Sukuk* in civil law jurisdictions

Recognising the promise of the *sukuk* market, some Muslim majority civil law jurisdictions have enacted specific legislation to provide for the introduction of common law enclaves so that their legal systems are better aligned with the requirements for developing Islamic capital markets. The United Arab Emirates has set up the common law-based Dubai International Financial Centre, while Qatar has set up the Qatar Financial Centre, both as common law jurisdictions. While these two GCC jurisdictions have created common law enclaves within civil law systems, Indonesia, another civil law jurisdiction, has recently passed a new *sukuk* law. Aiming to catch up with Malaysia, which has taken advantage of a common law-based legal system, Indonesia has explicitly sanctioned the sale of usufruct as well as the creation of special purpose vehicles, both of which are firsts for this civil law jurisdiction.

Another key civil law jurisdiction is France where, following a roundtable discussion with important industry participants in 2008, the Ministry of Economy and Industry has announced regulatory and tax changes to facilitate Islamic finance, including:

- changes related to *sukuk* listings in France;
- the tax treatment of Islamic finance transactions; and
- the introduction into French law of trusts (*fiducie*), which generally form the bedrock for *sukuk* transactions in other jurisdictions.

Since that announcement, there have been several important legal developments. The *fiducie* law was enacted to bridge the gap in French civil law created by the absence of the Anglo-American concept of trust. Although the initial 2007 law contained significant restrictions on the manner in which a *fiducie* can be created and the identity of both the constituent and the fiduciary, a 2008 law rendered the framework more flexible, whereby both natural persons and legal entities, including lawyers, will be permitted to constitute a *fiducie*.

The ministry also published a statement in July 2008 relating to the listing of *sukuk* on French-regulated markets, stating that *sukuk* issues may be structured as either asset based or asset backed. It also set out the level of disclosure and other requirements in relation to the prospectus for each type of *sukuk*. In 2009 France formally introduced tax neutrality laws for *sukuk*. The French legislation ensured that for tax purposes, Islamic transactions would be treated in the same manner as conventional offerings and would not be subject to additional taxes, despite the alternative vehicles used in *Sharia*-compliant transactions. The French tax administration also published guidelines listing the conditions with which *sukuk* must comply in order to qualify as debt instruments for tax purposes. If *sukuk* fulfil such characteristics, remunerations paid under such instruments will qualify as interest deductible from taxable income. Moreover, remuneration paid by the issuer to *sukuk* holders that are not French tax residents will be exempt from withholding tax in France. Additional measures were passed in 2010 to strengthen the tax treatment of *sukuk* under French regulations. Just as developments in the United Kingdom have set a precedent for common law jurisdictions, the French model may serve as a guiding light for civil law jurisdictions, including Muslim-majority countries which have historic ties with France.

10. Looking ahead

To the uninitiated, the lack of standardisation is something to decry. For those who are familiar with Islamic capital market transactions, their historical jurisprudence, their application (in a legal and regulatory environment – which, far from prohibiting the causes of the credit crunch, actually acted as a catalyst for them) in the contemporary financial markets and the need to avoid Islamic capital markets being hijacked by conventional lenders and a 'renting money' ethos, the examination by *Sharia* scholars occasioned by the absence of 'cookie cutter' documentation is to be welcomed. As the credit crunch has shown, scrutiny in all areas is compulsory, including ethical standards.

Although the many initiatives have come a long way in developing basic standards in Islamic capital markets transactions, they are used only as guides by practitioners and as yet do not yield definitive authority. If progress is to be made towards standardisation, more cooperation is needed between industry professionals, banks, Islamic financial institutions and governments. The Malaysian model demonstrates the effectiveness of a national level supervisory council to the application of *Sharia* to the Islamic capital markets – this is the fruit of well-coordinated, coherent policy and a supportive regulatory framework. However, sight should not be lost of the more profound question of whether it is appropriate to regulate Islamic financial institutions and their products in the same manner as conventional banks.

Listing *sukuk*

Roger Fankhauser
Hogan Lovells (Middle East) LLP

---

1. Introduction

The market for *sukuk* listing is a nascent and niche one. Up to 85% of the *sukuk* issued (in terms of the number of *sukuk* transactions) are issued without a listing of the certificates. However, multilaterals and sovereign and quasi-sovereign issuers usually arrange a listing for their *sukuk* – for instance, the $100 million International Finance Corporation *sukuk* is listed on Nasdaq Dubai and the Bahraini Stock Exchange, and the $750 million *sukuk* issued by the government of Bahrain is listed on the London Stock Exchange. The government of Dubai recently listed its $2.5 billion *sukuk* programme on both the Dubai Financial Market and the London Stock Exchange. In addition, an increasing number of corporate issuers of *sukuk* with large nominal amounts seek a listing of their *sukuk* on one or more stock exchanges. Petronas had a triple listing – it listed its $1.5 billion *sukuk* on the Luxembourg Stock Exchange, the Labuan Stock Exchange and the Bursa Malaysia.

This chapter explores the main reasons for listing *sukuk* and outlines the listing process in general, the eligibility criteria and the disclosure requirements. Based on recent experience, it highlights key issues to be addressed if an issuer is considering listing its *sukuk* and is choosing the stock exchange and platform on which the *sukuk* are to be listed.

In terms of numbers of listed *sukuk*, the London Stock Exchange shows a total of 25 *sukuk*. The Indonesian Stock Exchange has a total of 25 *sukuk* and Nasdaq Dubai lists 20 *sukuk* on its website. On the Luxembourg Stock Exchange and the Bahrain Stock Exchange, a total of 16 and 10 *sukuk* are listed, respectively. The London Stock Exchange and the Luxembourg Stock Exchange are the two hubs for cross-border listings of *sukuk* in Europe.

Despite a general harmonisation trend, listing procedures and disclosure standards still vary on different stock exchanges. Accordingly, this chapter provides a general overview rather than a detailed comparison of the listing rules of various stock exchanges.

For the purpose of this chapter, references to the 'issuer' mean the obligor of the *sukuk*, rather than the special purpose vehicle (SPV) which technically issues the *sukuk*.

2. Listing *sukuk* –why and where?

2.1 Reasons for listing *sukuk*

A listing of *sukuk* usually increases the issuer's reputation and prestige. As part of the listing application and thereafter until the *sukuk* are redeemed (or delisted, if earlier), the issuer subjects itself to a disclosure standard that displays a level of transparency as to the issuer's business, financial position and prospects. The prospectus is reviewed and approved by the listing authority, thereby ensuring that the disclosure in the prospectus as of the listing date meets the stock exchange's required minimum standard. On listing of the *sukuk* and for as long as they remain listed, the relevant authority of the stock exchange further supervises the issuer's compliance with any continuing disclosure obligations of the issuer under the listing rules.

Further, a listing of *sukuk* has the potential to help to diversify and extend the investor pool: regulations governing investment activities of pension funds, collective investment schemes and other professional investors include specific provisions as to the assets comprised in these investors' investment portfolio, and require that a certain proportion of the assets be listed securities.

A stock exchange with a listing authority and regulations which are respected grants investors comfort and protection, and attaining listed status may enhance the marketability of the *sukuk* on the secondary market. However, a deep secondary market for *sukuk* is yet to be established: *sukuk* are regularly structured as restricted or wholesale securities which may not be offered or sold to retail investors. Financial institutions and other professional investors conduct most trades in *sukuk* over the counter. Such transactions are not transparent to the public or other investors, so that the bid-ask spread for *sukuk* remains potentially significant – one of the reasons why the volume of trading activities is usually low.

2.2 Choice of stock exchange

Once the issuer opts for a listing of the *sukuk*, the question becomes which stock exchange is the most appropriate for listing.

For many issuers, the stock exchange in the jurisdiction where the issuer is incorporated still forms the exchange for first consideration. Issuers are most familiar with the legal and regulatory framework of their domestic stock exchange. Issuers in some emerging markets may feel pressure to list their *sukuk* on their home market to promote it and to provide local investors with more immediate access to their securities.

Capital markets are worldwide. Cross-border listings of *sukuk* are becoming increasingly popular, as is demonstrated by the number of *sukuk* listed on the London and Luxembourg Stock Exchanges. If issuers consider a cross-border listing on a foreign stock exchange, they need to understand fully the effect of the eligibility criteria and disclosure standards imposed by the listing rules. Issuers need to assess frankly whether they are able and – often more relevant – willing to comply with the level of disclosure until the *sukuk* matures or is redeemed. Any breach of continuing disclosure obligations may trigger severe consequences for the issuer: it may become liable for any damage or loss incurred by investors and face penalties or other legal consequences under the listing rules – all of which also affects the issuer's reputation significantly.

Issuers must choose the stock exchange at the start of the transaction. Financial and legal advisers often suggest specific stock exchanges in discussions with the issuer. This process usually involves a brief description of the main eligibility and disclosure requirements applicable under various listing rules. Accordingly, a predictable and consistent interpretation of the listing rules by the listing authorities becomes essential.

On some occasions particular listing authorities have altered their previous interpretation of the listing rules without giving any particular reason or warning to relevant market participants – for example, issuers were required to publish transaction documents on their website, even though waivers had previously been granted. Modified application of the listing rules is often caused by a high rate in personnel fluctuation. Eagerness to increase the stock exchange's reputation by complying with, or in many cases outperforming, international standards may also contribute to modifying a previous interpretation of the same rules. However, from the issuer's perspective, any change in previous practice triggers additional discussions with the listing authority, delays and additional costs. In some cases such changes may even put at risk the originally envisaged listing structure, as the new disclosure standard may not be compatible with requirements under the listing rules of a secondary listing stock exchange.

The efficiency of the relevant listing authority in processing listing applications, including reviewing drafts of the prospectus and dealing with queries regarding the required disclosure standards, is essential. Well-experienced staff familiar with *sukuk* structures make for a smooth listing process. A listing authority with the reputation of being approachable and flexible and reliably responding to specific issues of a particular transaction gives that stock exchange a significant competitive advantage.

Some stock exchanges also compete for new issuers by establishing specific platforms with lower entry barriers and/or less onerous disclosure regimes. For example, on the London Stock Exchange, *sukuk* and other securities can be listed on the exchange's main market platform, which is classified as a regulated market under the EU Markets in Financial Instruments Directive (2004/39/EC). On regulated markets, issuers must comply with the provisions set out in the EU Prospectus Directive (2003/71/EC) and the EU Transparency Directive (2004/109/EC). Alternatively, issuers choosing the London Stock Exchange may opt to list their *sukuk* on the Professional Securities Market, a platform reserved to professional investors that is not classified as a regulated market. Consequently, issuers need not comply with the stricter disclosure standards.

3. Overview of listing procedure

3.1 Primary versus secondary listing

Listing rules usually distinguish between a primary and a secondary listing. If the *sukuk* are not (and will not simultaneously be) listed on another stock exchange, the issuer must apply for a primary listing on the chosen stock exchange. The regulations applicable to this stock exchange then determine which eligibility criteria and disclosure requirements the issuer must adhere to in order to list the *sukuk*. Some stock exchanges require issuers seeking a primary listing to confirm that their domestic stock exchange has not previously refused to list their *sukuk*.

It is possible to opt for a primary listing on more than one stock exchange, in which case the issuer must comply with the listing rules of each primary stock exchange. A dual listing requires coordination with all listing authorities involved to ensure that the issuer and the listing documents adhere to all listing rules and, to the extent that the rules are inconsistent, waivers are granted.

Instead of several primary listings, issuers may, in addition to the listing on their domestic market, apply for a secondary listing of the *sukuk* on a foreign stock exchange (or *vice versa* – that is, apply for a cross-border primary listing and a secondary listing on the home market). Applications for secondary listings can be submitted simultaneously or within specific periods of attaining listing status on the primary stock exchange. Conditions for a secondary listing are often less strict than for a primary listing. The listing authority of the secondary market often relies on the review and approval by the authority of the primary market to the extent that it recognises the listing regime of the primary exchange as being at least equivalent to the standard set out in its own listing rules – the prospectus approved by the listing authority of the primary stock exchange is regularly recognised by the authority reviewing the application for the secondary listing as satisfactory for its purposes without extensive or substantive review.

3.2 Listing procedure

A listing application is an interactive process involving coordination and discussion between the issuer, its advisers and the listing authority. On some stock exchanges, such as Nasdaq Dubai, a listing must be approved by two different authorities: first by the Listing Committee, with that approval then confirmed by the Dubai Financial Services Authority.

The issuer and its legal advisers usually contact the listing authority as early as possible in a transaction to discuss the upcoming *sukuk* issue and timing for their listing. If the issuer opts for a simultaneous primary and secondary listing, the listing process must be coordinated with both listing authorities.

The critical document to be submitted to the listing authority is the prospectus. As soon as the draft of the prospectus is in a form that includes most of the information to be disclosed under the listing rules, it is sent to the listing authority for its review so that any amendments and additional disclosure requirements can be addressed and discussed as early as possible in the listing process. First submission usually includes an annotated version of the draft prospectus (ie, a version in which the information required by the listing rules is marked).

A formal listing application is usually submitted between launch and signing of the *sukuk* issue. Lodging the formal listing application marks the formal start of the listing procedure. Together with the listing application form and the preliminary prospectus, the issuer files ancillary documents evidencing that the issuer satisfies all eligibility criteria under the listing rules. Ancillary documents usually comprise:

- drafts of any agreement and other documents to be executed on closing;
- constitutional documents;
- the resolution of the issuer's board of directors approving the issue of the *sukuk*; and

- in some cases, a letter requesting waivers from such listing rules of which the issuer, or the *sukuk*, would otherwise be in breach.

Based on this information, the listing authority considers whether the application and documentation submitted fulfils all requirements and, subject to them being issued on the closing, approves the listing of the *sukuk* as of the date agreed with the issuer.

Depending on how familiar all parties involved are with the process and the structure of a particular *sukuk*, the listing process for the issuer's first *sukuk* takes approximately four to six weeks from the date on which the draft prospectus is submitted to the listing authority for the first time. If well organised and properly coordinated from the start, the listing process will usually fit into the scheduled transaction timetable without causing any delays. It is rare for the listing to hold up completion of a transaction.

3.3 Listing of a standalone issue versus a programme

Instead of issuing a standalone *sukuk*, issuers that anticipate raising funds on the capital markets through various tranches of *sukuk* have started to establish *sukuk* programmes, comprising a base prospectus and related documentation. Based on the programme documentation, multiple tranches can be issued within a period of one year simply by completing a 'final terms' form specifying the particular terms and conditions of the relevant tranche.

Drawing up a programme is usually more cost effective and time efficient than issuing and listing several standalone *sukuk*. Since documentation for each tranche relies on the programme documentation, a programme also provides more flexibility to react quickly to changing market conditions and to issue *sukuk* at the best possible time.

If a *sukuk* programme is listed, the listing authority will register the base prospectus and grant a pre-approval for the listing of a maximum amount of *sukuk* to be issued under the programme. For each tranche, only the final terms or pricing supplement for the particular *sukuk* need be submitted to the listing authority. A supplemental prospectus discloses any changes in the business or financial performance of the issuer that may have an effect on the investment decisions of investors.

4. Eligibility criteria

4.1 Classification of *sukuk*

The listing rules of each stock exchange set out eligibility criteria that an issuer and the securities must satisfy for the securities to be listed. Criteria differ depending on the nature of the securities to be listed: units in collective investment schemes are subject to eligibility criteria different from shares or conventional bonds.

Some stock exchanges incorporate specific provisions for the listing of *Sharia*-compliant debt instruments, and *sukuk* in particular, to address the specific characteristics of and disclosure requirements related to these financial instruments. Other stock exchanges, such as the London and the Luxembourg Stock Exchanges, do not include specific provisions for *sukuk* and they must first be classified in order to determine the applicable listing criteria.

Classifying *sukuk* under non-specific regulatory and legal frameworks poses challenges. Although many Islamic financial instruments commercially replicate or mirror conventional products, their legal structure and the means by which the return is achieved differ from their conventional counterparts. They often also involve other risk elements due to applicable *Sharia* principles.

Sukuk represent beneficial ownership interests in underlying assets and grant investors a right to the profit generated by these assets. From that perspective, *sukuk* show similarities to units in collective investment schemes. The commercial characteristics of *sukuk* are clearly of a financing nature as opposed to the investment nature of units in collective investment schemes. The purpose of issuing *sukuk* is the same as that of conventional bonds – the issuer seeks to raise funds on the capital markets for a pre-defined term and promises the investors, to the extent possible under *Sharia* principles, to periodically pay a pre-defined return.

In line with this financing nature, both the London and the Luxembourg Stock Exchanges classify *sukuk* for listing purposes as securities similar to conventional debt instruments. Accordingly, the criteria applicable to a listing of *sukuk* on these stock exchanges are the same as those for the listing of conventional bonds. This classification has recently been supported by various European jurisdictions such as England, Luxembourg and France, which have amended or are in the process of amending their tax, regulatory and other legal frameworks to create and ensure a level playing field for *sukuk* and conventional bonds. Accordingly, most eligibility criteria relevant for *sukuk* apply to debt instruments in general.

4.2 *Sukuk*-related and issuer-related criteria

Eligibility criteria related to *sukuk* include free transferability of the securities, the whole class of securities being listed and, depending on the applicable listing rules, a minimum market capitalisation.

Issuer-related eligibility criteria generally require that the issuer of the *sukuk* be duly incorporated and validly established and have a minimum track record of two to three years, depending on the stock exchange. Some listing rules further stipulate a minimum value for the net assets owned by the issuer.

Sukuk are regularly structured to be issued by an SPV incorporated offshore for the single purpose of issuing the *sukuk*. Accordingly, the SPV issuer cannot satisfy all issuer-related eligibility criteria. In particular, it will neither show a track record of at least two years nor have published audited financial statements for the same period. The listing rules of stock exchanges that include specific provisions relating to *Sharia*-compliant securities expressly address this particularity of *sukuk* and state that issuers may apply for a waiver to look through the SPV so that the real issuer or obligor will be the entity to satisfy eligibility criteria relating to the issuer. This possibility conforms to the situation of a conventional guaranteed bond issued by an SPV: in a typical *sukuk* structure, the obligor ultimately provides the funds and is responsible for fulfilling the issuer's payment obligations under the *sukuk*. Thus, the decision to invest in *sukuk* is mainly based on the obligor's credibility and ratings assigned to the obligor.

Based on this similarity of *sukuk* structures to conventional guaranteed bonds, the London Stock Exchange and other stock exchanges without particular provisions for *Sharia*-compliant financial instruments grant similar waivers and allow to look through the issuer to the obligor with respect to issuer-related eligibility criteria and (continuing) disclosure obligations.

4.3 Financial reporting standard

In order to attain listing status, issuers must have published audited accounts covering at least the past two years and copies of the (consolidated) financial statements must be included in the prospectus. Technically, the period to which the most recent annual financial statements relate must not end more than 18 months before the date on which the (listing) prospectus is published: if a listing is granted in April 2010 and the financial statements for 2009 have not been prepared and audited by then, the issuer may, at least in theory (marketing considerations usually require non-stale financial information), still submit financial statements for the two financial years ending on December 31, 2007 and 2008 – the grace period of six months from the end of the most recent financial year acknowledges that issuers need time to draw up, and arrange audit of, their financial statements.

Issuers need to establish whether the chosen stock exchange recognises and allows them to draw up their financial statements in accordance with the issuer's local accounting standards. For example, issuers from a non-EU country which seek to list *sukuk* on the London Stock Exchange are allowed to submit financial statements drawn up in accordance with their local generally accepted accounting principles (GAAP) if the *sukuk* represent wholesale debt instruments and must not be offered to retail investors. However, stock exchanges, at least for their main market platforms, regularly require that financial statements be drawn up in accordance with International Financial Reporting Standards (IFRS) or US GAAP. Issuers must then restate their financial statements for the last two years and any coming year to one of the internationally recognised accounting standards.

The requirement for restating financial statements not only causes additional costs, but also potentially deters issuers from seeking a listing on the relevant stock exchange: the fact that the US Securities and Exchange Commission refused to accept financial statements drawn up under IFRS has precluded many European issuers from applying for a secondary listing on stock exchanges in the United States.

4.4 Appointment of *Sharia* board

The listing rules of stock exchanges with separate platforms for *Sharia*-compliant instruments, such as Nasdaq Dubai, require the issuer to appoint a board of *Sharia* scholars with adequate qualifications, expertise and experience in Islamic jurisprudence and finance. The *Sharia* board shall advise the issuer, in respect of *Sharia* compliance, on all aspects of the offering of the *sukuk*. Since the appointment of a *Sharia* board is usually a costly requirement, issuers often mandate *Sharia* scholars of one of the lead managers to review the structure of the *sukuk* and issue the *fatwa* to confirm that the *sukuk* are *Sharia* compliant.

Stock exchanges without a specific regime for listing *Sharia*-compliant instruments, such as the London or Luxembourg Stock Exchanges, require neither the appointment of a *Sharia* board nor submission of a *fatwa* as part of the listing application. However, issuers listing their *sukuk* on any of those stock exchanges often seek the approval of *Sharia* scholars due to market and investor expectations. The related consideration is as to whether the scholars' credentials as experts must be disclosed.

5. Disclosure in prospectus

5.1 Two sets of rules – one prospectus

If *sukuk* are to be listed on a stock exchange, a disclosure document must be submitted as part of the listing application. The terminology used for these disclosure documents varies, but they are regularly referred to as a 'prospectus' or 'offering circular'. The latter term in particular indicates that in practice, one disclosure document is used for two processes that must be clearly distinguished from each other: the initial offering and the subsequent listing of the *sukuk*.

Before a listing, *sukuk* are issued on the primary market by way of an initial offering of the *sukuk* to investors. Initial offerings are generally subject to disclosure requirements set out in rules dealing with any offering of securities, a set of rules different from the listing rules. Even if *sukuk* are not listed, an issuer may be obliged to draw up an offering prospectus to satisfy disclosure standards under the offering rules.

The listing rules determine a minimal disclosure standard to be set out in the prospectus. The primary purpose of these disclosure requirements is to protect investors on the secondary market (ie, investors that trade *sukuk* previously issued), and to contribute to a fair pricing of the securities by ensuring that market participants are provided with equal information about the issuer, its business and the risks involved in an investment in the *sukuk*.

If issuers intend to list their *sukuk*, market practice and efficiency reasons dictate drawing up only one prospectus, which is used for the offering and the listing of the *sukuk*. Newer regulations such as the EU Prospectus Directive acknowledge that investors on the primary and the secondary markets need the same information to make a sound and informed investment decision. Accordingly, the directive stipulates a harmonised and uniform disclosure standard for the prospectus to be published in connection with a public offering of securities and for the listing of securities on a regulated market.

The level of required disclosure in the prospectus may be different for the initial offering of the *sukuk* and the listing of the same – whether due to the age of the offering or the listing rules, or to a lack of consistency of the exemptions set out in the two sets of rules. Issuers must then ensure that the form and content of the combined offering and listing prospectus follow the stricter disclosure standard.

5.2 Level of required disclosure standard

Generally, a prospectus must contain such details on the issuer, its business and the *sukuk* as a competent investor needs in order to reach an informed assessment of an investment in the *sukuk* (ie, sufficient information on the structure of, and rights attached to, the *sukuk* and on the issuer's assets and liabilities, financial position, profits and losses and prospects). A prospectus is usually divided into the following main sections:

- summary of the offering;
- risk factors;
- use of proceeds;
- business description of the issuer;
- terms and conditions of the *sukuk*;
- taxation;
- subscription and selling restrictions; and
- general information.

Copies of the most recent interim financial statements and the annual financial statements for the past two or three years, as applicable, are attached at the end of the prospectus.

The level of disclosure required depends on the addressees of the offer to buy the *sukuk*, be it on the primary or the secondary market. The rules applicable to initial offers usually distinguish public offerings addressed to retail investors from placements with professional and other qualified investors. Wholesale investors are deemed to have sufficient understanding of the risks involved in investing in *sukuk* and accordingly require less protection than retail investors. Disclosure regimes applicable to such placements are therefore less strict than the disclosure standard applicable in the course of a public offering of *sukuk* to retail investors. The same proposition is reflected in the listing rules of various stock exchanges: under the listing rules of Nasdaq Dubai, for example, a listing prospectus may include less information if an issuer seeks to list 'restricted securities', which are basically securities issued only to professional investors. Similarly, the listing rules of the London Stock Exchange stipulate a less onerous disclosure regime if the denomination of the *sukuk* is at least €50,000, thereby presuming that only qualified investors would be able to buy the securities. The same applies if the *sukuk* are listed on the Professional Securities Market.

5.3 Process of drafting the prospectus

Copies of a combined offering and listing prospectus in preliminary form must be available for the roadshow, at which the issuer and the joint lead managers present the issuer's business and the upcoming *sukuk* offering to potential investors to test market appetite. The preliminary prospectus must be in final form, save for the commercial terms which are determined at pricing, including aggregate nominal amount of the *sukuk*, the return to be paid and periodic payment dates.

Ideally, the listing authority has also confirmed by the start of the roadshow that the preliminary prospectus complies with all disclosure requirements under the listing rules, which is often achievable only if the listing authority has been involved from the beginning of the drafting process. To the extent that another authority must review and approve the prospectus under applicable offering rules, coordination of the two separate processes becomes another essential milestone.

Satisfying required disclosure standards is one thing. A different issue is that some first-time issuers tend to regard the prospectus as a forum for marketing speak – it is not. False, inaccurate or misleading information disclosed in a prospectus, or any failure to disclose material information in a prospectus, can cause loss to investors. Due diligence is usually conducted by the financial advisers and their legal counsel to obtain a better understanding of the issuer's business and related risks, and to ascertain that the information included in the prospectus is accurate and complete. Ultimately, the issuer knows its business, challenges and prospects best. Issuers remain responsible for disclosing all information that is material for investors, even if negative.

6. Continuing disclosure requirements

The prospectus submitted as part of the listing application provides investors with a snapshot of the issuer's business and financial performance as of the date of the prospectus. Additional and continuing disclosure obligations of the issuer stipulated in the listing rules ensure that investors on the secondary market are, on an ongoing basis, provided with any information that could have a material effect on the market price of the *sukuk*.

Continuing disclosure obligations may be broadly grouped in two categories: reporting obligations that must be satisfied on a periodic basis and *ad hoc* disclosure obligations that apply at all times.

6.1 Periodic reporting obligations

Under the periodic reporting obligations, issuers are obliged to publish certain information on the stock exchange or to report specific facts to the listing authority, irrespective of whether disclosure of the information may have a material effect on the market price of the *sukuk*.

Most importantly, issuers must publish annual reports including their audited annual consolidated financial statements and, during the financial year, (semi-annual or quarterly) interim financial statements. Those financial statements must be drawn up in accordance with accounting standards recognised by the relevant stock exchange.

In addition to reporting their financial performance, issuers are required to announce administrative information relating to the issuer itself (eg, a change in the issuer's name or its auditors) or to the *sukuk* (eg, appointment of new paying agents or periodic disclosure of profit rates).

6.2 *Ad hoc* publicity

The second category of ongoing disclosure obligations relates to the disclosure of price-sensitive information on an *ad hoc* basis. The purpose of *ad hoc* publicity is to ensure that issuers provide all market participants at the same time with accurate, clear and complete information on significant events. Accordingly, selective disclosure to only some investors is not permissible.

Price-sensitive information is generally described as any fact arising in the issuer's sphere of activity that is likely to cause a significant change in the market price of the *sukuk*. *Ad hoc* publicity applies only if the change in the market price triggered by a particular fact is greater than usual price fluctuations on the market.

Whether a specific development constitutes a price-sensitive fact must be assessed on a case-by-case basis. Listing authorities usually issue guidelines as to the interpretation of the term and provide examples of what they would consider typical price-sensitive facts. If a price-sensitive fact arises, related information must be announced on the market as soon as the issuer becomes aware of the relevant facts. Immediate disclosure may be omitted only if and for as long as the relevant facts are confidential and disclosure would prejudice interests of the issuer.

The decision as to whether a fact is actually price-sensitive information, or whether the conditions for postponing disclosure are fulfilled, is often difficult to make and issuers regularly seek professional legal advice. In these cases, issuers must contact their advisers as early as possible, as issuers may become liable for any damages or losses incurred by investors due to an unjustified delay in disclosing price-sensitive information.

7. Conclusion

A deep secondary market for *sukuk* is yet to be established. At present, the main benefit of a listing is the potential diversification and extension of the investor pool, particularly if the *sukuk* are rated.

Issuers that consider listing their *sukuk* need to weigh the benefits against the extra effort and cost. It is essential for each issuer to understand fully the legal and regulatory framework applicable on the chosen stock exchange and platform and its continuing disclosure obligations. Efficiency and reliability of the listing authority are further key elements to be considered.

Islamic treasury products: demystifying the *Tawarruq* controversy

Rafe Haneef
HSBC Amanah Malaysia

1. Introduction

The *tawarruq* transaction, which is also widely known as the 'reverse *murabaha* trade', is often perceived as the Achilles heel of Islamic finance. Many customers and practitioners alike find the *tawarruq* trade to be the least credible of the contemporary Islamic financial products, mainly due to its emphasis on form over substance. Despite being much criticised, it is still widely in use as an Islamic treasury product for liquidity management, as well as for credit, rate and currency hedging requirements. Accordingly, in order to gain a better understanding of the *tawarruq* controversy, it is essential to have a thorough understanding of the *tawarruq* contract and its various modes of operation.

Although there has been much criticism from various quarters against many other contemporary Islamic finance transactions, such as *murabaha lil amir bil shira* and, most recently, some *sukuk* structures, the *tawarruq* contract has undoubtedly faced the fiercest criticism. In response, the International Council of *Fiqh* Academy[1] commissioned research into the operations of contemporary *tawarruq*; in April 2009[2] it passed a ruling banning contemporary forms of organised *tawarruq*. In this chapter, '*tawarruq*' refers to organised *tawarruq* and 'classical *tawarruq*' refers to the form of *tawarruq* where the seller (*muwarriq*) sells goods already in its ownership directly to the buyer (*mustawriq* or *mutawarriq*) and the buyer then directly sells the goods to another party not connected to the *muwarriq*.

This chapter discusses and analyses the perspectives of both opponents and proponents of *tawarruq*, with a view to ascertaining the soundness of the *Fiqh* Academy ruling. Interestingly, the *tawarruq* ruling epitomises the growing divide between proponents and opponents of the contemporary Islamic finance industry as a whole. Generally, those who oppose *tawarruq* also oppose *murabaha lil amir bil shira*, *ijara muntahia bittamleek*, contemporary *sukuk al-mudaraba*, *musharaka*, *wakala* and many other contemporary Islamic finance products (hereinafter referred to as 'contemporary contracts'). Critics view the ban on *tawarruq* as the tip of the iceberg; they want the whole iceberg – the contemporary Islamic finance industry itself – to be exposed and transformed in its totality. Many critics believe that the

1 The academy is an initiative of the Organisation of Islamic Conferences.
2 The ruling was made in its 19th session, held in Sharjah, United Arab Emirates, from 1st to 5th of Jamadil Ula 1430 AH, corresponding to April 26 to 30 2009.

transformation can be realised only by banning all contemporary contracts and rejuvenating the classical *mudaraba* and *musharaka* contracts. Hence, it is important to discuss the *tawarruq* ban within the overall Islamic finance context.

2. Mechanics of classical *tawarruq*

The juristic meaning of '*tawarruq*' is "the act whereby a person purchases a commodity on credit and sells in cash to another third person at a lower price than the price at which he bought it, so that he may acquire cash".[3] In classical *tawarruq*, a customer will buy the commodity from a supplier on credit terms (eg, $100) and the customer will then sell the commodity in the market (but not to the original supplier) on a spot basis at a discount (eg, $90). The customer can utilise the $90 to meet its liquidity needs and will pay the $100 to the supplier on the deferred date.

All the four *madhahib*, except a few dissenting jurists such as Ibn Taymiyyah and Ibn Qayyim of the Hanbali school,[4] have approved the above classical *tawarruq* trade. Analysed from a purely contractual basis, the customer has merely entered into a valid classical *murabaha* contract with the supplier. The key distinction here is that at the point of entering into the *murabaha* trade, the customer had the intention of selling the goods immediately to another party at a discount to obtain cash. When buying with such intention, the customer is classified in *fiqh* as a *mutawarriq*. The supplier (*muwarriq*), on the other hand, may not be privy to the intention of the customer. Given that the nature of the transaction is essentially a *murabaha*, the majority of jurists have declared such contract to be valid even if it subsequently emerged that the customer had sold at a discount the *murabaha* goods to another party (that was not connected to the *muwarriq*). Hence, the majority of jurists have allowed the classical *tawarruq* contract since it is a valid trade and neither the supplier nor the customer has any intention to engage in *riba*.

In this respect, classical *tawarruq* can be contrasted with *inah*, where the supplier usually sells the goods to the customer on a *murabaha* basis (eg, $100), payable on deferred terms, and the customer then immediately sells them back to the same supplier (or another buyer which is connected to the first supplier) on a spot payment basis (eg, $90). Although, if viewed independently, the first trade is a valid *murabaha* and the second is a valid *wathiah*, the jurists have not allowed such trades when they are entered into between the same parties, as both parties were conniving to enter into the trades with the intention of engaging in *riba*.

3. Modes of contemporary *tawarruq*

3.1 *Tawarruq* as a liquidity placement facility

In contrast to classical *tawarruq*, the *muwarriq* in a contemporary *tawarruq* actively promotes the sale of commodities on deferred terms to the *mutawarriq* with the clear knowledge that the customer will re-sell the commodities for cash. In most cases the

---

3 See Muhammed Taqi Uthmani, *Verdicts on At-Tawarruq and Its Banking Applications* 1-2 (www.isra.my/index.php?option=com_content&view=article&id=360&Itemid=185), quoting *Al-Maws'at al-Fiqhiyyah al-Kuwaytiyyah*, 14/147.

4 See *id* at 5 for a discussion on the opinions of the two scholars.

financier will facilitate the customer to re-sell the commodities for cash. This form of active promotion and intermediation has been seen by the *tawarruq* opponents as a disguise to engage in *riba*; therefore, the initial part of this chapter focuses on the forms of promotion and intermediation prevailing in contemporary *tawarruq*.

In general, *tawarruq* contracts are used today as either liquidity facilities (eg, an inter-bank placement) or credit facilities (eg, a customer credit financing). Below, some of the prominent modes of *tawarruq* contracts prevailing in the Islamic finance industry today are discussed.

Tawarruq liquidity facility 1

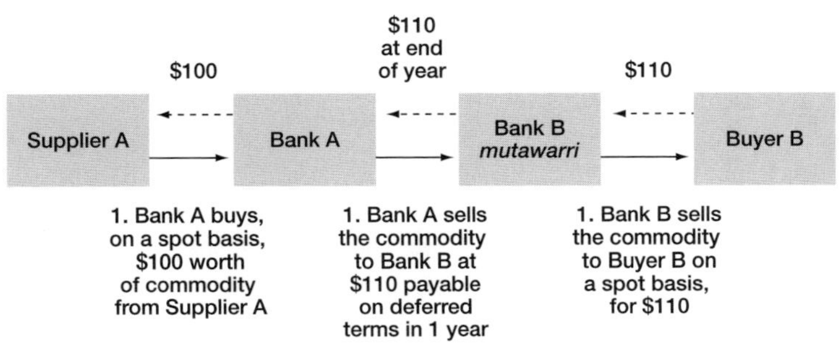

Usually both Bank A and Bank B will have negotiated the general terms of *tawarruq* inter-bank placements between them before any *tawarruq* contract is executed. Bank A (the *muwarriq*) with surplus cash will call on Bank B (the *mutawarriq*) to see whether it wants to buy a commodity on a *murabaha* basis from Bank A under the *tawarruq* arrangement. If Bank B does wish to buy a commodity on a *murabaha* basis, Bank A will buy the commodity from Supplier A and sell the commodity to Bank B. Bank B will then sell the commodity to Buyer B on a spot payment basis. From a *fiqh* perspective, Bank B has entered into a valid *murabaha* contract with Bank A and Bank B has independently sold the commodity to a third party, Buyer B, which is not connected to Bank A (the first seller). This transaction is hence very much similar to classical *tawarruq*, except that instead of the *mutawarriq* approaching the *muwarriq* for a *murabaha* transaction, the *muwarriq* is now approaching the *mutawarriq* first. But is this reverse approach prohibited by *Sharia*? None of the opponents to *tawarruq* have produced evidence to establish that a reverse approach is contrary to *Sharia*. Hence, unless clear *Sharia* evidence is produced against such reverse approach, this form of *tawarruq* should be considered permissible under *Sharia*.

However, prominent Islamic jurist Sheikh Taqi Usmani recently stated that: "*At-Tawarruq*, which was conceived and ruled in favour of its permissibility by the jurists, is that the commodity is available with the seller as his real owned possessions. Then, its possession right will transfer to the buyer by the term of real sale, which all the rules of sale will follow."[5] This statement is perhaps true from a historical perspective,

5 *Supra* note 3, at 15.

where usually the *mutawarriq* in classical *tawarruq* approaches a local supplier (the *muwarriq*) to sell certain commodities on *murabaha* terms, and the *muwarriq* will usually sell the commodities that it already has in its possession.

However, with due respect to Usmani, is it contrary to *Sharia* if the supplier first goes out and buys some commodities from the market and then sells them on a *murabaha* basis to the *mutawarriq*? Such activities have clearly been allowed under *murabaha* contracts and are still practised by Islamic banks globally. For example, when a customer approaches an Islamic bank to finance a car purchase, the bank first buys the car from the supplier and then sells it to the customer at a higher price under a *murabaha* contract. Clearly, the Islamic bank did not own the car at the time the customer first approached it. Are the *tawarruq* opponents now saying that a *murabaha* contract is not valid unless the Islamic bank already owns the car from the beginning? The same analysis will apply for an *ijara* transaction where a customer approaches an Islamic bank to finance a house purchase. The Islamic bank first buys the house chosen by the customer from the seller and then leases the house to the customer on an *ijara muntahia bittamleek* basis. The Islamic bank clearly does not own the house when the customer first approaches it for financing. Why then are contemporary *murabaha* and *ijara muntahia bittamleek* allowed under *Sharia*? If contemporary *tawarruq* is prohibited on this ground, should not the prohibition equally apply to *murabaha* and *ijara* contracts? Surprisingly, this requirement was imposed only on *tawarruq* – the reasons for this become clear later in this chapter.

Tawarruq liquidity facility 2

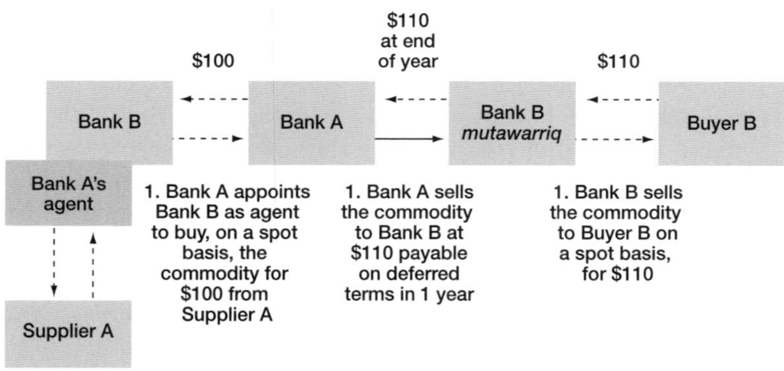

In this mode of *tawarruq*, Bank A (the *muwarriq*) with surplus funds appoints Bank B (the *mutawarriq*) first to buy the commodity as Bank A's agent. On Bank A paying Supplier A, Bank A will then enter into the *murabaha* trade with Bank B. Usually, this form of *tawarruq* is conducted when Bank B does not have the expertise or resources to deal directly with the commodity suppliers. The rest of the transaction is identical to *tawarruq* liquidity facility 1. Interestingly, this form of agency has also been prohibited by the recent ruling on *tawarruq* by the *Fiqh* Academy.

Usmani also stated that:

[M]any of the banks and the institutions add another agreement, which is At-Tawkil (authorization). For instance, if one of the bankers requests for the financing on the basis of At-Tawarruq, surely the bank will not sell a commodity available under their [sic] possession, but rather will only be required to buy it from the market. But if the bank buys it themselves through one of their workers [sic], then this may be possibly accepted. However, in most cases, the bank will not buy it themselves. It will authorize the agent who is himself Al-Mutawarriq to buy it from the market on behalf of the bank. Then, the Al-Mutawarriq will buy it from the bank at a delayed price. He will later sell it to a third party. The custom adopted in many banks is that the bank will not pay the price to the original seller, but rather pays the amount to Al-Mutawarriq, as he is an agent for them in buying and selling the commodity.

Because of the addition of this At-Tawkil (authorization)' to At-Tawarruq, the procedure becomes something similar to usurious financing, because the Al-Mutawarriq will take the smaller amount from the bank, while the higher amount will be paid to him [sic, should be 'by him'] when the fixed time lapses. If he takes it for a lesser amount, then that only occurs as a result of his being an agent for the purchase, and not as loan seeker. But this accurate difference cannot distance the procedure from the similitude of usurious finance, as this issue of At-Tawkil (authorization) may turn the contract agreement to either Mazhur (prohibited) or Makruh (disliked).[6]

It is intriguing why similar agency agreements have been allowed and are still being practised in contemporary *murabaha* and *ijara* contracts. Rarely will the financiers buy *murabaha* goods themselves, for various reasons. The financiers will usually appoint the customers to buy the goods required under an agency arrangement and, on the customers acquiring title to the goods as agent, will immediately sell such goods on a *murabaha* basis. The same *modus operandi* is adopted in contemporary *ijara* transactions. The financiers will appoint the customers as agents to buy the assets required and, on the customers acquiring title to the assets, will lease such assets to the customers. In most such *murabaha* and *ijara* contracts, the financiers will pay the consideration for such goods or assets directly to the customers as agents and the customers will make the payment to the seller of such goods or assets. If this type of agency is *Sharia* permissible in *murabaha* and *ijara* contracts, why is such agency not permitted for *tawarruq* contracts? The opponents of *tawarruq* have been unable to support their stand with any specific evidence from the *Quran, Sunnah* or *ijma*. Their only key evidence seems to be that in classical *tawarruq* contracts, the seller sells only goods already in its possession to the *mutawarriq* and does not buy from the market after the *mutawarriq* has approached the seller or appoint the *mutawarriq* to buy the goods on its behalf.

With respect to the learned *tawarruq* opponents, this line of reasoning lacks any merit. The *Sharia* principle *in muamalat* is that everything is permissible (*mubah*) unless clearly prohibited by *Sharia*. The fact that something was not done in the past

6 *Supra* 3, at 15. The typos highlighted in the paragraphs quoted may have arisen during the English translation of the original paper, which was in Arabic.

does not create a barrier to innovation in the future. Is there any evidence from the *Quran, Sunnah* or *ijma* that unequivocally prohibits a seller from appointing an agent (the *mutawarriq*-to-be) to buy certain goods and then selling such goods to the *mutawarriq*? If there is any such evidence, surely that evidence will be extended to contemporary *murabaha* contracts as well where the customer is acting as agent to buy the goods on behalf of the financiers. Why are the *tawarruq* opponents then relying painstakingly on such remote points to prohibit *tawarruq*? Again, the rationale for this narrow juristic approach becomes clearer in the latter part of this chapter.

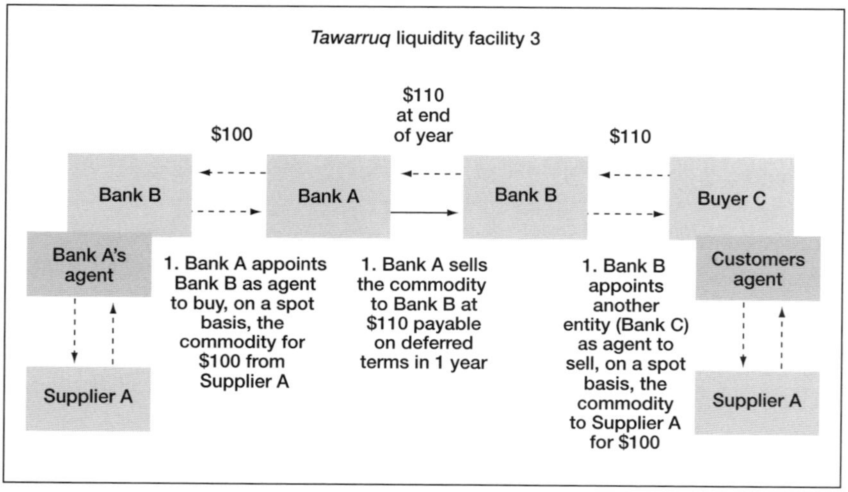

The above mode of *tawarruq*, although not very prevalent, is being practised in some jurisdictions. Most scholars have not allowed this mode of *tawarruq*, given that it closely resembles the prohibited inah contract as stated by the learned Sheikh Taqi Usmani: "[The p]ermissibility of this type of sale is conditioned with the fact that the buyer should not sell (to the first seller) the commodity at the price lower than the price of its purchase from its first seller, whether directly or through an intermediary. If he does, then both of them would eventually fall into the unlawful credit sale (bay'u al-Inah), according to the legal ruling, because of its embodiment of the trick of Ar-Riba (interest), and it may so become an unlawful contract/agreement."[7]

3.2 *Tawarruq* as credit facility

This mode of *tawarruq* is similar to classical *tawarruq*, where the *mutawarriq* approaches the *muwarriq* for a credit sale or *murabaha* trade and on such trade the *mutawarriq* sells the commodity to a third party in the market. The key distinction between the contemporary mode and classical mode of *tawarruq* is that, in the contemporary mode, the financier does not have the commodity in its possession at

7 Resolutions of the Islamic Jurisprudential Assembly, 321-322, Muslim World League 1421 AH/2000 AD, at 16.

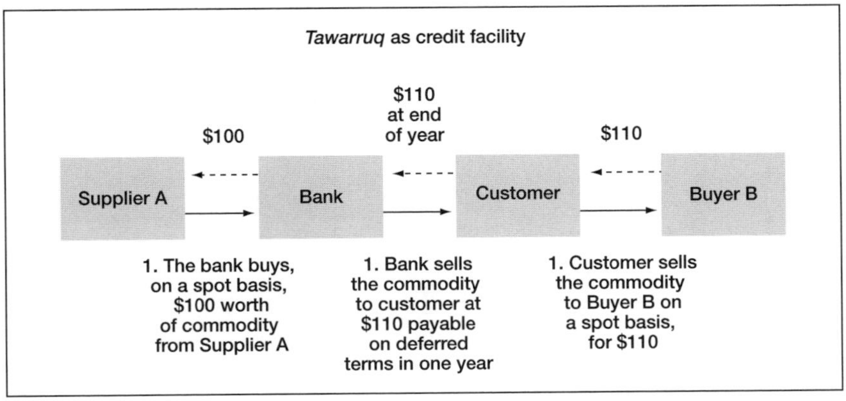

the very inception. The *tawarruq* opponents have again used this difference as grounds to ban contemporary *tawarruq*. As analysed above, this line of reasoning is not supported by any clear evidence from the *Quran, Sunnah* or *ijma*. This mode of *tawarruq* should be considered as in compliance with the standards of *Sharia* as applied to other contemporary contracts.

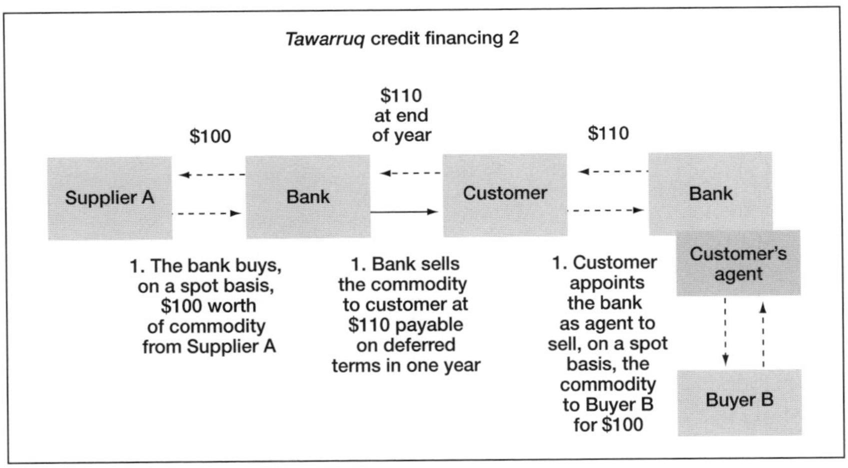

Under this mode of *tawarruq*, the customer (*mutawarriq*) appoints the bank (*muwarriq*) as its agent to sell the commodity to a third party (ie, Buyer B); this is usually due to the *mutawarriq*'s lack of experience or expertise to sell down the commodity. As discussed above, given that agency arrangement is not allowed by the *tawarruq* opponents, this mode of *tawarruq* was also banned. As analysed above, it is intriguing that this form of agency has been prohibited only in *tawarruq* transactions, and not in *murabaha* and other contemporary contracts.

Like the *tawarruq* liquidity facility 3, this form of *tawarruq* bears close resemblance to *inah* and should be considered as not permissible under *Sharia*.

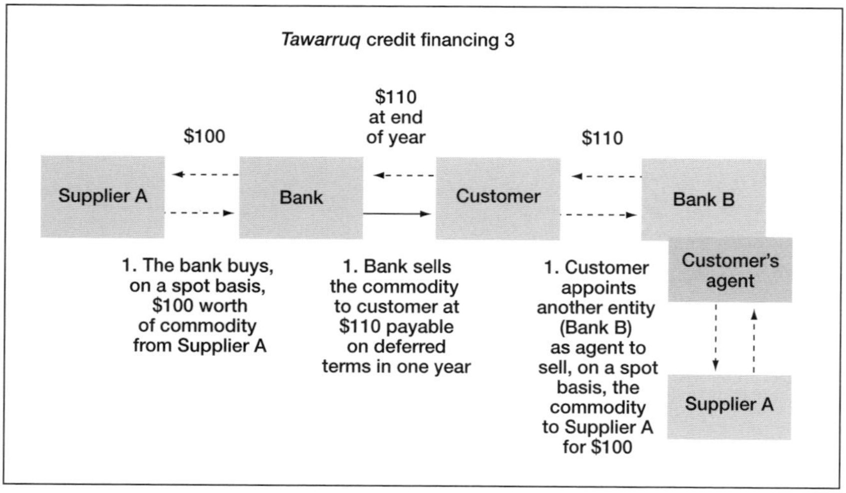

4. Analysis of rationale for banning *tawarruq*

The above discussion clearly evinces the following:

- From a *fiqh* perspective, the *tawarruq* opponents have applied a different standard to *tawarruq* from that applied to other contemporary contracts;
- The *tawarruq* opponents have not allowed the *muwarriq* to buy the commodity after being approached by the *mutawarriq*, but clearly they have allowed similar practices for the sellers and lessors in contemporary *murabaha* and *ijara* contracts; and
- While the *tawarruq* opponents have not allowed the *muwarriq* to appoint the *mutawarriq* as agent to buy the commodity, evidently they have allowed similar practices in contemporary *murabaha* and *ijara* contracts.

The author strongly believes that the *tawarruq* ruling is a direct result of mounting disappointment among Islamic jurists regarding development – or rather, the lack of positive development – in the Islamic finance industry. The *tawarruq* ban appears to many as just the tip of the iceberg. By targeting *tawarruq*, the *tawarruq* opponents hope that the Islamic finance industry will receive a strong message that it must seriously transform itself from the prevailing 'conventional' platform to a truly Islamic platform. *Tawarruq* was unfortunately an easy target, given the outwardly superficial nature of the transaction. Unlike *murabaha* and *ijara* contracts, where the customers require the goods or assets to be financed, *tawarruq* customers require the commodity only as a means to raise cash and do not usually bother with whether the commodity is a hard commodity (eg, copper), a soft commodity (eg, cotton), a security (eg, shares) or even an intangible commodity (eg, airtime). The lack of material association with the underlying commodity makes *tawarruq* appear to be an artificial contract resulting in a *ribawi* transaction.

Hence, to understand the rationale for banning *tawarruq*, we first need to understand the concerns and frustrations of the *tawarruq* opponents regarding the Islamic finance industry as a whole.

Again, the true concerns of the *tawarruq* opponents can be gleaned from the following statement of the learned Sheikh Taqi Usmani:

More than thirty years have passed since the establishment of Islamic financial institutions, with an increase in its number, growth in shape and multiplicity of the number of those who transact with them during the time. The time has now come for the legal monitoring organizations of these institutions to emphasize on minimizing the procedures of shared profit and At-Tawarruq, and opting for more concentration on the preferred procedures of Ash-Sharkah and Al-Murabaha, as the origin of various procedures in the totality of their transactions should be under a permanent monitoring, so that the Islamic banks can move towards the purposes of Islamic legal legislation that can portray the Islamic economy with its bright integrated form, not to appear to the world as absolute partnerships for the way outs and tricks, because that will lead to bad reputation or notoriety for these institutions and the Islamic economy that they represent.[8]

The above statement, which is profoundly important, expresses the growing frustration with the contemporary approach of Islamic finance which conforms to the ways of conventional debt finance through "way-outs and tricks"[9] or legal stratagems. Such conformist approach will "lead to bad reputation or notoriety (disrepute) for these institutions and the Islamic economy that they represent". Only by minimising *tawarruq* and maximising *musharaka* and *mudaraba* transactions can the Islamic banks "move towards the purposes of Islamic legislation that can portray the Islamic economy with its bright integrated form".[10]

It is evident from this statement that the real focus of the *tawarruq* opponents is on the lack of positive development in the Islamic finance industry. Instead of deploying more *musharaka* and *mudaraba*ha contracts in commercial transactions,

---

8 *Supra* note 3, at 18. Interestingly, the learned Sheikh Taqi Usmani also shared a similar perspective in "*Sukuk* and their Contemporary Applications" (www.failaka.com/downloads/Usmani_Sukuk Applications.pdf), which subsequently gave birth to a ruling by the *Sharia* Committee of the Accounting and Auditing Organisation for Islamic Financial Institutions that banned contemporary *sukuk al-mudaraba* and *sukuk al-musharaka*. Explaining the irregularities and the need to ban contemporary *sukuk al-mudaraba* and *sukuk al-musharaka*, the learned jurist stated the following (at 14): "Actually, the number of Islamic banks and financial institutions today is not to be overlooked, and thank God! The numbers increase day after day; and the growth of Islamic banks in many countries is greater than that of conventional banks. It is now incumbent upon these Islamic banks and financial institutions to cooperate among themselves for the purpose of developing authentic products that are far removed from empty stratagems, free from all association with riba, and that aim to serve the higher purposes of Islamic law in the spheres of economics, development, and social justice. None of this will come about without the guidance and encouragement of *Sharia* supervisory boards. If these boards continue with their present policies, however, Islamic banks will stumble on the road, and there is a danger, God forbid, that this virtuous movement will fail."

9 Which in this context refer to *makharij* and *hiyal*.

10 In "*Sukuk* and their Contemporary Applications" (see *supra* note 8 at 7-8) the learned jurist emphatically stated: "From the perspective of the higher purposes of Islamic economics, such [irregularities] in today's *Sukuk* actually defeat the purpose of an Islamic economic system in which wealth is equitably distributed among investors. *Sukuk* that are based on such [irregularities] distribute profits to investors on the basis of prevalent interest rates, and not on the basis of actual returns from an enterprise... If *Sharia* supervisory boards have tolerated such irregularities (mafasid) when *Sukuk* began to be issued, and at a time when Islamic financial institutions were few in number, the time has now come to revisit the matter... and to rid *Sukuk* from now on from such blemishes. Either *Sukuk* should be free of all such [irregularities] or these should be based on the enterprise's expected profits. These should certainly not be based on prevalent interest rates. This will then become a truly distinguishing characteristic of Islamic financial institutions, and one that sets them apart from their conventional, interest-based counterparts."

the Islamic finance industry is relying predominantly on debt contracts based on "way-outs and tricks". The learned Sheikh Taqi Usmani also advocated that: "if the seller knows that the buyer of *at-tawarruq* (*al-mutawarriq*) is in need of cash liquidity for his commercial purposes, where his aim is to achieve the means of financing, then the best thing for the buyer is for him to engage in the contract of *ash-sharkah* (partnership) or *al-mudarabah* (profit sharing) with him, because both are the two ways preferred for financing and capitalization."[11]

The prominent scholar also emphasised that: "The ideal way for commercial financings in the *Sharia* is financing on the basis of *ash-sharkah* (partnership) and *al-mudarabah* (profit sharing), because it is the one that incorporates fair distribution of wealth among the people, guides the excess of money from the rich to balance with the generality of the people. So, the expansion in the procedures of shared profit, *at-tawarruq* and the like, especially when the evaluation of those procedures are on the basis of the interest indication narrowing the domain of the partnership and *mudarabah* operations and encouraging the usurious mentality, which aims at profit seeking without bearing any risk where there will be no basic change in the current prevalent capitalistic method."[12]

In discussing the permissibility of *tawarruq* contracts in the past, the scholar stated as follows:

> *Verily, the jurisprudential assemblies, seminars and the organizations of legal monitoring for the Islamic financial institutions have all passed legal personal opinion (fatwa) in favor of the permissibility of the shared profit for one who commands purchasing and at-tawarruq, and so on and so forth in the legal ways out in terms of the situations surrounding the Islamic banks at their inception. It started working in the market crowded with complete usurious procedures, as it is very difficult that its activities should be sincere in financing on the basis of partnership and al-mudarabah, to the extent that it would resort to this type of procedures, in order to be able to adopt its fundamental steps to run away from clear usury and enable the general population of Muslims to benefit from the monetary channels that are included in clear prohibition.*[13]

Therefore, the *tawarruq* was approved at the beginning, when Islamic banking was in its embryonic stage, on the basis of necessity given the surrounding circumstances where Islamic banks were competing in a "market crowded with

11 *Supra* note 3, at 15.

12 *Id* at 18.

13 *Id* at 18. Again, the learned jurist expounded a similar line of thought in his "*Sukuk* and their Contemporary Applications", see *supra* note 8 at 13:

> *Undoubtedly, Sharia supervisory boards, academic councils, and legal seminars have given permission to Islamic banks to carry out certain operations that more closely resemble stratagems than actual transactions. Such permission, however, was granted in order to facilitate, under difficult circumstances, the figurative turning of the wheels for those institutions when they were few in number [and short of capital and human resources]. It was expected that Islamic banks would progress in time to genuine operations based on the objectives of an Islamic economic system and that they would distance themselves, even step by step, from what resembled interest-based enterprises. What is happening at the present time, however, is the opposite. Islamic financial institutions have now begun competing to present themselves with all of the same characteristics of the conventional, interest-based marketplace, and to offer new products that march backwards towards interest-based enterprises rather than away from these. Oftentimes these products are rushed to market using ploys that sound minds reject and bring laughter to enemies.*

complete usurious procedures" and where *mudaraba* and *musharaka* practices were difficult to implement. However, after 30 years "it was not in the calculation of the jurists who ruled to permit these procedures that these institutions would sit contentedly satisfied with these way outs for an unlimited time, adopting it as the targeted goal for the establishment of Islamic banks and the basic activity, which centers around their dealings forever".[14]

4.1 *Tawarruq* as *makhraj*

From the writings of the learned jurist and other Islamic scholars, it appears that the *tawarruq* opponents acquiesced to the use of stratagems such as *makharij* to permit organised *tawarruq* during the initial stage of the Islamic finance industry in order to facilitate the industry's growth. Certain allowances were made at the inception of the Islamic finance industry to kickstart its development; however, this did not mean that the leeway provided dispensed with the requirements of the higher objectives of *Sharia* ('*maqasid al Sharia*'). The noble objectives of *Sharia* are critical requirements which must be nurtured and applied gradually due to the overwhelming reach and influence of the prevailing interest-bearing systems. However, these allowances should be ended when the Islamic finance industry has reached a mature stage. The *tawarruq* opponents seem to believe that the industry has now reached that stage. Based on this belief, they ruled that the higher objectives of *Sharia* should now be the overriding consideration in Islamic financial products and consequently organised *tawarruq* should not be permitted.

Based on the learned jurist's line of reasoning, contemporary *murabaha lil-amir bil shira*, *ijara muntahia bittamleek* and other contemporary contracts would also be categorised as stratagems because all these products also closely resemble the risk-reward profile of a conventional loan, and neither conform to nor promote the profit-and-loss sharing ideals of *Sharia*. Does this mean that all these contemporary contracts will suffer the same fate as the organised *tawarruq*?

The author would like to differ from the views taken by the *tawarruq* opponents. The author strongly disagrees with the fundamental assumption made by the *tawarruq* opponents, based purely on the number of Islamic banks operating today, that the Islamic finance industry has now reached a stage of maturity that could invoke the full force of the higher objectives of *Sharia*. The author appeals to the learned jurists not to consider the number or even growth rate of Islamic banks in the world, but rather to compare the current market share of Islamic banking versus conventional banking in the Muslim world. Numbers and growth figures are often misleading, particularly when the base level of the Islamic finance industry is very low. On the other hand, market share offers a true indication of where the industry is today.

4.2 Why size matters

The development of Islamic banking in Malaysia provides a clear illustration of the true state of maturity of the industry. Islamic banking has been actively promoted by

14 *Id* at 18.

the Malaysian government since the 1980s and, after more than two decades, the size of the Islamic banking market is merely 13% of the total banking market size. The Islamic banking market aims to hold 20% of the total banking market share in 2010. In the same period, the number of dedicated Islamic banks has increased from one bank (from 1983 to 1993) to 17 full-service Islamic banks (from 1993 to 2009). The number of banks has increased rapidly, but the market share has grown only marginally. With a 13% market share, it is hardly surprising that Islamic banks are forced to play second fiddle to conventional banks. Islamic banks currently have no power, among other things, to:

- dictate the pricing benchmark in the market;
- influence the shift in consumer behaviour in terms of pricing and risk appetite for profit and loss-sharing products;
- pressurise the regulators to make meaningful changes to the legal, regulatory and other infrastructure, which has been shaped towards promoting a debt-based financial system; and
- offer truly indigenous Islamic products such as the classical *mudaraba* or *musharaka*, due to the well-entrenched conventional financial system.

All of these hurdles are ultimately forcing the Islamic banks to modify their Islamic products to match the pricing and risk-reward profiles of the dominant conventional market products.

A similar scenario is found in Bahrain, which is the hub of Islamic finance in the Middle East and the home to institutional and regulatory bodies including the Accounting and Auditing Organisation for Islamic Financial Institutions, the International Islamic Finance Market and the Islamic Rating Agency and the Liquidity Management Centre. After almost three decades, the market share of Islamic banking assets is just 10% of all banking assets. Even in Pakistan, the market share of Islamic banks is less than 10% of the total banking market. In Indonesia, the largest Muslim country in the world by population, the Islamic finance industry has barely 2% of the market share.

How can the learned jurists reasonably expect the Islamic banks in these countries with such low penetration to change radically the mindset and behaviour of the regulators and consumers? How can they be expected to revolutionise the market by replacing the debt-based system with a new system based on profit-and-loss sharing? Such a radical shift, as advocated by the respected jurists, would render Islamic financial products less attractive compared to conventional products (mainly due to the higher pricing of the profit-and-loss sharing products) and may eventually even erode the current paltry market share of the Islamic finance industry.

The reality in these markets is that customers are attracted to Islamic financial products due to pricing parity with conventional products, in addition to *Sharia* compliance. Without pricing parity with conventional products, the industry faces a grave danger that many existing Islamic finance consumers would shift back to conventional products. It is undoubtedly clear that the foundations of the Islamic finance industry in these countries are still weak and need much more support, particularly from a competitive pricing perspective. The sad reality is that the Islamic finance industry must first focus on increasing its market share – even at the expense of the ideal platform based on the profit-and-loss sharing system – if it wants to survive in the contemporary world.

5. Is *tawarruq* stunting the growth of other products?

A key criticism levelled at *tawarruq* is that the spread of *tawarruq* has curtailed the growth of other products, such as *ijara* or *musharaka*, in some markets. However, a deeper analysis of the situation reveals that the *tawarruq* trades grew mainly because the other alternatives were simply not feasible. In many Muslim countries, for example, the property laws are not as well developed, and in many instances the financiers end up taking huge risks when dealing with properties. For example, the contract of *ijara* requires the financiers to own the properties, which creates a lot of legal hurdles. Hence, in some markets the financiers and customers will end up carrying out a *tawarruq* trade to facilitate a home financing. In some markets the law allows a conventional bank to give a home loan and to take a mortgage over the native land, such as Arab land or Malay reserve land. However, an Islamic bank must own the land in order to offer an *ijara* facility and local laws do not allow such ownership of native land unless all shareholders of the Islamic bank are natives. Most Islamic banks, however, are publicly listed and have non-native shareholders. Hence, they are barred from such ownership and prevented from offering *ijara* or *musharaka* solutions. The critics would recommend that the law be changed. But these things take time, so what should Islamic banks do in the interim? Should they recommend that customers opt for a conventional loan or offer them a *tawarruq* solution? Some critics have in fact recommended that a conventional loan is preferable. However, the Islamic finance industry has taken a stand to offer the *tawarruq* solution and most customers have also chosen the *tawarruq* option.

In another instance, a corporate won a licence to run a mobile phone business and needed a major financing within a short period. The shareholders of the corporate wanted only an Islamic facility. The financiers offered a simple *murabaha* solution: the financiers would buy the licence from the regulator and then sell it immediately to the corporate at cost plus profit payable on deferred terms. The regulator rejected this proposal, stating that the law provided for the sale of the licence only to the corporate and not to the financiers. The financiers then offered an alternative structure whereby the corporate would act as an agent of the financiers to buy the licence directly from the regulator and the financiers (as principal) would immediately sell the licence to the customer on issuance on a *murabaha* basis. Again, this option was rejected, for the same reason. A third alternative was proposed whereby the corporate would set up a special purpose company (SPC) and would hold the shares of the SPC as an undisclosed agent of the financiers. The SPC would then buy the licence and the financiers (as principal) would sell the shares in the SPC to the corporate on a *murabaha* basis. Again, this option was rejected. The financiers then offered a *tawarruq* facility and it was approved. What more can financiers do other than suggesting a conventional loan (instead of *tawarruq*)? Importantly, this incident happened in Saudi Arabia. Critics must be conscious of the challenges and hurdles faced by the Islamic finance industry before offering their sweeping remarks.

The laws do need to be changed and the industry is working towards that, but these things do not happen overnight. Until then, the *tawarruq* option is often the only viable solution and this situation is likely to continue for some time.[15]

6. The way forward

One of the main factors that contribute to *tawarruq* abuses is the currently limited role played by the *Sharia* committee of Islamic financiers. The *Sharia* committee's role often ends with the approval of the *tawarruq* structure and documentation and the periodic review of the operational aspects of the *tawarruq* contracts. The committee plays hardly any role in defining the scope of marketing and credit offering, or customer suitability or use of proceeds standards. Financiers have been given a free hand to define all of these and to practise as they deem fit. These practices must stop immediately. The *Sharia* supervisors must play an active role in ensuring, for example, that financiers educate customers on the true cost of financing and avoid aggressive marketing strategies that entice customers into debt. They must also ensure that financiers educate customers on the potential downside of debt and highlight that *Sharia* tolerates debt only as a last resort and when there is a genuine need. The opponents and proponents of *tawarruq* should focus their energy on educating the financiers on the terms of responsible marketing and scope of credit offering, and customer suitability or use of proceeds standards, and provide measures to ensure their full compliance.

As discussed above, whether classical *tawarruq* or organised *tawarruq* comply with *Sharia* depends greatly on the end use. If used responsibly for a genuine need, both classical and organised *tawarruq* should be permissible under *Sharia*. If used irresponsibly or to satisfy a profligate desire, *tawarruq* should be prohibited regardless of whether it is classical or organised. If we fully understand and accept this distinction, there should probably be no more *tawarruq* controversy.

This chapter represents solely the views of the author and does not necessarily reflect the views of HSBC Amanah Malaysia. An extended version of this chapter was initially published as Research Paper 2 by the International Shari'ah Research Academy for Islamic Finance.

15 Some may wonder why the Islamic finance industry cannot offer *mudaraba* or *musharaka* solutions to the customers. Although *mudaraba* or *musharaka* solutions would work from a structural perspective, such financing is not attractive to customers that can command competitively priced debt financing in the market.

Equity-linked *sukuk*

Imran Mufti
Hogan Lovells (Middle East) LLP

1. Introduction

Demand for Islamic finance structured products and transactions has experienced unprecedented growth over the past decade. This demand began to show signs of slowing down only when the global money markets were hindered by the effects of the worldwide recession in the latter part of the decade. Unsurprisingly, the initial period of demand came hand in hand with significant innovation and development in the complexity and sophistication of *sukuk* structures. This development was perhaps most pronounced with the introduction of the equity-linked *sukuk*.

Some of the largest and best-publicised *sukuk* issuances to date, including the $3.5 billion issue for Ports Customs & Free Zone Corporation (PCFC) and the $3.52 billion issue for Nakheel, both issued in 2006, have incorporated equity-linked features. The structures of these two *sukuk* issues, in particular, are analysed below. These landmark *sukuk* issues also attracted a significant amount of interest from western financial institutions, no doubt because of the way in which the structures could accommodate something more exotic than the equivalent of a straight conventional debt instrument.

However, since the onset of the worldwide recession, there have been relatively few *sukuk* issues, and consequently there has also been a relative reduction in terms of both volume and innovation in the sector during that period. The development of *sukuk* has arguably also been hindered by a February 2008 ruling of the Accounting and Auditing Organisation for Islamic Financial Institutions (AAOIFI) which ostensibly restricted the way in which *sukuk* could be structured in the future, primarily addressing fundamental concerns around *musharaka* and *mudarabah sukuk* – two principal structures which had commonly been used for convertible *sukuk* issues. However, the effects of the AAOIFI ruling should not be overstated – ultimately, economics have been the prime substantive reason for the relative lack of activity in the *sukuk* market, caused by the credit crunch and exacerbated by the fact that the Gulf Cooperation Council (GCC) state economies are in a different cycle from the US economy, against whose currency the GCC local currencies are predominantly pegged.

Following the AAOIFI ruling, and in conjunction with the beginnings of a gradual upturn in the global money markets, financial advisers have been working to develop methods in order to circumvent these restrictions. As evidenced by the recent *sukuk* issue by Saudi Hollandi Bank, innovation appears to be re-occurring, with a shift from a hybrid instrument to a method for capital raising which, some may argue, is more akin to the true spirit of *sukuk*.

This chapter analyses the structure of convertible *sukuk* prior to the AAOIFI ruling and the structure utilised by Saudi Hollandi Bank, which will no doubt reinvigorate issuers' appetites to issue *sukuk* with more of an equity-linked flavour where such financing is suitable.

2. Overview

To understand the function and purpose of the equity-linked *sukuk* properly, one must first appreciate the nature of convertible bonds, whose function equity-linked *sukuk* are designed to replicate. A convertible bond is a bond that can be converted at the option of the holder into shares of the issuer at a pre-agreed price. From the issuer's perspective, convertible bonds offer the prospect of obtaining debt finance at a lower interest rate than would otherwise be possible, as well as the prospect of the debt not having to be repaid, but instead being converted into the issuer's shares at a premium to the market value of the shares at the time of issuance of the bonds. Convertible bonds also improve the issuer's balance sheet and gearing if the debt is ultimately converted to equity. In addition, convertible bonds rank above equity in the order of priority for the distribution of the issuer's assets if it becomes insolvent. From an investor's perspective, a convertible bond typically has a low yield, but offers the investor the prospect of participating in any significant increase in the issuer's share price, with the protection that if the share price does not perform as anticipated, the investor's principal is safeguarded by the ability to redeem the bonds instead of converting.

The PCFC *sukuk*, which adopted a *musharaka* structure, heralded the advent of the 'true' convertible *sukuk*. It featured *sukuk* convertibility and a lookback for the *sukuk* holders, which gave them the opportunity to participate in a qualifying public offering (QPO) up to 12 months after the scheduled maturity date of the *sukuk* should no QPO occur within two years of the issue date.

Historically, *sukuk* transactions relied on the tried and tested *ijara* – an easily understood structure with almost universal *Sharia* acceptance. However, one of the inherent restrictions with the *ijara* structure is its lack of redemption flexibility. This inflexibility led to the development of structures, such as *musharaka* and *mudarabah sukuk*, which permitted the kind of redemption scenarios required for an equity-linked instrument.

Case studies in respect of each of the *ijara*, *musharaka* and *mudarabah* structures are provided below, illustrating how the equity-linked *sukuk* market has developed.

3. *Sukuk al-ijara*

The predominant structure utilised in *sukuk* in general is that of the *al-ijara*. Its common use is explained and justified by the need to present investors with familiar structures: a sale and leaseback structure is easily understood even by those less well versed in Islamic financing. There is an appreciation that even the most attractive of *sukuk* that are investment grade, or are perceived as being akin to that, can receive negative uptakes from investors due to overly complex structuring. While there is no such thing as a 'cookie-cutter' *sukuk*, repeat structures epitomise a market seeking to

Nakheel sukuk

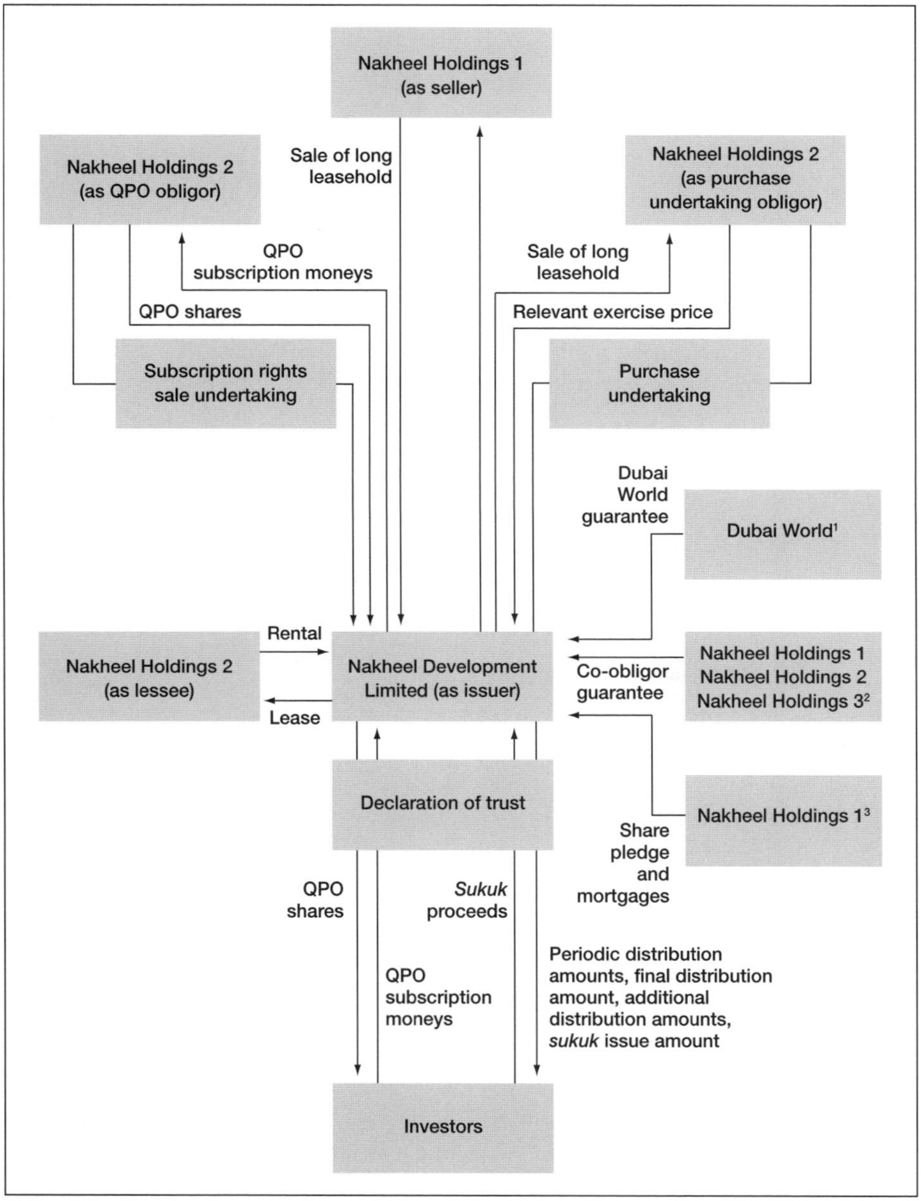

1 The Dubai World guarantee guarantees all of the co-obligors' payment obligations under the transaction documents.

2 The co-obligor guarantee guarantees the obligations of each co-obligor under the transaction documents.

3 Mortgages granted by Nakheel Holdings 1 over the property and share pledge granted by Nakheel Holdings 1 over shares to secure the payment obligations of the co-obligors under the transaction documents.

create benchmark structures and yield curves. Standardisation is a good thing because a deal which has return on assets as its core, as is the case with *sukuk*, must be highly structured.

3.1 Nakheel *sukuk*

The Nakheel development *sukuk* received much press attention following the recent financial troubles experienced by the Dubai government. Indeed, it was the announcement of the Dubai Ministry of Finance indicating that the issuer would be unable to redeem the certificates that played a significant part in the pandemic.

The Nakheel *sukuk* is notable as it utilises an *al-ijara* structure where the terms and conditions of the *sukuk* provide *sukuk* holders with the option to redeem all or part of their *sukuk* in exchange for shares in certain eligible Nakheel subsidiaries and affiliates which make primary or secondary equity offerings. The *sukuk* received *Sharia* approval despite the lack of certainty regarding which entity a certificate holder could subscribe for shares in. Notably, as is the case with most convertible bonds, the amount that certificate holders could subscribe amounted to a maximum of 25% of the certificates issued ($880 million).

Key terms of the *sukuk*

Structure	*Sukuk al-ijara* in registered global form
Issue amount	$3.52 billion
Redemption	36 months on maturity or earlier (at the option of the *sukuk* holders) either in cash or shares (at the option of the issuer)
Profit rate	6.345% – commencing on June 14 2007, the issuer will pay 'periodic distribution amounts' (as defined herein) to each certificate holder calculated as the product of 50% of the QPO yield and the principal amount of the certificates on a 30/360 basis

3.2 Limitations of *al-ijara*

Despite the advantages of the *ijara* structure due to the presence of a tangible or certain asset which reflects – at least in principle (an obvious limitation in the Nakheel *sukuk* was the fact that the value of the assets had plummeted due to a crash in the Dubai real estate market) – an amount at least equal to the certificates in issue, using such a structure can give added headaches to those involved. Interposing asset ownership into any financing requires full due diligence for deal viability. The *Sharia* concern with an *ijara*-based structure is linked to the requirement that the sale of assets be for an asset of value, and also more generally to ensure that there is no disguised *riba* (a loose Arabic translation of the word 'interest') transaction.

Other *sukuk* structures, primarily *musharaka* and *mudarabah*, have been developed to overcome the disadvantages of the *sukuk al-ijara* structure – namely, that the *sukuk* issue amount cannot be justified because the value of the assets earmarked to be the subject of the sale and leaseback structure is insufficient to approximate to the issue amount, or the leased position of those assets does not permit *sukuk* structural flexibility (eg, periodic redemptions). Of course, redemption flexibility is vital for equity-linked *sukuk* offerings such as convertible and exchangeable *sukuk* offerings. The *sukuk* structure needs to accommodate the commercial deal where the *sukuk* may be redeemed in the same scenarios as a conventional convertible bond (eg, voluntary redemption, change of control, elective tax redemption, clean-up).

4. *Sukuk al-musharaka*

Sukuk al-ijara can be structured only if the issuer owns the asset which it leases to a third party in order to pay back the certificate holders' principal. If an issuer does not own sufficient assets or if their value is insufficient to justify the *sukuk* issue amount because the value of the assets is less than the target *sukuk* issue amount, or there is a need for the assets to be created for a sale and leaseback to occur, then, before the AAOIFI ruling, issuers would enter into *sukuk al-musharaka*.

AAOIFI Standard 17, 3/6 provides that: "These are certificates of equal value issued with the aim of using the mobilized funds for establishing a new project, developing an existing project or financing a business activity on the basis of any partnership contracts so that the certificate holders become the owners of the project or the assets of the activity as per their respective shares, with the *musharaka* certificates being managed on the basis of participation or *mudaraba* or an investment agency."

4.1 *Musharaka* structure

The first international *musharaka sukuk* structure was the 2005 $200 million Dubai Multi-Commodities Centre (DMCC) *sukuk*. A sale and leaseback was not viable as the land available for the *sukuk* was undeveloped and consequently did not have the value to justify the targeted issue amount. That *sukuk* received widespread acclaim for a number of reasons – it was

- the first international *sukuk* based on a *musharaka* structure;
- the first-rated *sukuk* coming out of Dubai; and
- the first *sukuk* to offer investors an option for settlement in commodities (here gold) rather than cash.

The DMCC *sukuk* is also distinguishable for the fact that its proceeds were to finance construction. The DMCC *sukuk*, with its unprecedented level of creativity, showed that it is possible to fund a construction using a *musharaka sukuk* structure, rather than the usual *istisna/ijara* or forward lease route, with the complexity that entails in terms of trying to generate acceptable periodic returns during construction. In fact, the DMCC *sukuk* was A rated by Standard & Poor's.

What happens when there is a huge acquisition, a buoyant initial public offering

Musharaka structure

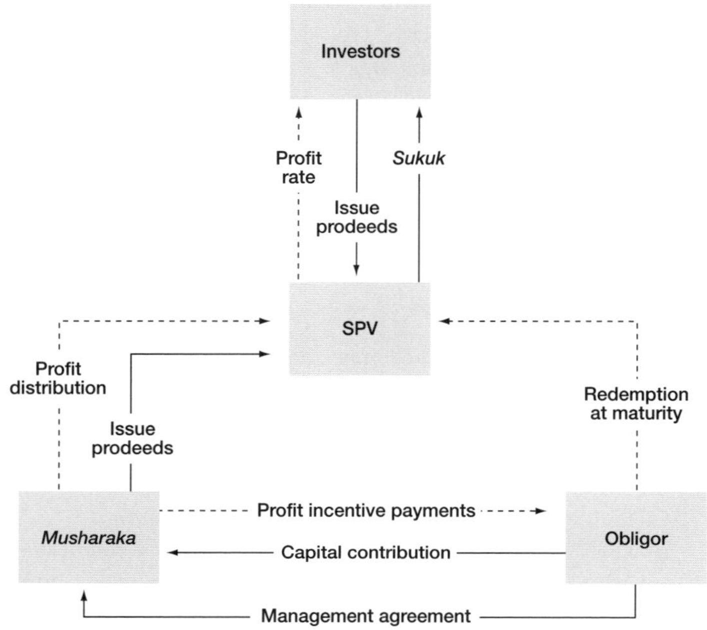

Structure highlights

- Issuer is a special purpose vehicle (SPV).
- SPV issues *sukuk*.
- SPV contributes the proceeds of the *sukuk* to the *musharaka*.
- Obligor makes a contribution in kind to the capital of the *musharaka* and manages the *musharaka*.
- Obligor executes a purchase undertaking in favour of the SPV.
- Profit generated from the *musharaka* is distributed between the SPV and the obligor in the agreed percentages, with profits in excess of the return to the *sukuk* holders paid to the obligor as manager of the *musharaka* as incentive fees for its management performance of the *musharaka*.
- SPV distributes profits to *sukuk* holders.
- *Sukuk* are redeemed at maturity or at early redemption following *sukuk* dissolution pursuant to the purchase undertaking.

(IPO) market (as is the case in the GCC) and the need for *sukuk* financing on an unprecedented scale? These considerations led to the structuring of the PCFC *sukuk*, which constituted the world's first convertible *sukuk*.

4.2 PCFC *sukuk*

(a) Redemption 1

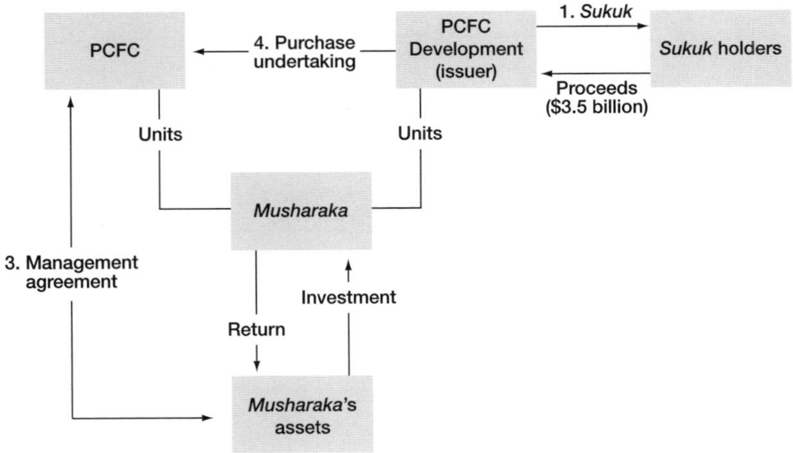

1 Issuer is PCFC Development.
2 PCFC Development invests the proceeds of the *sukuk* into a *musharaka* formed between PCFC Development and PCFC.
3 PCFC manages the *musharaka* pursuant to the terms of a management agreement.
4 PCFC executes a purchase undertaking in favour of PCFC Development, under which PCFC commits to purchase the issuer's units in the *musharaka* at the relevant exercise price on the relevant redemption date.

(b) Redemption in case of no public offering

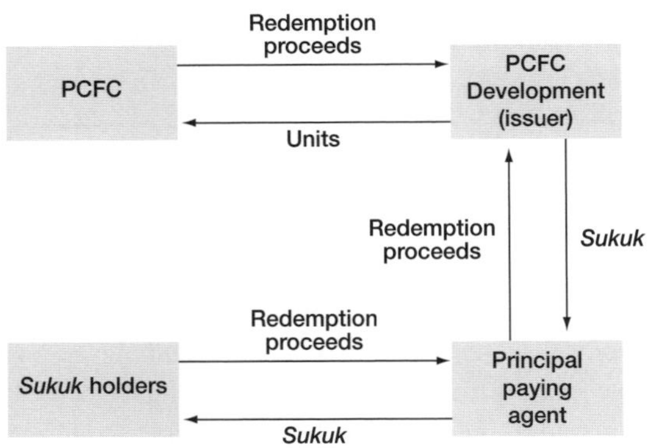

Sukuk will be redeemed in cash with higher yield.

(c) Redemption in case of a public offering

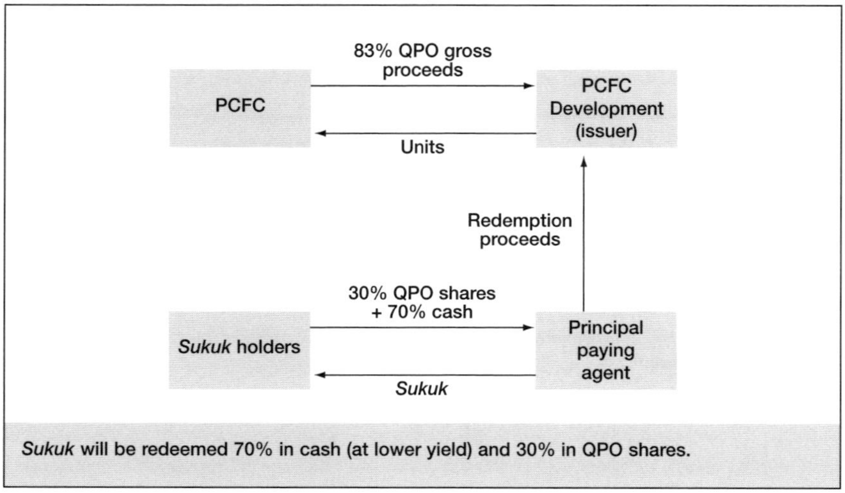

Key terms of the *sukuk*

Structure	*Sukuk al-musharaka* in registered global form
Issue amount	$3.5 billion
Redemption	24 months to final maturity (January 23 2008) (partial) mandatory redemption upon a QPO event. Additional 12-month lookback option on the amount redeemed in cash at maturity
QPO yield	7.125%
Maturity yield (if no QPO)	10.125%
Redemption in shares	On a QPO redemption, 30% redemption through QPO shares

The PCFC *sukuk* can be considered groundbreaking for a number of reasons. It was not only one of the world's largest *sukuk* closed to date, but also the first convertible *sukuk*. Although most of the headlines focused on the issue amount of $3.5 billion and the fact that the *sukuk* was linked to DP World's acquisition of P&O, the *sukuk* also incorporated a number of innovations which perhaps received less attention than they deserved.

Its main innovative features were the convertibility of the *sukuk* and the 'lookback' for the *sukuk* holders. This gave the *sukuk* holders the opportunity to participate in a QPO up to 12 months after the *sukuk* was redeemed, should no QPO occur within the two-year tenor of the *sukuk*. The lookback option gave rise to complicated, but surmounted, issues resulting from the need to identify *sukuk* holders so that they would repay their higher-yield return.

In October 2007 DP World announced its IPO, which was the largest ever in the Middle East and allowed the company to raise $3.2 billion through the issuance of 3.2 billion shares to investors. Exercise of the lookback option resulted in 25% of these shares being allocated to PCFC *sukuk* holders. As a result of the IPO, the government's indirect ownership in DP World was reduced to 80%, with the remaining 20% of the shares held by public shareholders and listed on the DIFX (which subsequently changed its name to Nasdaq Dubai).

5. *Sukuk al-mudarabah*

The *mudarabah* structure is another method to structure *sukuk* where an issuer has insufficient assets to adopt an *ijara* structure.

A *mudarabah* is a partnership in profit (akin to a non-discretionary investment management arrangement) between a capital provider and a person that applies its skill and expertise in investing that capital – put differently, one partner, the *rab-ul-maal* (or investor), contributes money and the other, the *mudarib* (or investment trustee), invests its time and skill with a view to generating profit on that capital.

The Dana Gas *sukuk*, which closed in in mid-2007, was one of a number of *sukuk* issues around that time to adopt a *mudarabah* structure, again because of the redemption flexibility that was afforded to it.

5.1 *Dana Gas* sukuk

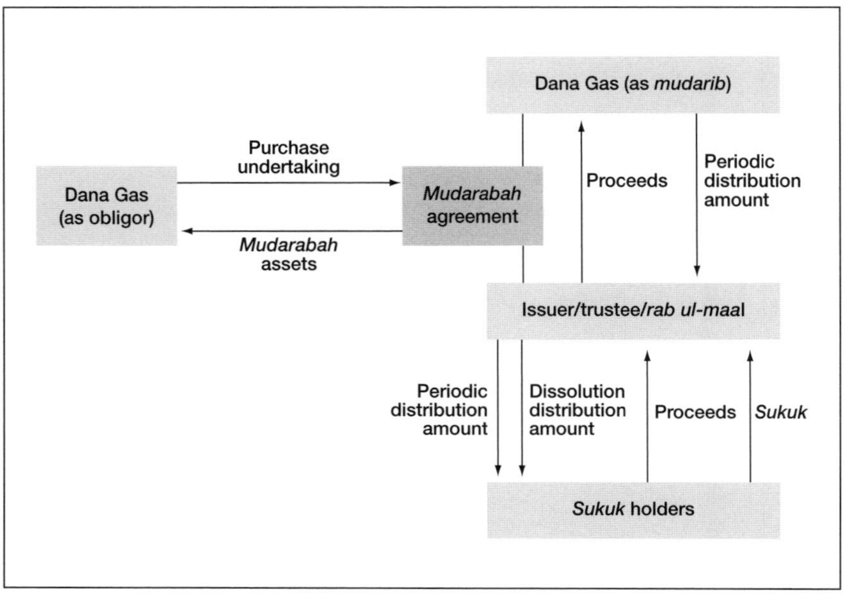

Key terms of the *sukuk*

Structure	*Sukuk al-mudarabah* in registered global form
Issue amount	$1 billion
Redemption	October 2012, on maturity or earlier (at the option of the *sukuk* holders) either in cash or shares (at the option of Dana Gas)
Yield	7.5%

Transaction structure

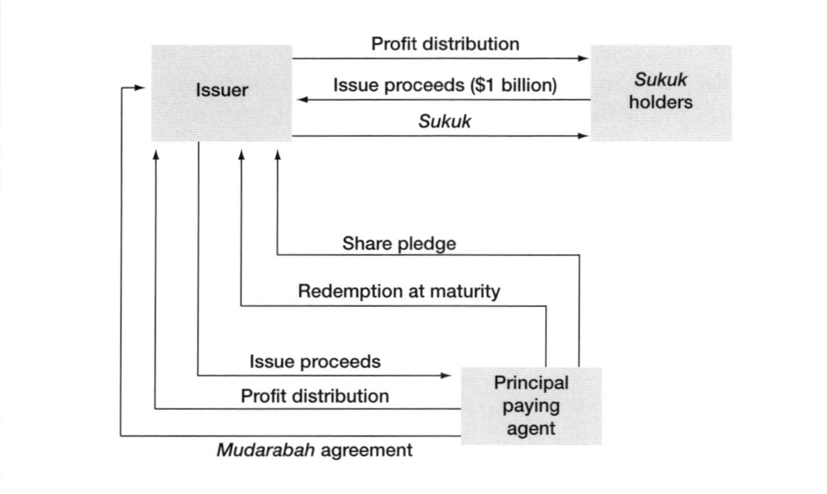

Structure highlights

- Issuer issues *sukuk.*
- Dana Gas is appointed as *mudarib* under the *mudaraba* agreement
- Profit generated from *mudaraba* is distributed to issuer (for *sukuk* holders) and *mudarib*.
- *Sukuk* redeemed either at the option of the *sukuk* holders at quarterly intervals or on scheduled maturity, in each case in the prescribed manner (ie, in cash and/or shares).

The Dana Gas *sukuk* was issued through an offshore SPV, with the proceeds of those *sukuk* being applied as capital of the *mudarabah*. The *mudarabah* agreement provided that those proceeds will be invested by Dana Gas PJSC (as *mudarib*) in its business activities in accordance with a pre-determined investment plan prepared by Dana Gas. Returns to the *sukuk* holders were generated through profit payments to the issuer and distributed by Dana Gas on quarterly periodic distribution dates.

The flexibility which the *mudarabah* structure offers made it a natural choice for issuers looking to convertible bond investors. It formed the basis for a number of convertible *sukuk*, including Aldar Properties. However, despite its obvious benefits for issuers seeking to issue convertible *sukuk*, the *mudarabah* structure has not been without its critics among the *Sharia* scholar fraternity. At first glance, the cash-flow characteristics of the *mudarabah* structure seem to mimic very closely the calculations, periodic payments and redemption mechanics of a conventional bond, with the obligor ultimately underwriting the return due to *sukuk* holders through the purchase undertaking. That concern fell under an international spotlight towards the end of 2007.

6. AAOIFI ruling

All entities issuing and advising in relation to Islamic finance products abide by the guidance and rules of the AAOIFI. Although the AAOIFI's rules are not legally binding, Islamic institutions commonly seek to offer Islamic finance products that abide by the AAOIFI's rules and guidance.

In February 2008 the AAOIFI issued a ruling relating to *sukuk* structures. This AAOIFI ruling restricts the ability of an issuer to repurchase its *mudaraba* and *musharaka sukuk*. The ruling specifically stated: "It is not permissible for the manager of *sukuk*, whether the manager acts as *mudarib* (investment manager) or *sharik* (partner) or *wakil* (agent) for investment, to undertake to offer loans to *sukuk* holders, when actual earnings fall short of expected earnings. It is permissible, however, to establish a reserve account for the purpose of covering such shortfalls to the extent possible, provided the same is mentioned in the prospectus."

Regarding the redemption amount, the ruling stated that: "It is not permissible for the *mudarib* (investment manager), *sharik* (partner) or *wakil* (agent) to undertake [now] to re-purchase the assets from *sukuk* holders or from one who holds them, for its nominal value, when the *sukuk* are extinguished, at the end of its maturity. It is, however, permissible to undertake the purchase on the basis of the net value of assets, its market value, fair value or a price to be agreed, at the time of their actual purchase."

Consequently, one of the major uncertainties for Islamic issuers and financial institutions over the last few years has been how a convertible *sukuk* can be structured without offending the AAOIFI ruling.

7. Saudi Hollandi Bank *sukuk*

In November 2009 and January 2010 Saudi Hollandi Bank issued Saudi riyal-denominated *sukuk* which represented a paradigm shift in the way in which *sukuk* have historically been structured. These *sukuk* represent the first *sukuk* issued since the AAOIFI ruling which attempt to attach a form of equity-linked product (a callable subordinated *sukuk*) without offending the AAOIFI ruling. Indeed, this innovative structure is also supported by the fact that the *sukuk* represents the first time in which a financial institution has raised finance in order to support its capital adequacy requirements in a *Sharia*-compliant manner.

Key terms of the *sukuk*

Structure	*Sukuk al-mudarabah* in registered global form
Issue amount	Sr775 million
Redemption	2014
Yield	Singapore Interbank Offered Rate (SIBOR) plus 1.9% (if the *sukuk* is not called in 2014, the expected profit payments are increased by a step-up margin for the final five years).

The *sukuk* was based on a *mudarabah* structure, was issued to finance the expansion of the bank's Islamic finance business and constitutes Tier II capital under the Basel Regulations.

The important aspect of the Saudi Hollandi Bank *sukuk* from the perspective of the AAOIFI ruling is how the periodic payments and redemption value are determined. Under normal circumstances (ie, outside a default or winding-up of the bank), the capital provided will be used in the Islamic banking business of Saudi Hollandi Bank and can be combined with the bank's assets. The net income constitutes the income of the bank's operations minus the direct costs of its operations, any allocated costs and the current year provisions of its operations. This income is divided according to a profit-sharing ratio between the bank (10%) and *sukuk* holders (90%).

If the net income exceeds the periodic distribution amount (the SIBOR+190 basis points/360 days), the periodic payment amount is made and the excess is placed in a reserve account. If there is a shortfall, the difference is paid from the reserve account. If there are insufficient funds in the reserve account, the issuer is still required to pay the distribution amount. At the redemption of the *sukuk*, if a positive amount remains in the reserve account, it will first be used to cover any shortfalls in the redemption amount, with any remaining amounts paid to Saudi Hollandi Bank as an incentive payment.

This is a significant difference from how *mudaraba sukuk* worked before the AAOIFI ruling, where the issuer would make an interest-free loan to cover any shortfalls in the periodic payments (the AAOIFI ruling specifically prevents issuers from doing this). There is also a difference in the redemption amount calculation. The redemption value at maturity in 2019 will be the aggregate face value of the *mudaraba sukuk* payable upon the redemption of the *mudaraba sukuk* by the issuer on the occurrence of a redeeming event, less any loss relating to the *mudaraba* assets not covered by the credit of the reserve. There are some restrictions on redemption under the call provisions that protect the *sukuk* holders relating to the value of the *mudaraba* assets. The bank can call the *sukuk* between 2014 and 2018, but only if the redemption amount is not below the face value of the *sukuk*.

However, things can become difficult for investors in case of default. Because the *sukuk* was issued as Tier II capital and is subordinated debt, the investors do not have primary recourse against the assets of the *mudaraba*.

The Saudi Hollandi Bank *sukuk* represents a new look for the *mudaraba sukuk*. There are changes that shift some of the risk that the *mudaraba* will not generate sufficient income to cover what are otherwise fixed payments and a reserve account is used to smooth payments over the term of the *sukuk*. One area of concern is that the *sukuk* creates greater risk for the investors without any corresponding potential return.

That caveat aside, the *mudaraba* structure used by Saudi Hollandi Bank is probably preferable from an 'authenticity' perspective to the 'old' *mudaraba* structure, which used a repurchase undertaking at par to redeem the *sukuk* regardless of how the assets backing the *sukuk* perform.

8. Conclusion

Following the AAOIFI ruling and the effects of the global recession on the capital markets worldwide, it is evident that a revolution in the structure of Islamic financial products will not happen immediately. Since the recession, markets have seen a general trend against exotic structures and products. Consequently, products such as the Saudi Hollandi *sukuk*, while innovative, will continue to copy existing conventional products to the best of their ability. However, investors demand diversity in the products that they invest in and conformity with *Sharia* principles. The Saudi Hollandi *sukuk* is a step in that direction, coupling the *Sharia* concept of risk sharing with a capital markets instrument that works commercially.

Project *sukuk*

Shibeer Ahmed
White & Case LLP

1. Introduction

The *sukuk* market has the potential to play a major role in the financing of infrastructure, power and energy projects. This chapter provides a brief overview of the history of Islamic project finance and provides details of possible *sukuk* structures which may be adopted to refinance existing and finance new projects.

The nature of Islamic finance makes it highly appropriate for use in the development of infrastructure, power, water and other capital-intensive projects. As in project finance generally, contractual certainty and clearly defined risk-sharing mechanisms are key to Islamic project finance. Asset-based Islamic finance structures, particularly those involving *istisna* and *ijara* arrangements, are ideal for use in project financings.

There is an existing track record of Islamic finance techniques being successfully employed in the power and petrochemical sectors. The $1.8 billion Hub River Power Project in Pakistan was the first major internationally financed project to include an Islamic finance component. The financing involved a $92 million *istisna* facility, which was used towards financing the turbines for the project.

The $2 billion Equate Petrochemical Project in Kuwait, which followed soon after the Hub River Power Project, included a $200 million Islamic project finance tranche. Unlike the *istisna* structure used in the Hub River Power Project, an *ijara* financing structure was used in the Equate Petrochemical Project to finance existing equipment which was incorporated into the petrochemical plant. The use of Islamic finance tranches in the context of multi-sourced project financings raised a number of intercreditor issues between the conventional and Islamic banks. These included the treatment of project assets in which the Islamic banks had an ownership interest by virtue of using an *ijara* financing structure, and the methods for calculating the Islamic banks' exposure and voting rights in the bank decision-making process.

From 1996 to 2006 the value of Islamic project finance tranches in major projects continued to grow, with one of the largest being the $847 million Islamic finance tranche raised by SABIC subsidiary Yanbu National Petrochemical Company for a greenfield petrochemical facility.

The first greenfield petrochemical project financed on a purely Islamic finance basis was the 2006 financing for the Al-Waha Petrochemical Company. This involved a combination of a *musharaka*, procurement and a forward lease (*ijara mawsufah fi al dimmah*) arrangement. The financing involved a co-purchase agreement between the investment agent (on behalf of the banks) and Al-Waha, under which Al-Waha assumed responsibility for construction of the plant. The banks agreed to fund a portion of the costs incurred by Al-Waha under the turnkey construction arrangement and took a proportionate share in the ownership of the project assets reflecting their investment in the project. The operating phase involves the banks leasing their ownership interest in the project assets to Al-Waha for a period of 11 years. The structure provides for the purchase by Al-Waha of portions of the project assets owned by the banks at semi-annual intervals during the operating phase pursuant to a purchase undertaking.

The increased demand by governments to involve private finance in the development of public infrastructure presents considerable opportunities for Islamic finance to be employed in capital-intensive projects developed using the public-private partnership model.

One of the first concession-based transport infrastructure projects to be financed using purely Islamic finance was the Doraleh Container Terminal Project, which achieved financial close in 2007. The project involves the development, design, construction, management, operation and maintenance of a new container terminal at Doraleh, Republic of Djibouti. This project demonstrates how far Islamic project finance has developed within a relatively short period of time. The financing has one of the longest tenors in the history of Islamic finance and was the first Islamic project financing to benefit from the World Bank Group's Multilateral Investment Guarantee Agency political risk guarantee.

The next phase in the development of Islamic project finance will involve the use of *sukuk* structures to finance greenfield projects and to refinance existing projects. The advantages of using project finance *sukuk* for project companies and sponsors will be better pricing and longer tenors than those currently available in the Islamic commercial bank market, and less oversight compared with the active management of projects by investment agents acting on behalf of Islamic commercial banks. The recent conventional project bond issues by Dolphin Energy and RasGas have shown that there is considerable market appetite for well-structured projects developed and operated by financially strong and technically experienced sponsors.

Project finance *sukuk* has an important role to play in resolving the liquidity and maturity mismatch issues faced by most Islamic banks. The lack of a mature debt capital market in the Gulf Cooperation Council region means that Islamic banks must rely heavily on relatively short-term customer deposits. This, together with the impact of the global credit crunch on the availability of inter-bank financing, makes it difficult for them to fund project finance facilities with long tenors. Being able to issue a well-structured and contractually robust *sukuk* will provide project sponsors with access to investors, such as pension funds, which need to match their long-term liabilities with long-term investments.

2. Refinancing existing projects

It is possible to structure a *sukuk* for the refinancing of a project in its operating phase, provided that the *sukuk* investors are satisfied with the economic and technical performance of the project and the level of support provided by creditworthy and technically capable sponsors.

The *sukuk al-ijara* structure, in particular, can be easily adapted for use in the refinancing of existing projects. The structure is commonly used and easily understood, even by those not familiar with Islamic finance. This is because an *ijara* transaction is similar to a conventional lease (with elements of both an operating lease and a finance lease), as it involves the transfer of an interest akin to leasehold in an asset by one person (the lessor) to another (the lessee) for payment of rental by the lessee.

The structure relies on the sale and purchase of the project assets. If the legal title to the project assets cannot be transferred – either because the project company itself does not have legal ownership of the project assets under the terms of a concession or other licence granted to it in relation to the project, or because it would not be cost effective (due to the cost of transfer of the legal title or any property registration tax payable in relation to the transfer of the legal title) – it will be necessary to structure the transaction in such a way that only the project company's limited interest in the project assets is sold and leased back. Whether the project company's interest in the project assets can be used in a *sukuk al-ijara* structure will depend on the legal and regulatory regime of the jurisdiction in which the project is located and the acceptability of the overall structure to the *Sharia* scholars responsible for approving the financing.

To avoid the need for changes to the project documents at the time of the refinancing, it is advisable to include provisions in the project documents (particularly in any build-operate-transfer contract, concession agreement or other licence agreement with the host government) at the time of the initial financing which allow for the transfer of an interest in the project assets for the purposes of a *Sharia*-compliant refinancing.

In jurisdictions that recognise a distinction between legal interests and beneficial interests, it may be possible for the structure to involve the sale and leaseback of only the beneficial interest in the project assets. Alternatively, where usufruct interests are recognised, the usufructuary can sell its interest in the project assets and lease it back. This would include, for example, a *musataha* interest under UAE law, which provides the beneficiary of the *musataha* interest with the right to build and retain ownership of the project assets for a fixed period of time, with the ownership of the underlying land remaining with the grantor of the *musataha* interest.

For the purposes of this chapter, it is assumed that an ownership interest in the project assets other than the legal or registered ownership will be sold and leased back.

The figure below shows the contractual structure which may be used in the refinancing of an operating project. The structure involves the proceeds of the *sukuk* issue being used by the issuer as consideration for the purchase of an interest in the project assets from the project company and the subsequent leasing of those assets back to the project company in return for rental payment by it to the issuer. The rental is paid by the project company from the project revenue. The revenue stream from the operation of the project is thus used to generate returns for *sukuk* investors. As with any conventional project finance structure, the strength of the *sukuk al-ijara* structure relies on the bankability of the underlying project documents and the

Refinancing project contractual structure

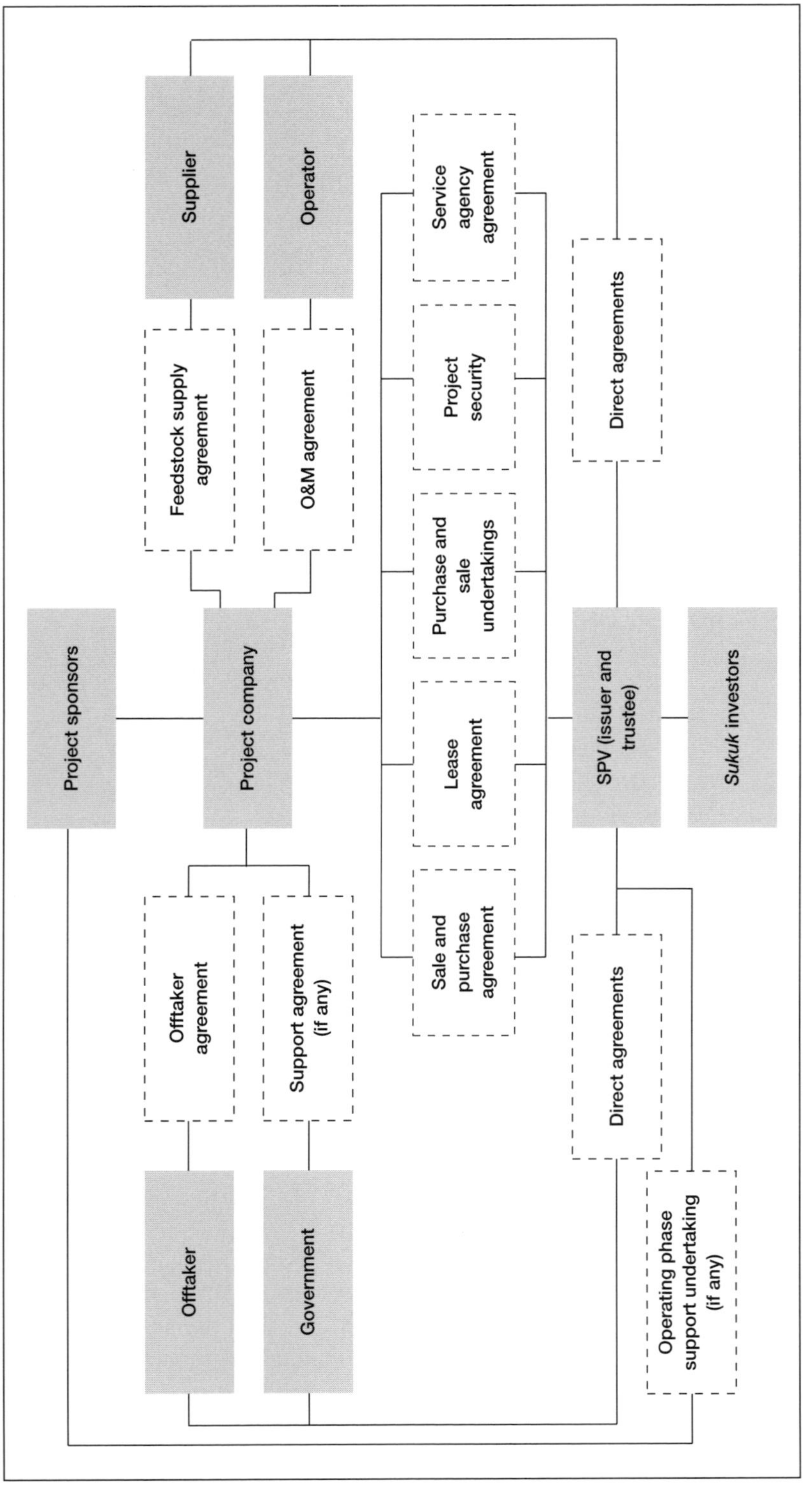

ability of the project company to comply with its financial and contractual covenants. The rental payment profile can be sculpted to fit the project's revenue profile. This is particularly important for projects with a seasonally variable revenue stream.

The rental payments by the project company (as lessee) at any time will be equal to the *sukuk* return payable at that time. This amount may be calculated by reference to a fixed rate or variable rate (eg, by using the London Interbank Offered Rate as a benchmark), depending on the currency of the *sukuk*.

The contractual structure involves the issuer issuing the *sukuk* certificates to the *sukuk* investors for payment by them of the issue price to the issuer. The *sukuk* certificates prove that:

- each *sukuk* investor has an undivided ownership interest in the project assets (or the relevant interest in the project assets) financed by the *sukuk* issue; and
- the *sukuk* holders have the right to receive the *sukuk* return and the *sukuk* maturity payment from the issuer.

The proceeds of the issue (and the interest in the project assets acquired using the proceeds) are held by the issuer (as trustee) on trust for the *sukuk* investors.

In addition to the *sukuk* offering, issue and listing documents, a *sukuk al-ijara* transaction involves the following main finance documents.

2.1 Sale and purchase agreement

The sale and purchase agreement is concluded between the project company (as seller) and the issuer (as purchaser). The sale and purchase agreement provides for the sale of an interest in the project assets by the project company and the purchase of that interest by the issuer in consideration for payment of the sale price to the project company.

In the context of a refinancing, the project company will use the funds to repay (or pre-pay) the existing project development financing.

2.2 Lease (*ijara*) agreement

Once the sale and purchase is completed, the issuer (as lessor) leases its interest in the project assets to the project company (as lessee) under the terms of a lease (*ijara*) agreement between the issuer (as lessor) and the project company (as lessee). The *ijara* agreement provides for the lease of the interest in the project assets acquired by the issuer under the sale and purchase agreement to the project company and gives the project company possession and use of the project assets so that the project can continue to operate without interruption. It also specifies the method for calculating the fixed and variable components of the rental. The issuer applies the rental that it receives to make payments of the *sukuk* return to the *sukuk* investors. In order to satisfy the certainty principle of Islamic finance, the rental must be determined at the time of execution of the *ijara* agreement for the term of the *ijara*. As this would make the structure impractical, it is possible to split the term of the *ijara* into shorter rental periods with different amounts of rental for each such period (as mentioned above, this would allow for sculpting of the rental payments to reflect the projected profile of the project revenue). If the overall *ijara* term is broken into rental periods, the amount of rental will need to be fixed at the start of each rental period because, from a *Sharia* perspective, each such period will be treated as a separate lease contract.

2.3 Service agency agreement

Although any liabilities arising from the use of the project assets must be met by the project company (as lessee), in contrast to a conventional lease, the lessor under an *ijara* contract is also required to assume certain responsibilities in relation to the leased assets. These include responsibility for major maintenance and structural repairs, insurance of the assets and payment of any taxes relating to the assets. Obviously, these are not the types of obligation which the issuer would be able to perform in the context of a complex project. In order to transfer these obligations back to the project company, the issuer (as lessor) and the project company (as servicing agent) enter into a service agency agreement, under which the project company takes on those responsibilities in consideration for payment of a service agency fee. To make the arrangement under the service agency agreement cost neutral for the issuer, the amount payable to the project company (as servicing agent) is netted against an increase in the supplemental rental (by an equivalent amount) under the *ijara* agreement.

If, as a result of a natural catastrophe or an accident, the project assets are destroyed or damaged to such an extent that they no longer have any economic use, this will constitute a termination of the *ijara* agreement. As a consequence, the purchase undertaking (see below) in respect of the project assets will also become ineffective. The issuer (as lessor) will have the right to receive the insurance proceeds under the policies taken out by the project company (as servicing agent). If the proceeds are less than the full replacement value of the assets, the project company (as servicing agent) will have failed to satisfy its strict liability and will be liable to indemnify the banks for any shortfall.

2.4 Purchase undertaking

In order to provide the issuer with a mechanism to accelerate the project company's payment obligations and take enforcement action following an event of default, and to trigger payment on the maturity of the *sukuk*, the project company (as obligor) grants a purchase undertaking in favour of the issuer. The purchase undertaking contains a put option in favour of the issuer allowing the issuer to sell its interest in the project assets to the project company following the occurrence of an event of default or on maturity of the *sukuk*, in return for which the project company is required to pay all outstanding amounts (through the purchase undertaking exercise price) so that the issuer can make the equivalent payment to the *sukuk* investors. Unlike the *musharaka* and *mudaraba* structures, the use of a purchase undertaking in an *ijara* structure is not controversial from a *Sharia* perspective.

2.5 Sale undertaking

The sale undertaking is granted by the issuer in favour of the project company (as obligor). The purchase undertaking contains a call option allowing the project company to buy the issuer's interest in the project assets in certain circumstances (including occurrence of a tax event), in return for which the project company is required to pay all outstanding amounts (through the sale undertaking exercise price) so that the issuer can make that payment to the *sukuk* investors.

The exercise price under the purchase undertaking and the sale undertaking will be equal to the principal amount of the *sukuk* certificates plus any accrued but unpaid *sukuk* return owing to the *sukuk* investors. The issuer will apply any exercise price received from the project company to pay the *sukuk* maturity payment to the *sukuk* investors.

2.6 Security documents

Security documents provide the issuer or a security agent (on behalf of the issuer and the *sukuk* investors) with comprehensive security over the project company's contractual rights and assets (to the extent not sold by it to the issuer as purchaser under the sale and purchase agreement) securing the project company's obligations under the finance documents.

2.7 Direct agreements

Direct agreements can be made between the issuer or a security agent (on behalf of the issuer and the *sukuk* investors) and each major project counterparty. The underlying major project contracts should provide the project company with the right to substitute another entity in place of the security agent (representing the original project funders) on a refinancing of the project.

In addition to the financing documents described above, the documentation package for the project will include a full suite of bankable project documents appropriate for the industry sector of the project. The project documents will need to be reviewed in order to ensure that they contain no provisions which may be deemed repugnant to *Sharia* by the particular scholar(s) who will be issuing the *Sharia* approval in respect of the financing structure.

The project may have the benefit of operating phase sponsor support (particularly for the early and start-up phase of the project), which is necessary in order to make the project bankable (this may be particularly important if the *sukuk* issue is to be rated by one or more of the rating agencies). The sponsor support undertaking may take the form of either a revenue shortfall guarantee in favour of the issuer (as lessor), or an undertaking by the sponsors to inject additional equity into the project company, in each case to ensure that the project company continues to meets its rental payment obligations and to comply with the financial covenants in accordance with the financial model for the project.

3. Financing greenfield projects

Although it is possible to structure the financing for the development of a greenfield project using a *sukuk* al-*musharaka* (particularly where the project company has some existing assets that it can contribute to the *musharaka*) or a *sukuk al-mudaraba*, the most appropriate structure for a project payment financing for a greenfield development is an *istisna* with an *ijara*.

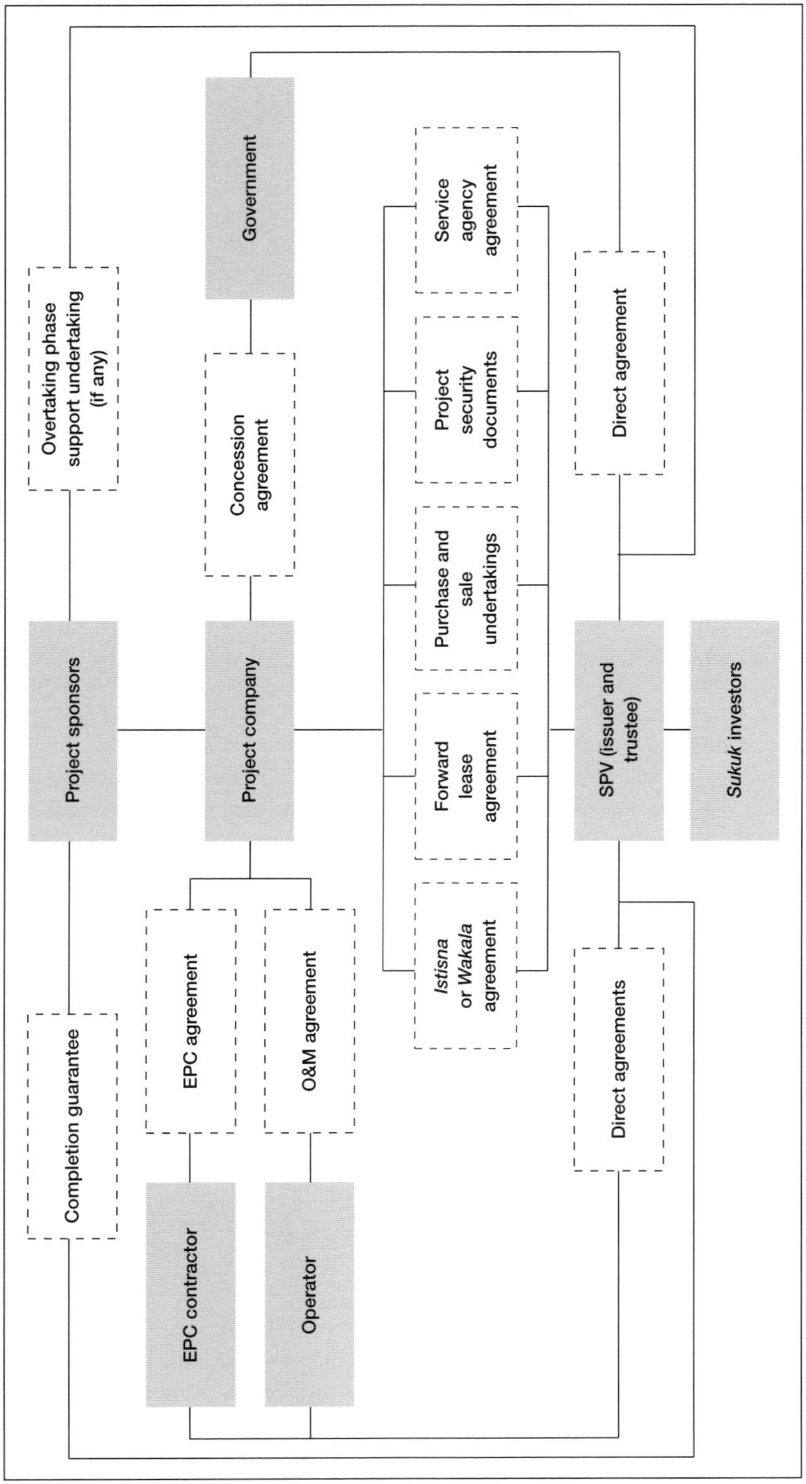

Greenfield project contractual structure

Istisna is one of two *Sharia*-compliant transactions in which an asset can be sold before it comes into existence; the other is *salam* (where a seller agrees to supply a specified asset at a fixed date in the future, with the price being paid in full upfront). In an *istisna* the price and specification of the project assets to be constructed must be agreed at the time of entering into the *istisna* agreement but, unlike *salam*, the price can be paid in instalments during the construction period. This allows for the payment of *sukuk* issue proceeds to the project company to be linked to satisfaction of construction milestones by the project company (as seller) under the *istisna* agreement. As with conventional project bonds for greenfield projects, the proceeds of the *sukuk* issue will need to be invested (in the case of *sukuk* proceeds) in liquid *Sharia*-compliant investments until they are paid to the project company in instalments linked to the satisfaction of agreed construction milestones.[1]

The *ijara* part of the structure is necessary for two reasons. First, it allows for payments to be made by the project company during the construction phase under an *ijara mawsufah fi al dimmah* (or forward lease), thereby allowing the *sukuk* investors to receive a return during that period. Second, it allows for the structure described above (in the section on refinancing existing projects) to be implemented for the operating phase of the project.

An important issue to bear in mind when structuring a project finance *sukuk* for a new project is that a *sukuk* cannot be traded unless, for instance, at least 50% of the proceeds of the *sukuk* issue have been invested in tangible assets. This will mean that a *sukuk* issued to finance the development of a greenfield project may not be tradable until a substantial part of the project has been developed. As with conventional project finance bond issues, the proceeds of the *sukuk* issue will need to be invested until applied to make stage payments on satisfaction of construction milestones. In order to limit the negative carry of holding the *sukuk* proceeds, they will need to be invested in *Sharia*-compliant investments.In addition to the *sukuk* offering, issue and listing documents, the combined *sukuk* structure will involve the following main finance documents.

3.1 *Istisna* and *wakala* agreements

The *istisna* agreement is made between the project company (as seller) and the issuer (as purchaser). Under the *istisna* agreement, the project company (as seller) undertakes to construct and deliver the project assets. In order to ensure that the structure is bankable, the project company will subcontract the works to an experienced engineering, procurement and construction (EPC) contractor under a fixed-price turnkey EPC contract. Even though it subcontracts the works to a third-party EPC contractor, for the purposes of the *istisna* the project company (as seller)

1 The proceeds of the *sukuk* issue will be provided by the *sukuk* investors at financial close, even if all the funds are not required until later in the construction programme. This will require the *sukuk* proceeds to be invested until the funds are required. In general, the return received on the invested *sukuk* proceeds will be lower than that paid to the *sukuk* investors, resulting in negative carry. Because a greenfield project will not generate cash flows until the project assets are completed, the negative carry phenomenon is likely to require the project to raise more money in a *sukuk*-financed project than in the equivalent bank-financed project to cover the payments to the *sukuk* investors during the construction period. In this respect, a *sukuk* financing is likely to be less efficient than a bank financing.

remains strictly liable to deliver the project assets to the issuer (as purchaser) in accordance with the terms of the *istisna* agreement. The *istisna* contract will, among other things, contain the detailed specifications of the project assets to be delivered by the project company (as seller) (these will usually reflect the detailed specification contained in the EPC contract). The sale and purchase of the project assets or an interest in the project assets takes place at the time of signing of the *istisna* agreement, with the project assets being delivered to the issuer (as purchaser) once the relevant project completion tests are satisfied. Although it is not necessary to fix the time of delivery under an *istisna*, a construction completion longstop is nevertheless included in project-financed *istisna* arrangements with liquidated damages payable for late delivery (this liability is usually passed on by the project company to the EPC contactor on a back-to-back basis).

As an alternative to the project company (as seller) and the issuer (as purchaser) entering into an *istisna* agreement, the parties may instead employ an agency (*wakala*) agreement. Under this arrangement the issuer appoints the project company as its agent to procure the construction and delivery of the project assets. In turn, the project company appoints an EPC contractor to undertake its works, but remains strictly liable to deliver the project assets to the issuer on time and to specification. The *wakala* agreement need not contain the detailed specifications of the project assets to be developed, but will usually cross-refer to the specifications set out in the EPC contract. The *wakala* agreement structure is preferred by those *Sharia* scholars who expect the purchaser of the project assets (ie, the issuer) to enter into the EPC contract with the contractor either directly or though an agent under a *wakala* agreement. If a *wakala* agreement is used, the EPC contract must be structured to accommodate the *wakala* provisions.

As the purchase undertaking and sale undertaking can be used only once the project assets are delivered to the issuer, any event of default and termination event occurring before delivery of the project assets must be dealt with under the *istisna* agreement. If an event of default or a termination event occurs during the construction phase, the issuer will have the right to require the project company to:

- procure a refund all of the instalments made by it under the *istisna* agreement; and
- procure payment of a compensation amount equal to an amount sufficient to cover the *sukuk* maturity payment.

The calculation of the compensation amount will need to take into account the fact that the issuer (as lessor) under the forward lease agreement (see below) will also be required to refund all the advance rental received from the project company (as lessee) during the construction period.

3.2 Forward lease (*ijara mawsufah fi al dimmah*) agreement

A forward lease (*ijara mawsufah fi al dimmah*) agreement is entered into between the issuer (as lessor) and the project company (as lessee). A traditional *ijara* (involving leasing of assets already in existence) will not provide the *sukuk* investors with a return during the construction phase, as the project assets to be leased will not be in existence. As a result, the *istisna* is usually combined with a forward lease for the lease of the project assets which will come into existence on the project completion date. Although the actual lease period does not start until the project assets are delivered to the issuer, the project company pays advance rental to ensure that the *sukuk* investors receive a return during the construction period. Since the advance rental represents payment on account of the rental for a future actual lease period, it is necessary for the forward lease agreement to state clearly that the issuer (as lessor) will reimburse all the advance rental received by it during the construction period if the project assets are not delivered, and therefore cannot actually be leased by the project company. The advance and actual rentals payable by the project company (as lessee) will be equal to the *sukuk* return payable under the *sukuk* during the construction and the operating phases of the project. The rentals may be calculated by reference to a fixed or variable rate. The concept of a forward lease is not universally accepted by *Sharia* scholars.

From a *Sharia* perspective, it is usually necessary to document separately the contractual arrangements for the construction of a project from those related to the operating phase of the project (in order to ensure that capacities in which the parties are transacting with each other during the two phases are clearly specified). As a result, it is important to ensure that the forward lease agreement contains only provisions (including representation, covenants and defaults) that relate to the operating phase of the project, and that the *istisna* agreement contains only construction-related provisions. The contractually complex nature of project financings means that it is not always possible to separate clearly the construction-related contractual obligations from those related to the operating phase. One way to deal with this issue is to document all the definitions, representations, covenants, defaults and other provisions which are common to both phases of the project in a common terms agreement, and limit the contents of the *istisna* agreement and the forward lease agreement to specific construction phase and operating phase provisions, respectively.

3.3 Purchase undertaking and sale undertaking

The purchase undertaking and sale undertaking operate in the same way as for a project refinancing structure described above. Each will apply to the project assets following their delivery to the issuer under the *istisna* agreement.

3.4 Service agency agreement

Following delivery of the project assets (or the relevant interest in the project assets) to the issuer (as purchaser) under the *istisna* agreement, the issuer (as lessor) transfers responsibility for major maintenance, insurance and payment of taxes back to the project company (as servicing agent) under the terms of a service agency agreement.

3.5 Sponsor support

In the event that the project does not benefit from a fixed-price turnkey EPC contract, or the creditworthiness of the EPC contractor (or any EPC contract guarantor) is not acceptable from a general bankability perspective or to the rating agencies (in the case of a rated *sukuk*), the project is likely to benefit from a project completion guarantee to protect the *sukuk* investors against construction and start-up risks. Any completion guarantee will be expected to stay in place until the project has satisfied financial covenants in accordance with the financial model for the project.

4. Ratings and credit support

Investors in the *sukuk* market generally invest in financings involving obligors which are either established and financially strong private sector corporations or creditworthy government-owned or supported entities. In producing a rating for a project finance *sukuk*, rating agencies will need to satisfy themselves of the efficacy of the *Sharia* structuring and documentation in addition to undertaking the usual rating analysis in relation to the underlying transaction documents and the project as a whole. This will involve the rating agencies undertaking an analysis of, among other things:

- the financial strength and experience of the project sponsors in developing similar projects;
- the capabilities of the EPC contractor and the project operator;
- mechanisms for funding and maintaining the project reserve accounts; and
- in the case of concession-based projects, the concession termination provisions and methods for calculation and payment of concession termination compensation.

In the conventional project bond market, monoline insurers[2] have historically played a major role in providing credit enhancement for bond investors by guaranteeing the payment obligations of the issuer. This allows the rating agencies to apply the monoline insurer's rating to the bonds guaranteed by it. Involving monoline insurers in project bonds means that the investors can rely on the creditworthiness of the monoline and not the underlying project. This is particularly important for greenfield projects where the investors may be unable to take completion risk. The monoline will be actively involved in negotiating the transaction documents and be responsible for dealing with any requests for consents and waivers under the transaction documents. Without having the monoline perform such a controlling creditor or financier role, it would be difficult to obtain the consents and waivers which may be required during the construction and early operating phases of a complex project. Provided that the monoline maintains its minimum required rating, the investors will continue to rely on the monoline's balance sheet rather than taking project risk. In order to issue a financial guarantee, monoline insurers usually require the bonds (and thereby the underlying project) to obtain a rating (known as a 'shadow rating') of at least investment grade as a condition of issuing the financial guarantee.

As conventional insurance involves *gharar* (uncertainty), and because the investment activities of conventional insurance companies often contravene the

---

2 A monoline insurer is an insurance company that provides guarantees to bond issuers under the terms of financial guarantees issued by them that enhance the credit rating of the project bond issuer.

principles of *Sharia*, the involvement of a monoline insurer may not be acceptable to all *sukuk* investors. The Islamic insurance (*takaful*)[3] industry is insufficiently developed for operators in that industry to perform a credit enhancement role similar to that performed by monoline insurers. The Islamic Corporation for the Insurance of Investment and Export Credit[4] is, however, able to offer commercial and political risk cover for project *sukuk* – particularly where the purpose of the underlying project is to manufacture products (eg, petrochemicals) for export from Organisation of Islamic Conference member countries.

The absence of a monoline wrap or credit enhancement provided through a *takaful* insurance structure means that in rating a project finance *sukuk*, rating agencies will (as well as undertaking their usual analysis of the project risks) place much importance on the level of project sponsor (or third-party) support (in the form of completion guarantees and operating phase shortfall undertaking) in their ratings analysis. Any demand for a tight covenants package will need to be weighed up against the relative difficulty and expense of obtaining waivers and consents from *sukuk* investors. Any project sponsor (or third-party) guarantor could either provide a guarantee direct to the issuer (for the benefit of the *sukuk* investors) or assume the project company's obligations by granting a purchase undertaking in favour of the issuer (for the benefit of the *sukuk* investors). For rated projects, *sukuk* investors may require regular rating reaffirmations as a way of monitoring their investment without having to be involved in detailed analysis of the independent advisers' reports on the progress and performance of the project.

5. Multi-sourced projects

In multi-sourced projects where the *sukuk* tranche is only one part of the overall senior project financing package, all of the *sukuk* investors and the other financiers will need to enter into an intercreditor agreement to regulate their relationship, and to ensure that they share in any payments (whether voluntary or mandatory) on a *pro rata* basis and that the facilities rank on a *pari passu* basis. The *sukuk* investors will be represented by the issuer. The intercreditor agreement will contain provisions relating to the sharing of the project security between the *sukuk* investors and the other senior financiers and provisions relating to rights of the parties to instruct the security agent to take enforcement action following an event of default. It will also contain the voting and decision-making controls in relation to the project documents. In a rated *sukuk* transaction where the *sukuk* investors benefit from regular rating reaffirmations, they may agree to allow the banks to control the day-to-day operation of the project and (provided that the required *sukuk* rating is maintained) have voting rights only in relation to certain reserve matters such as:

- material amendments to the transaction documents;
- raising of additional finance; and

---

3 '*Takaful*' is an Arabic work which means "guaranteeing each other". This system of Islamic insurance is based on the principle of mutual assistance where risks are shared between the participants collectively.

4 This is a multilateral credit and political risk insurer operating in accordance with *Sharia* principles and is a member of the Islamic Development Bank Group.

- changes to the tenor, payment profile or interest rate applicable to any of the other tranches of the senior finance.

If the *sukuk* issue is used to develop part of the project facilities, there may be restrictions on how the proceeds of enforcement of security over those project assets is shared between the *sukuk* investors and any conventional banks participating in the overall financing of the project. The *Sharia* scholar(s) approving the transaction may, among other things, require that under the enforcement waterfall of payments, the sale proceeds relating to the *sukuk* assets be applied only towards payment of the principal, but not the interest component of the amounts due to the conventional banks.

6. Conclusion

The last decade has seen increased emphasis by project sponsors on the use of Islamic project finance for the development of major power, petrochemical and infrastructure projects in the Middle East and Southeast Asia. The inability of Islamic banks to provide long-term finance has constrained the number of transactions which have been financed on a purely *Sharia*-compliant basis. The *sukuk* market, which has also seen considerable development over the last decade, has the potential to provide project sponsors with an important alternative source of long-term finance for limited recourse projects.

Islamic securitisation

Debashis Dey
Stuart Ure
Clifford Chance LLP

1. Introduction

Since its debut on the international financial market, *sukuk* issuance has grown and developed significantly year on year. Despite this, in 2008 the number of *sukuk* issued globally declined for the first time. Market commentators attributed this to a number of factors, including the global financial turbulence and resulting market conditions. The default by Kuwaiti firm Investment Dar on a $100 million *sukuk* and the headlines relating to Nakheel may have led to investor uncertainty and a re-evaluation of the treatment of *sukuk* in a default scenario. In the majority of *sukuk* transactions investors ultimately have no direct recourse to the assets themselves and, as with a conventional bond, investors take credit risk on the obligor which granted a purchase undertaking. In a case study of the Sun Finance Limited securitisation, the largest *Sharia*-compliant securitisation to date, this chapter examines a transaction which was structured to provide investors with direct recourse to securitised assets for the repayment of their investment. Given the compatibility of *Sharia* principles with the principles of asset-backed securitisation, this chapter then considers the future evolution of Islamic debt structures and the development of hybrid structures sitting somewhere between current corporate *sukuk* structures and true asset-backed transactions.

2. Background

The laws and techniques of Islamic finance have been established for hundreds of years, but it is only in the last decade that the Islamic finance industry has seen an unprecedented level of wider interest and expansion into transaction structures that provide capital for projects that might have sought conventional finance in the past. Not only have major financial centres such as Paris, London and Hong Kong declared their intention to develop themselves as Islamic financial centres, but traditional centres of the Islamic finance industry, such as the United Arab Emirates, Malaysia and Saudi Arabia, have seen escalating levels of innovation and activity.

A number of different Islamic financing techniques and products have been developed in accordance with Islamic principles and jurisprudence (*Sharia*), one of the most high-profile of which has been the *sukuk*, which has become synonymous with the Islamic capital markets. The *Sharia*-compliant alternative to conventional interest-bearing investment certificates or fixed-income securities has unfortunately led to the product commonly being referred to as the 'Islamic bond', in recognition of its ability to offer Islamic investors a means of subscribing to trust certificates which represent a right to receive a share of profits generated by an underlying asset base and that is capable of being traded on the secondary market. However, it is more accurate to refer to the *sukuk* as an asset-based investment, as each investor owns an undivided interest in an underlying tangible asset which can be structured to give a fixed-income economic return in a *Sharia*-compliant manner. The *sukuk* certificate evidences this ownership interest, but is not a debt or bond in the 'IOU' sense. In short, moneys raised by the issue of the *sukuk* certificates are used to invest in an underlying asset, a trust or agency is declared over the asset and the investor thereby becomes an owner in a beneficial or indirect interest in that asset in proportion to its investment, and is thus entitled to all benefits that this entails, including a proportion of the return generated by that asset.

Before the development of the *sukuk* product, there was a scarcity of Islamic capital markets products that could provide mid to long-term investment and which could readily be traded in the secondary market, both from a practical perspective and from a *Sharia* perspective. Therefore, the *sukuk* has opened up a new alternative from the perspective of the Islamic investor and, given that the instrument is an ownership interest in a real underlying asset and not a debt instrument, it is freely tradable under *Sharia* – trading in debt at a discount or, as the case may be, premium is prohibited by *Sharia*. Accordingly, this has made *sukuk* an attractive fundraising tool for sovereign, quasi-sovereign and corporate issuers alike, which have used *sukuk* to tap into a wider range of financing sources for their increasingly sophisticated financing and investment purposes.

The *sukuk* market experienced phenomenal growth from 2001 to 2007, growing from being worth less than $500 million in 2001 to more than $60 billion in 2007. In a report published in 2008,[1] Standard & Poor's commented that as long as market conditions returned to normal, it expected this growth to continue and predicted that over the next few years, the total value of *sukuk* issuances outstanding would exceed $100 billion.

However, despite this recent growth and the positive forecasts, in 2008 the number of *sukuk* issued globally declined for the first time. This slowdown in the issuance of *sukuk* has been attributed to a number of different factors, including the global financial crisis and resulting market conditions, the lack of standardisation in the market and a tightening of standards published by the Accounting and Auditing Organisation for Islamic Financial Institutions (AAOIFI) made in February 2008.

Additionally, the default by Kuwaiti firm Investment Dar Company on a $100 million *sukuk* and the headlines relating to Nakheel, the master property developer in Dubai, may have increased investor uncertainty as to the treatment of *sukuk* in a default scenario. In particular, recent events may have left some investors confused as to whether they have a claim over the assets underlying the issuance and whether *sukuk* are more 'secure' than conventional bonds because they are backed by tangible assets. If indeed there is a claim over the assets, investors could expect priority in realising their investment in a default scenario (priority because the trust assets

---

1 Source: Standard & Poor's, "The *Sukuk* Market Continues To Soar and Diversify, Held Aloft By Huge Financing Needs".

would belong to the investors and would not, therefore, be available to creditors of the obligor generally). However, if this were not the case, investors would be unsecured creditors in the bankruptcy of an obligor. This uncertainty may have arisen because a number of structural features are typically present in *sukuk* (see below) that are linked to tangible assets (eg, land, real estate or machinery and equipment). However, the vast majority of *sukuk* to date are not 'true securitisations', meaning that investors have no claim against the assets during a default (unless there has been a pledge of an asset) – this is the commercial basis on which the end investment is made. This leads to the question: can securitisation be adapted for *Sharia*-compliant transactions?

In 2008 the Sun Finance Limited securitisation successfully closed – this was a securitisation of proceeds derived from the sale of plots of land by Sorouh Real Estate PJSC in Abu Dhabi and the world's largest *Sharia*-compliant securitisation to date.

This seems to be proof that true securitisation can be made to be *Sharia* compliant. However, before discussing in detail the features of asset-backed securitisation and the Sun Finance securitisation in particular, it is first important to understand fully the inherent differences between 'asset-based' and 'asset-backed' Islamic structures.

3. Asset-based *sukuk* structures

The basic premise for a *Sharia*-compliant structure used in a capital markets transaction, such as the issuance of *sukuk*, is that there must be a direct link between the assets that underpin the cash flows on the *sukuk* and the indirect ownership of the underlying asset by the investors. For this reason, *sukuk* structures involving the sale of an asset are predicated on transferring title to the underlying assets (there are many forms of what constitutes title) from the obligor (typically, the entity which owns the assets and wishes to raise funds) to a newly formed special purpose vehicle that will hold such assets on trust or as agent for the investors.

To date, the issuers of *sukuk* and the financial intermediaries that assist in selling such securities have tried to meet the requirements of *Sharia*-compliant investors that have sought a similar fixed-income risk and performance profile to a conventional bond based on the obligor's creditworthiness with which they are familiar and in which they wish to invest. In the majority of unsecured *sukuk* transactions, although the investment is *prima facie* also an indirect investment in assets, ultimately the investors have no direct recourse to the assets themselves and the repayment of their investment is ultimately dependent on the exercise of a purchase undertaking by the obligor of the assets at maturity or on the occurrence of a default. Thus, as with a conventional bond, the investors are taking credit risk on the party which grants the purchase undertaking. While typically there is a physical asset in the structure as described above, it is present primarily to generate periodic profit payments, not to enhance the credit quality of the deal or provide investors with recourse to such assets on a default. As a result, offering documents prepared for most *sukuk* transactions have very little disclosure (if any) in respect of the physical asset (they do not need to); instead, disclosure focuses principally on the balance sheet and business and risks of the obligor. Accordingly, most entities that wish to raise finance through *sukuk* structures essentially put forth their own credit rating to the *sukuk*.

While we have highlighted that *Sharia* principles require a transfer of control and risk (as well as reward) in relation to an asset from the seller of the asset to the investors, to date the actual analysis as to whether a transfer of the asset is perfected and immune from the bankruptcy of the seller (a typical feature of conventional asset-backed securitisation) has not been a necessary feature of most *sukuk*. This is because the majority of *Sharia*-compliant investors in the Gulf Cooperation Council states and Malaysia which currently make up the market appear to prefer taking risk on the corporate rather than taking true control of (and risk on) the assets, which would require detailed disclosure and analysis in the offering document of statistical data on the underlying assets. This naturally evokes the question of what alternative *Sharia*-compliant structures exist for an investor that wants exposure to asset risk and direct recourse to those assets.

4. Asset-backed securitisation structures

Typically, conventional securitisations are structured finance transactions through which corporates (including companies and banks) can obtain funding from the capital markets other than by issuing full recourse corporate bonds. Securitisations are generally limited recourse transactions, whereby investors ultimately invest their capital in the credit or performance of a pool of assets, rather than the credit of a corporate or other entity. The investors therefore take risk on the performance of the assets themselves, as opposed to on the performance of the corporate entity which previously owned the assets (thus, their risk and reward are limited in recourse to the assets only). As a result, this is a very different credit analysis from that described above in respect of conventional bonds or unsecured *sukuk*.

One motivation of the originating entity to enter into a true-sale securitisation may be balance-sheet driven, with the aim of removing the asset risk from its balance sheet and raising the future value of an income stream arising from such assets on a present value basis. Another reason can be to obtain financing at a price or from a source that would otherwise be unavailable to the originating entity. If the originating entity is a bank or other financial institution, the intention may also be to obtain capital or other regulatory relief from its regulator.

In order for the instruments ultimately evidencing an investment in an asset-backed transaction to achieve the appropriate credit rating, the transfer or sale of assets must be a sale which would survive the insolvency of the original obligor (ie, the assets must be isolated from the bankruptcy estate of the obligor). This is achievable only to the extent that the transfer represents a true transfer of ownership which is legally perfected. Accordingly, in a conventional true sale securitisation transaction, a pool of assets is typically sold and transferred (hence, 'true sale') by the company or the bank originating the assets (the obligor) to a special purpose vehicle typically established in an offshore jurisdiction for the sole purpose of the securitisation. The special purpose vehicle issues securities to obtain the funds used by it to pay the purchase price for the pool of receivables to the obligor. Repayment of the principal and interest due under the securities issued by the special purpose vehicle will be provided for by the cash flow arising from the purchased pool of assets.

Under *Sharia* principles (and as a distinction from the structure described in the preceding paragraph), it is difficult to separate a receivable (eg, arising from conventional automobile loans), which under conventional finance one would consider an asset itself, from the asset that generates such receivable (ie, the automobile loan). By way of example, in order for receivables such as payments from customers under automobile loans to be utilised to pay amounts to investors in a *Sharia*-compliant structure, the ownership of the underlying automobile portfolio (ie, the actual title to the automobiles) would ordinarily need to be transferred by way of a true sale into the direct ownership of a special purpose vehicle that would issue *sukuk* and declare a trust or agency over the acquired assets for the benefit of the investors.

This direct link to title to the underlying assets (which may not be perfected legally and thus may be an indirect title only) is essential as receivables on their own are, under *Sharia* principles,[2] considered a debt rather than an asset (as they are a right to receive money). Therefore, if one owns an asset that generates a receivable, one has the right to the receivable and is thus exploiting the asset (eg, the automobile portfolio) rather than trading in debt (ie, purely buying and selling the receivables).

In each of the conventional and Islamic scenarios above, however, the recourse of the investors is limited to recourse against the special purpose vehicle and its assets (ie, there will generally be no direct recourse against the obligor). The investors in the securities issued by the special purpose vehicle ultimately take credit risk on the pool of purchased assets and the ability to collect the receivables generated by those assets.

For some financial experts and commentators, Islamic securitisation is the next stage of evolution for Islamic capital markets. Indeed, commentators have argued that the use of securitisation will bring much-needed liquidity to Islamic institutions, thereby enabling them to free up capital which is currently attached to presently illiquid assets, such as real estate.

The Sun Finance Limited securitisation, launched in 2008, represented a novel securitisation of proceeds derived from the sale of plots of land by Sorouh Real Estate PJSC in Abu Dhabi and reflected the fact that current methods exist to structure Islamic true sale securitisations. This transaction broke new ground in the Islamic capital markets as the largest *Sharia*-compliant securitisation to date, while the *sukuk* certificates issued by Sun Finance Limited (a special purpose vehicle incorporated in Jersey and the issuer of the *sukuk* certificates) represented (at the time of issue) the highest-rated non-sovereign instruments to be issued in the Middle East and North Africa region.

---

2 Malaysian Islamic finance products do not always conform to the Gulf Cooperation Council (GCC) concept of *Sharia* compliance, as a divergence has evolved in the industry between the GCC model and the Malaysian model. This lack of convergence of *Sharia* interpretations is one of the issues facing the development of the Islamic capital markets.

5. Sun Finance securitisation: a case study

5.1 Islamic structure

When structuring the Sun Finance securitisation, the first step was to identify an Islamic structure satisfactory to *Sharia* scholars. In the Islamic finance industry, the term '*mudaraba*' is broadly understood to refer to a form of equity-based partnership arrangement whereby one partner provides capital (the *rab-ul-maal*) and the other provides managerial skills (the *mudareb*) (to enable the manager to develop its business), premised on a profit-sharing basis according to pre-determined ratios, provided that any losses are borne by the provider of the funds. The features of this Islamic structure were utilised in the Sun Finance securitisation as they fit the risk sharing in securitisation structures ideally.

5.2 Diagrammatic overview

An abbreviated diagram of the Sun Finance securitisation structure is provided opposite.

5.3 True sale

In order to achieve the true transfer of ownership required for an Islamic securitisation, plots of land which formed parts of the Shams, Reem Island, Abu Dhabi development and the Saraya, Abu Dhabi development were sold by Sorouh Real Estate PJSC to a newly established limited liability company in Abu Dhabi, Sorouh Abu Dhabi Real Estate LLC ('PropCo'). The sale of such land was legally perfected by registering the land in the name of PropCo at the Abu Dhabi Lands Department.

Sorouh had previously entered into contracts of sale with or granted *musataha* rights (a right to use and develop) to sub-developers with respect to the plots. Under these sale and purchase agreements, the sub-developers were obliged to make periodic payments to Sorouh in respect of the initial purchase or grant of the plots from Sorouh. In return, Sorouh was obliged to develop certain items of infrastructure on the master developments and to transfer title to the plots on payment in full of the amounts outstanding under the relevant sale and purchase agreements by the sub-developers. Title to the land was not transferred to the sub-developers and would be transferred only on the final payment.

In accordance with the terms of a *mudaraba* asset sale agreement between Sorouh and PropCo, pending payment in full by the sub-developers of the purchase price with respect to the plots, PropCo (as *mudareb*) purchased from Sorouh, by way of a true sale, the legal title to the plots and all the rights, title and benefit of Sorouh under the sale and purchase agreements entered into with the sub-developers, including the right to receive the periodic sub-developer payments. In addition, Sorouh granted to PropCo the right to exercise all rights and interests of Sorouh against the sub-developers under the sale and purchase agreements, such that PropCo would have recourse against the sub-developers (using Sorouh as its agent).

In consideration for entering into the *mudaraba* asset sale agreement, PropCo paid to Sorouh the proceeds of issuance of the *sukuk* certificates.

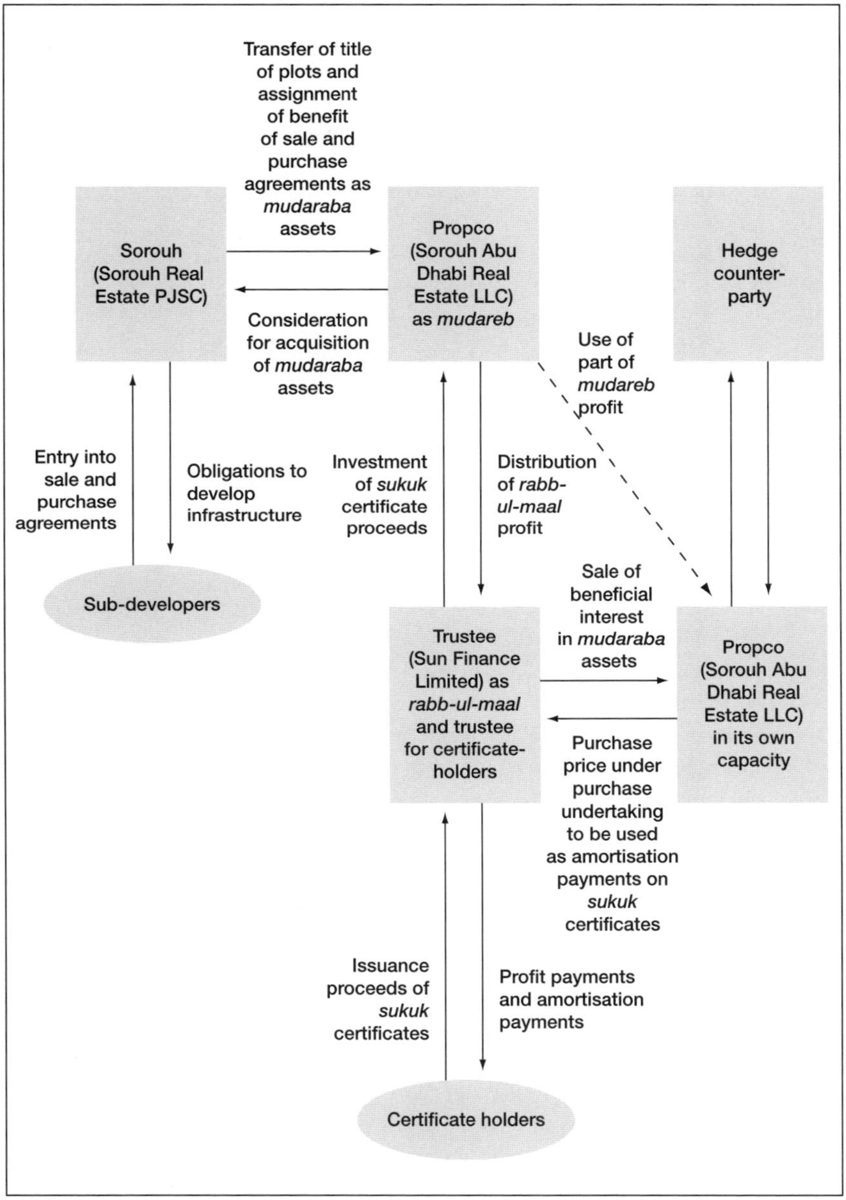

5.4 *Mudaraba* arrangements

As described above, a *mudaraba* is a form of Islamic investment arrangement whereby an investor, the *rab-ul-maal*, provides capital (in this case, the proceeds) to the investment manager, the *mudareb*, to invest and manage for the benefit of both parties for an agreed profit ratio.

While a *mudaraba* is an arrangement recognised by the principles of *Sharia*, under the UAE Civil Code, it is also an enforceable legal contractual arrangement. In addition, as the *mudaraba* established was constituted in Abu Dhabi, it conformed to and complied with the articles of the UAE Civil Code which provide that if, before the insolvency of the *mudareb*, the capital is identifiable and the identifiable capital forms part of the bankruptcy estate of the *mudareb*, the *rab-ul-maal* maintains the exclusive right to the capital in priority over other ordinary or unsecured creditors of the *mudareb*. Each of these legislative provisions assisted in the development of a robust legal structure for an Islamic securitisation.

For a *mudaraba* to be valid, the following conditions must be satisfied:

- The *rab-ul-maal* must be competent to grant a power of attorney[3] and the *mudareb* competent to hold one;
- The capital must be known, such that it can be properly dealt in (ie, the proceeds);
- The capital must not be a debt or a deposit with the *rab-ul-maal* which is owed by the *mudareb* to the *rab-ul-maal*;
- The capital must be delivered to the *mudareb*; and
- The share of each contracting party in the profit must be ascertained.

The *mudaraba* entered into between PropCo (in its capacity as *mudareb*) and Sun Finance Limited (in its capacity as *rab-ul-maal*) constituted a 'restricted *mudaraba*', as the *rab-ul-maal* specified certain conditions to be adhered to in a pre-agreed investment plan.

On the closing date, the proceeds were applied as the capital of the restricted *mudaraba* and invested in accordance with the investment plan, including to purchase, among other things, the plots and all rights, title and benefit of Sorouh under the sale and purchase agreements. In turn, in consideration for the investment of the proceeds with the *mudareb*, the *mudareb* agreed to hold and manage the *mudaraba* assets in favour of the *rab-ul-maal* for the duration of the restricted *mudaraba*.

The total amount of profit to which the *rab-ul-maal* would be entitled to be paid under the restricted *mudaraba* was calculated by reference to, among other things, the sum of the aggregate amount of all profit payments on the *sukuk* certificates. In turn, the amount of profit to be distributed to the *mudareb* was calculated as an amount equal to the aggregate amount of profit, less the *rab-ul-maal* profit amount.

In this structure the *mudareb* profit periodically distributed to the *mudareb* amounted to a significant proportion of the payments received under the sale and purchase agreements in relation to the plots. From this profit amount, PropCo was contractually obliged to utilise the *mudareb* profit to pay, among other things, the exercise price under a 'purchase undertaking' (as defined below).

5.5 Purchase undertaking

In order to facilitate the transfer of the plots from PropCo to the sub-developers on

3 Under the terms of the *mudaraba*, the *mudareb* agrees to contribute its expertise and management skills to the *Sharia*-compliant mudaraba enterprise, with responsibility for managing the *rab-ul-maal's* cash contribution in accordance with specified investment parameters. In order to do this, as a matter of company law, the *rab-ul-maal* must have the corporate capacity to grant a power of attorney to the *mudareb*.

payment in full by the sub-developers of the purchase price with respect to the plots, PropCo, in its own capacity (and not as *mudareb*), granted an irrevocable purchase undertaking in favour of the *rab-ul-maal* such that PropCo undertook, on periodic distribution dates, to purchase a portion of the *rab-ul-maal*'s beneficial interest in the plots forming part of the *mudaraba* assets until the redemption date or, as the case may be, the maturity date.

It is important to recognise that the purchase undertaking was not a guarantee by PropCo of the face value of the *mudaraba* assets. The funds available to PropCo to meet its payment obligation under the purchase undertaking were limited in recourse to any funds which PropCo had earned (in its capacity as *mudareb*) as *mudareb* profit (as described above). Accordingly, PropCo would earn only sufficient *mudareb* profit to meet its obligations under the purchase undertaking to the extent that the sub-developers had made sufficient payments under the sale and purchase agreements. To the extent that the sub-developers had made insufficient payments, it would potentially be the case that investors would ultimately not receive all amounts which were due to them under the *sukuk* certificates. This point is particularly pertinent because, as a result of the AAOIFI ruling of February 2008, some *Sharia* scholars took the view that it is not permissible for an obligor to grant a purchase undertaking to the special purpose vehicle (in its capacity as trustee) to purchase the *mudaraba* assets for any amount other than the trustee's share of the value of the *mudaraba* assets at the time of sale.

Since the proceeds which Sun Finance Limited received from the issuance of the *sukuk* certificates were invested in the initial *mudaraba* assets in return for an interest in the *mudaraba* assets, in order for the *rab-ul-maal*'s interest in the *mudaraba* assets to match the amounts outstanding under the *sukuk* certificates, any reduction of the *rab-ul-maal*'s interest in the *mudaraba* assets was accompanied by a corresponding return of capital under the *sukuk* certificates. In turn, on each purchase of *mudaraba* assets in accordance with the terms of the purchase undertaking, the amount of the *rab-ul-maal* profit earned by the *rab-ul-maal* with respect to the *rab-ul-maal*'s interest in the *mudaraba* assets was correspondingly reduced in accordance with the reduction in the *rab-ul-maal*'s interest in the *mudaraba* assets.

The mechanism of this asset reduction and return of capital is essential to an understanding of how this securitisation differs from *sukuk-al-mudaraba* done previously, where the corporate obligor had a purchase undertaking to purchase the assets back upon the dissolution date of the *sukuk* (the date that the capital was to be returned).

In those 'non-securitisation' *sukuk* transactions, the key difference from a true securitisation was that the price paid under the purchase undertaking would reflect the outstanding face value of the *sukuk* and was being paid by the corporate obligor. In the Sun Finance securitisation the price paid was:

- not being paid by the original seller of the assets; and
- dependent on the collection of payments from sub-developers which were purchasing the *mudaraba* assets from the *mudareb* at the market price for land in Abu Dhabi.

Finally, another important distinction was that in case of default, investors had the right to take control of the sale of assets to maximise their return.

5.6 Comment

Notably, by perfecting the sale and structuring of the transaction such that investors had access to (and risk on) the direct sale proceeds of the land, the rating of the *sukuk* was based on asset performance rather than Sorouh's creditworthiness. The result was that the investors in the *sukuk* certificates maintained sole recourse to the securitised assets for the repayment of their investment. If the assets do not perform and do not generate sufficient profit, the investors do not receive the expected profit on their *sukuk* certificates. In this way, the transaction represents a fully asset-backed, *Sharia*-compliant, non-recourse financing.

As discussed above, the exercise of the purchase undertaking in the majority of corporate *sukuk* transactions is dependent on the credit of the obligor. In contrast, in the Sun Finance securitisation the funds which were required to return capital to the investors were ultimately derived from performance of the securitised assets themselves. Therefore, to the extent that the assets do not perform, there will be insufficient funds available and, as a consequence, the investors will not receive the full capital back on their investment. Therefore, the investors are ultimately taking full credit risk on the performance of the assets for the realisation of their investment in compliance with both the *Sharia* and rating agency requirements.

In order for existing *sukuk* transactions to embrace fully the concept of risk following transfer of asset ownership, the structures require, among other things, a true or perfected sale of assets by the owner of such assets and also for the investors to take true economic risk on performance of the assets themselves. These are also two principles which underpin asset-backed securitisation transactions:

- a true and perfected sale of assets by the obligor of such assets in order to ensure that they are isolated from the bankrupt estate of the obligor; and
- the fact that the rating on the instruments can be delinked from the credit rating of the obligor only to the extent that the investors are taking true economic risk solely on the performance of the securitised assets.

Accordingly, the Sun Finance securitisation is an example of the way in which the two principles discussed above can satisfy the requirements of a *Sharia* advisory board, as well as the rating requirements of the rating agencies, in order to allow for the issuance of *sukuk* certificates which not only are *Sharia* compliant, but also represent a credit rating several notches higher than the credit rating of the obligor.

6. Will the Islamic finance industry embrace securitisation?

Given the compatibility of *Sharia* principles with the principles of asset-backed securitisation, as well as the emergence of transactions which have combined the two in practice, the logical question is whether the Islamic finance industry will embrace securitisation as the future of the *sukuk* industry. For securitisation to become more mainstream in the GCC, three prerequisites will be required:

- Investors will need to demonstrate a commercial desire to take the risk (and reward) associated with the true sale of assets in an asset-backed structure, including the management of those assets in a default scenario;

- Those companies seeking finance will need to demonstrate a desire to sell their assets (which will have accounting and shareholder equity implications); and
- A robust legal framework will need to evolve, as currently bankruptcy and asset-selling laws in many jurisdictions in the GCC remain opaque and militate against securitisation structures.

These issues are also accentuated by the fact that there can be a lack of convergence or uniformity in *Sharia* interpretations, as different countries have different interpretations in relation to various capital markets structures and products. Clearly, a convergence of *Sharia* interpretations would facilitate the evolution (and liquidity) of the Islamic capital market.

Furthermore, notwithstanding the fact that asset-backed securitisation is itself a sound product and a useful tool for financial institutions and corporate entities to diversify risk and free up other funding lines, it is complex and not widely understood among regional investors, and thus – rightly or wrongly – at present there is a degree of nervousness about asset-backed securitisation, accentuated by unfamiliarity.

7. Where does the future lie?

Given some of the recent criticism from some scholars of *musharaka*, *mudaraba* and *wakala sukuk* structures, as well as the factors discussed above, which may hinder a move by the Islamic finance community towards a product that appears to be consistent with the principles of *Sharia*, it will be interesting to see what the future of the *sukuk* market will be going forward.

One possibility may well be that the *sukuk* industry will move towards a hybrid asset class structure which lies somewhere between the current corporate *sukuk* structures and true asset-backed transactions. In order to accommodate both investor appetite and the requirements of *Sharia*, it may be that structures develop which provide investors with recourse to both the corporate credit of the obligor (which they desire) and the assets themselves, to the extent that the obligor fails to fulfil its obligations - the so-called 'dual-recourse' structures.

There is certainly precedent for similar transactions in the conventional 'covered bond' industry across North America and Europe. In covered bond transactions, investors have initial recourse to the corporate credit of the issuer of the covered bonds. However, to the extent that the issuer fails to fulfil its obligations, the investor will also have recourse to a segregated pool of assets.

While the global financial turbulence has resulted in a number of high-profile defaults, this has generated a timely debate among market participants as to the nature of investors' recourse to the underlying assets (if any) and the type of recourse which investors will require in the future. In turn, this inevitably results in a better understanding by investors, bankers, originators and lawyers alike of what the consequences of a default are, leading to further innovation and development of existing *sukuk* structures and products (both asset based and asset backed) and the further evolution of Islamic debt structures.

Ultimately, well-developed and diverse product offerings in Islamic capital markets will not only be beneficial for issuers and investors, but should also enhance the stability of Islamic financial institutions by providing them with improved portfolio, liquidity and risk management tools. In this regard, product innovation is crucial in the process of deepening and broadening the Islamic financial industry and this remains a critical emphasis in the development of the Islamic capital markets.

Restructuring and buy-back of *sukuk*

Daniel Rankin
Hogan Lovells (Middle East) LLP

1. Introduction

Sukuk are now a global financial instrument, with two jurisdictions dominating the market: Malaysia and the Gulf Cooperation Council (GCC) countries. Each of these jurisdictions has formulated its own consensus on the rules and policies for the issuance of *sukuk*. Neither the Malaysian nor the GCC consensus provides a set of formal rules for *sukuk* issuances. Instead, they consist of an omnibus of legislation, guidance from *Sharia* scholars and market practice used by issuers, regulators, investors and their advisers that continues to evolve with the issuance of new and more innovative *sukuk* structures. Each jurisdiction has a separate tradition of interpretation of *Sharia* requirements, its own governing laws and unrelated insolvency regimes. A global overview of the restructuring of *sukuk* inside both these regimes is beyond the scope of this chapter. Instead, this chapter focuses on the process of restructuring *sukuk* that have been issued under the GCC consensus.

Sukuk restructurings are typically part of a broader process whereby a company in financial difficulties looks to reorganise all of its liabilities, allowing it to continue to carry on business and avoid insolvency. The framework of this reorganisation is most often implemented by way of a contract between the restructuring company and its creditors. When the obligor of a *sukuk* issuance is restructuring its financial obligations, the rights of *sukuk* holders can be properly considered only in the context of that broader restructuring and in comparison to those of the other stakeholders (the most notable being the senior lenders, the trade creditors and the equity holders, as applicable). The relationships are fairly well defined: the obligor's obligations to *sukuk* holders rank *pari passu* with the other unsecured creditors, but senior to the equity holders.

Each restructuring is dependent on its own specific set of circumstances, and the decisions of *sukuk* holders regarding the way that a restructuring progresses, like those of the other creditors, will in large part be determined by the value of the obligor's business and whether it is likely to be less than the aggregate value of its outstanding obligations. While the conventional bond market has seen defaults and restructurings before, these are a relatively new phenomenon in the GCC *sukuk* market. Following the default of a number of high-profile *sukuk*, the process of *sukuk* restructuring has now been attempted, with varying results. The scarcity of completed *sukuk* restructurings means that the legal and regulatory systems governing Islamic finance in the GCC are still adapting to their first tests in relation to many aspects of the restructuring process.

The use of *sukuk* structures in the GCC gained popularity during a period when the seemingly endless liquidity of the Gulf region acted as a shield against the ebbs and flows of corporate insolvency. In this environment, as much emphasis was placed on making the best use of the liquidity available as on securing investors against potential defaults. The credit crunch of 2008 brought this period to an end and shifted the focus of both investors and obligors on the process of restructuring distressed *sukuk*. When Investment Dar Company become the first GCC issuer to default on a *sukuk* by failing to pay a periodic distribution due on April 27 2010, it became a test case for what the legal rights of *sukuk* holders would be. In addition to the Investment Dar *sukuk*, there have been defaults from obligors located in the United States (East Cameron Gas Company), Saudi Arabia (Golden Belt) and Kuwait (IIG), each issued under the GCC consensus. The process followed during the course of the restructuring of these *sukuk* provides some guidance, but not a template, for future restructurings. What is clear is that, given the various structures and asset classes that may be involved in a particular *sukuk*, each restructuring must be dealt with based on the specific facts and circumstances surrounding that *sukuk* and its obligor.

2. Restructuring process

Although no formal standardisation of *sukuk* documents or structures has been agreed, even within the GCC, market practice has given rise to a similarity in the operating parameters of most *sukuk*. The most important of these operating parameters during the restructuring process are the way that *sukuk* holders make decisions regarding the *sukuk* and their legal rights to the asset on which the *sukuk* is based.

Due to uncertainty as to how *sukuk* holders' rights would be viewed and enforced, the trend during the initial round of *sukuk* restructurings has been for *sukuk* holders of distressed obligors to pursue a consensus-based restructuring, as opposed to an adjudicated resolution. There are many factors which mitigate toward *sukuk* restructuring:

- It minimises publicity for the obligor;
- Restructurings tend to be more expedient than formal proceedings;
- A restructuring company can continue to operate as a going concern; and
- Perhaps most importantly, restructuring agreements generally fall outside of GCC insolvency regimes, which are still underdeveloped, uncertain and creditor unfriendly.

All of these factors have the potential to increase the value of the obligor's business beyond the value of its constituent assets and, by extension, the amount of recovery for *sukuk* holders.

Each *sukuk* restructuring is carried out against a legal, jurisdictional and operational background which is unique to that restructuring. There are nonetheless a number of steps which must be followed during the restructuring of a *sukuk*.

2.1 Convening a meeting of *sukuk* holders

A *sukuk* holder cannot recover from an obligor on an individual basis. The *sukuk* holders are required by the terms of the *sukuk* documentation to act only through a trustee. In most *sukuk* structures the trustee is a special purpose vehicle which has in turn vested all enforcement powers in a corporate services company that will act as its delegate. The delegate is responsible for convening *sukuk* holder meetings, determining whether a dissolution event has occurred, making amendments to the *sukuk* documents and appointing new trustees (if necessary). However, the delegate is not bound to act unless it has been properly indemnified by the *sukuk* holders.

The delegate will take action in relation to a *sukuk* only following an instruction from the *sukuk* holders that is in compliance with the *sukuk* documentation. In the event of a default or other event which would initiate a restructuring of the *sukuk*, the first step must be for a group of *sukuk* holders (typically holders of not less than 10% of the face value of the *sukuk*) to provide the delegate with a request in writing for a meeting of all *sukuk* holders to decide what should be done. The *sukuk* holders requesting the meeting can typically set the time and place, but most *sukuk* will require that at least 21 days' notice of the meeting be given to the remaining *sukuk* holders. To instruct the delegate, a decision must be taken by a minimum number of *sukuk* holders (typically 25% of the value of the *sukuk* certificates). Certain important decisions, such as changes to the *sukuk* redemption date, require a larger share of the *sukuk* holders (often 75% of the *sukuk* certificates) and may even require unanimity. Achieving such levels of support from *sukuk* holders is often difficult.

2.2 Determining *sukuk* holder support for a restructuring

The *sukuk* holders' negotiating position is often put forward to the obligor by a group of *sukuk* holders that form an *ad hoc* committee and retain their own independent legal and financial advisers. The larger the group, the more effective it will be. A group that consists of holders of 75% of the face value of the *sukuk* will typically be sufficient to pass an extraordinary resolution allowing for a change in terms of the *sukuk* or the passing of a scheme of arrangement, putting such a group in a strong negotiating position. One difficulty with *sukuk* holders formulating and executing a strategy for a restructuring is that although establishing a group of sufficient size is often vital to the chances of success for the *sukuk* holders, there are a number of hurdles to doing so. Notably, for a *sukuk* whose obligor is looking to reorganise, the *sukuk* holders will include both investors that purchased the *sukuk* at the time of issuance at full price and other investors that have purchased their *sukuk* in the secondary market, at a substantial discount. These two groups of *sukuk* holders will have different goals and, in particular, different minimum price thresholds for recovery. This disparity can complicate the formulation of any *sukuk* holder strategy and may prevent *sukuk* holders from obtaining the necessary support to execute their strategy. A further complication arises from that fact that *sukuk* holders are often difficult to identify because the *sukuk* are usually held in the clearing systems. Accordingly, *sukuk* holder groups in discussions with the other stakeholders in a restructuring may be working at a disadvantage, due to their inability to commit without convening a formal *sukuk* holder meeting.

2.3 Negotiation with other stakeholders

Most restructurings will involve negotiations between the company and the other stakeholders in its restructuring, with the senior lenders taking the lead. The senior lenders will attempt to form a steering committee which may or may not include representatives of the *sukuk* holders. Once established, the steering committee will act as the liaison between the obligor and its creditors, appoint accountants and legal advisers and seek to negotiate a standstill agreement. The accountants and legal advisers will review the obligor's cash flow and other financial information, assess the company's management and consider the viability of the company's continued operations. The information gathered by these teams will be used as the basis for the steering committee's restructuring negotiations.

Sukuk holders will scrutinise the financial documents available to them to gain a view of the relative strengths of the company, but they are unlikely to have the same access to the obligor's financial information as the steering committee if they are not represented as part of the steering committee.

The protections offered by the covenants in a *sukuk* are unlikely to offer as much protection as those in the senior lenders' transaction. For most *sukuk* issued in the GCC before 2008, the covenants negotiated were of a type that would be breached only if certain 'fatal' events occurred, such as non-payment or insolvency. As such, the structure of most *sukuk* provides a right to accelerate and enforce remedies only on the actual occurrence of an event of default and the lapse of any remedy period. If such an event has not occurred, there will be little leverage for the *sukuk* holders to use in negotiations with the other stakeholders.

If an event of default has occurred, the *sukuk* holders will be able to leverage the threat of enforcement to gain an advantage in restructuring negotiations and attempt to force a payment. This type of aggressive tactic is more characteristic of *sukuk* holders than senior lenders, because while *sukuk* investors are looking to the short term and repayment of their investment, financial institutions may have medium to long-term relationship concerns with the obligor. This is one of the reasons that bank syndicates tend to place a great deal of importance on trying to ensure that the obligor remains a going concern rather than breaking it into parts or liquidating its assets.

There has also been increasing consensus among financial institutions that, as creditors, they can achieve better returns (and balance-sheet treatment) through supporting a restructuring of the debt of a company than by forcing it into insolvency proceedings. In contrast to *sukuk*, loan documentation typically contains covenants (eg, requiring that a company maintain certain financial ratios) which gives them, on the early signs of financial problems, the ability to call a default, accelerate their loans and enforce any security interests which may exist. This gives the banks a first-mover advantage over *sukuk* holders and other creditors, which they can use to force the obligor company into consensual restructuring discussions before any rights arise for *sukuk* holders. The standstill agreement that will be signed usually includes a date on which exposures are frozen, a moratorium on acceleration, demand, termination, enforcement, set-off and the instigation of insolvency proceedings, and an agreement not to improve any individual position that would not be available to all other stakeholders.

(a) *Negotiating a settlement*

Sukuk holders have several options when approaching a restructuring and a request to enter into a standstill agreement:

- They can isolate themselves in an attempt to make use of a strategic advantage;
- They can try to make a claim on the *sukuk* assets; or
- They can attempt to join the steering committee and negotiate as one of the obligor's unsecured creditors.

Utilisation of a strategic advantage: An example of this strategy is the way that the potential default of Nakheel PJSC's $3.52 billion *sukuk* was approached in November 2009. It was anticipated that the *sukuk* would be subject to a general restructuring. However, a group of *sukuk* holders holding approximately 25% of the face value of the *sukuk* were able, through an aggressive negotiating stance, to block any potential restructuring and push for full repayment of the *sukuk* by Nakheel. These *sukuk* holders were able to take this position because:

- unless payment was made, a default was imminent;
- the *sukuk* had a guarantee from Dubai World PJSC, Nakheel's parent company;
- Dubai World has international assets that would be appealing for the *sukuk* holders to enforce against; and
- cash was available for repayment of the *sukuk* in full.

This particular factual matrix will not be replicated in most restructurings, but it is an example of how a group of *sukuk* holders can use a strategic advantage to increase their return from an obligor that is looking to restructure its obligations by reducing the return on their *sukuk* holders' investment.

Claim against *sukuk* assets: While the above strategy depends on a correct analysis of the *sukuk* holders' negotiating position, this strategy depends on a interpretation of the *sukuk* holders' rights which is still somewhat uncertain. The risk in making a claim against the obligor as a *de facto* secured creditor with a right to the underlying *sukuk* assets is that if it fails, *sukuk* holders will be left in a position where senior lenders and other creditors, the equity investors and the company's management can negotiate among themselves with little urgency, while the *sukuk* holders will be left without a seat at the table. If it is successful, however, *sukuk* holders will have the right to force the sale of the *sukuk* assets and be paid out of the proceeds. If the obligor cannot meet its obligations under the *sukuk* documentation, the *sukuk* holders will retain their interest in the *sukuk* assets and therefore hold a significant strategic advantage when negotiating with the other stakeholders in the obligor's restructuring. While *sukuk* holders are clearly restrained from taking any action to enforce directly against the *sukuk* assets, the other creditors will also be unable to enforce against those assets and they will remain out of the reach of the obligor as well. *Sukuk* holders will retain the rights to the assets' cash flows and can therefore, in certain circumstances, opt to sit out the standstill negotiations altogether.

This strategy was successfully implemented during the bankruptcy of East Cameron Gas Company. In October 2008 East Cameron filed for bankruptcy protection. During the bankruptcy proceedings the *sukuk* holders claimed the right to keep the portion of the company's oil and gas that was transferred to the issuer special purpose vehicle (SPV) as the *sukuk* asset. East Cameron argued that:

- there had been no real transfer of ownership of the royalties;
- the *sukuk* was merely a loan; and
- the royalties would have to be shared by all of its creditors.

The bankruptcy court held that *sukuk* holders "invested in the *sukuk* certificates in reliance of the characterization of the transfer of the royalty interest as a true sale" and the asset was transferred to an SPV controlled by the *sukuk* holders. The applicability of this precedent to other *sukuks* will have to be considered on a case-by-case basis.

One factor in favour of this type of claim by *sukuk* holders is that according to a March 2008 Accounting and Auditing Organisation for Islamic Financial Institutions (AAOIFI) ruling, only *sukuk* structures involving a true transfer of asset ownership will be seen as *Sharia* compliant. Accordingly, all *sukuk* holders will have the same expectation of an asset transfer that the holders of the East Cameron *sukuk* had.

If *sukuk* holders do decide to make a claim on the *sukuk* assets, this will involve the initiation of a legal action. The process that will be followed will be determined by the *sukuk* documentation. However, any court hearing such a case will need to weigh up not just the commercial and legal aspects of the claim, but also the *Sharia* considerations. While the commercial agreement may have been that the *sukuk* was to act like a fixed-income security with no recourse to the *sukuk* assets, the *Sharia* position will be that the contract governs and that title to the assets will pass in accordance with the contract. This could result in a quasi-secured interest being created for *sukuk* holders. The lack of precedent in this area makes it difficult to navigate potential conflicts between the law governing the *sukuk* and the *Sharia*. In addition, the question of who is even qualified to provide rulings on such *sukuk* issues has yet to be definitively answered. Finally, the question of how enforceable any judgment in favour of the *sukuk* holders would be in the jurisdiction in which the assets are located and how such a claim would interact with the insolvency regime to which the obligor is subject will be key considerations in any decisions made by *sukuk* holders to pursue a claim against the *sukuk* assets.

Entering into a standstill agreement with other creditors: Entering into a standstill agreement avoids a situation where each creditor acts unilaterally in its own interests. If each creditor tries to get paid ahead of all the others and the obligor does not have the cash to make the necessary payments, it is likely that the obligor will be forced into insolvency. In the GCC, where the insolvency regimes are uncertain, this could be one of the worst results for *sukuk* holders attempting to have a claim enforced against the obligor. Insolvency laws in the GCC have developed unevenly and are generally untested and therefore unpredictable. Importantly, due to the lack of precedent, there exists no definitive priority ranking of creditors and no way to determine how creditors will be paid in the event of a liquidation of the obligor's assets. There is also little guidance on the relative length of an insolvency proceeding or how it will be carried out in practice. Companies that have assets located in a number of jurisdictions in the region with different insolvency regimes present an additional problem for *sukuk* holders looking to enforce against *sukuk* assets. Accordingly, if no standstill agreement has been entered into, the *sukuk* holders will run the risk that another creditor may force the obligor into insolvency proceedings. In all likelihood, it would be far better for all stakeholders to negotiate with the creditors and to try to reach an accommodation with the obligor as part of a restructuring agreement.

(b) Negotiating a restructuring agreement

Following the execution of a standstill agreement, the creditors will have to work with the obligor to establish the terms on which they will be repaid. The crucial questions will include whether there needs to be a deferment or rescheduling of coupon amounts, an extension of maturity dates or a capitalisation of profit payments. The restructuring agreement may consolidate all outstanding obligations into one master agreement or operate as an override agreement setting out additional terms and providing appropriate variations to the existing documents.

Due to the nature of Islamic finance structures, careful consideration must be given to the timing and structure of any refinancing or restructuring of *sukuk*. Thought must be given to the availability of assets and use of proceeds. Some structures will not allow for an extension of the term of the *sukuk*, and therefore the compliance of the restructuring agreement must be carefully considered.

The obligor may look for new funding as part of the restructuring and *sukuk* holders will have the option to inject further capital into the obligor. This may improve the *sukuk* holders' ability to influence the restructuring if the new capital is used to remove some of the senior lenders and therefore decrease the number of parties entitled to payment ahead of the *sukuk* holders. If the *sukuk* holders are the only parties willing to inject further capital, the investors and the senior lenders may be forced to accept a restructuring proposal that favours the *sukuk* holders. However, given the risk of losing this additional capital in addition to their original investment and the difficulty of getting a large percentage of the *sukuk* holders to take action, a cash injection by the *sukuk* holders would be a fairly unusual step.

Whether *sukuk* holders provide further funding or not, new undertakings and financial covenants can be added to the terms of the *sukuk* to act as early warning signs of impending problems in case of future issues with the obligor. The new covenants become tools for the *sukuk* holders to control what the company may and may not do in terms of the cash it has, both immediately and going forward. These covenants include restrictions on dividends, capital expenditure, acquisitions, further borrowings and investments, close monitoring of warranties about information, restrictions on disposals, security and changes in business and management.

The obligor will typically need to provide the *sukuk* holders with an incentive to agree to a restructuring which may put the *sukuk* holders' investment at risk or delay payment. This incentive may be simple, such as an increase in the rate of return or even a cash payment; or may be a more complicated offer, such as a *sukuk* buy-back or an exchange offer.

***Sukuk* buy-back:** The relative illiquidity of the secondary market in *sukuk* may lead to *sukuk* certificate pricing which may make it attractive for an obligor to purchase existing certificates. This would reduce the obligors' overall obligation under the *sukuk* at a discount to the cost of repayment. Dubai Islamic Bank performed a successful buy-back of certificates issued during its $750,000 offering from March 2007. However, this buy-back was not connected to a restructuring.

A *sukuk* buy-back offer must be extended to all *sukuk* holders. The obligor will typically appoint an investment bank to act as manager to oversee the tender process and serve as the primary liaison with *sukuk* holders. The length of the offer period will be set with the objective of ensuring that there is enough time for a maximum number of *sukuk* holders to accept the offer while minimising the risk to the issuer of *sukuk* holders subsequently withdrawing acceptances.

As part of the *sukuk* buy-back offer, the obligor can request that *sukuk* holders consent to amendments to the terms of the *sukuk* (eg, an extension of payment terms). In order for *sukuk* holders to accept the offer, they must vote in favour of the proposed amendments at a *sukuk* holders' meeting.

One way to make the offer more attractive to *sukuk* holders is to make the tender in the form of a 'Dutch auction'. This format allows *sukuk* holders to determine the purchase price of the *sukuk* certificates that are tendered. The *sukuk* holders tender their certificates within a specified price range and tenders are accepted by the obligor, beginning with those for which the lowest price has been specified, until the obligor has purchased the desired number of *sukuk*. In a modified Dutch auction the purchase price is determined based on the lowest price that allows the obligor to buy the number of *sukuk* sought in the offer and the obligor pays that price to all *sukuk* holders that tendered at or below that price on a *pro rata* basis.

There are numerous legal considerations for a transaction of this type, including stock exchange requirements (if applicable), the corporate and securities laws to which the obligor and the issuer are subject and applicable tax law. The rules of the relevant clearing systems must also be considered.

Exchange offers: Another option for obligors that may provide an incentive to *sukuk* holders is an exchange offer, whereby the obligor offers to exchange existing *sukuk* for new *sukuk* with modified (typically beneficial) terms or, in some cases, shares of the obligor. Exchange offers are an attractive option when the obligor remains a fundamentally sound investment, but does not have the cash resources available to fund a *sukuk* buy-back. As *sukuk* structures comprise assets which must be disposed of when dissolving a trust, exchange offers may be somewhat more difficult to structure. *Sukuk* documentation anticipates dissolution of the trust by and full redemption of the *sukuk*, which makes a partial exchange difficult, and a number of issues must be considered, including:

- details of the rights and interests to be conferred to each *sukuk* holder that participates in the exchange offer;

- the mechanism and timing for exchanging *sukuk* holders' interests under the *sukuk* for such entitlements;
- details of the dissolution of the trust and of the calculation of the interests of each *sukuk* holder that are to be exchanged for entitlements; and
- the rights of those *sukuk* holders that do not wish to participate in the exchange.

3. Conclusion

As *sukuk* restructurings typically take place as part of a wider restructuring of an obligor's liabilities, when the obligor of a *sukuk* issuance is restructuring its financial obligations, the rights of *sukuk* holders can be properly considered only in the context of the broader restructuring and in comparison to those of the other stakeholders. The defaults which have occurred to date in the GCC *sukuk* market are providing the first test of the *Sharia* and legal regulations governing *sukuk* restructuring. The onset of restructurings for the Investment Dar, East Cameron, Golden Belt and IIG *sukuks* has provided some guidance for future restructurings, but the picture is far from complete. Each restructuring must be dealt with based on the specific facts and circumstances surrounding the *sukuk* and its obligor. Due to the nature of restructuring as contractual agreements between a company in financial difficulties and its creditors, the nature of the rights held by *sukuk* holders in the event of a restructuring is unclear. The bond market provides limited guidance, as unlike conventional bonds, *sukuk* are asset based and any restructuring must be consistent with *Sharia*. Accordingly, due to uncertainty caused by the relative scarcity of restructuring issuers in the *sukuk* market and the questions of how *sukuk* holders rights would be viewed and enforced, the initial trend of *sukuk* holders of distressed companies pursuing consensus-based restructuring, as opposed to court judgments, is likely to continue in the short to medium term. Many factors mitigate towards a *sukuk* restructuring and relatively few incentives for *sukuk* holders to risk isolating themselves, except in the most strategically advantageous of circumstances.

The future of *sukuk*: Islamic capital markets

Moinuddin Malim
Mashreq Al-Islami

1. Introduction

Sukuk have been the focus of much debate since the 2008 Accounting and Auditing Organisation for Islamic Financial Institutions (AAOIFI) ruling on *sukuk* and the subsequent global financial meltdown. Many issues have been raised challenging *sukuk's raison d'être* as 'Islamic bonds' on account of them having the same economic outcome as conventional bonds. Some scholars have asserted that contemporary *sukuk* are not compliant with the original purpose of *Sharia*. The notion that *sukuk* and Islamic finance were not susceptible to the general economic downturn and financial crisis has also been tested. While a consensus has emerged that Islamic finance and its products are more secure, particularly given the prohibition on speculative instruments (particularly those that are derivative based), it has also been accepted that Islamic finance cannot shield itself completely from a general economic downturn.

The future of the Islamic capital market will be based on investors' ability to comprehend and comply with *Sharia* requirements fully, with all its benefits following from its ethical restrictions. Despite the AAOIFI recognising 14 *Sharia*-compliant *sukuk* structures, global data shows that just five of those (*ijarah, mudarabah, musharaka, murabaha* and *istithmar*) hold up to 90% of the *sukuk* market share as per the diagram below. Of those, *ijarah* has been the most popular structure used by international *sukuk* issuers. The *musharaka* structure has been very popular with Malaysian issuers. Other *sukuk* structures include *al salaam, bai bithaman, ajil, bai inah, al istithmar* and *manfa'a*.

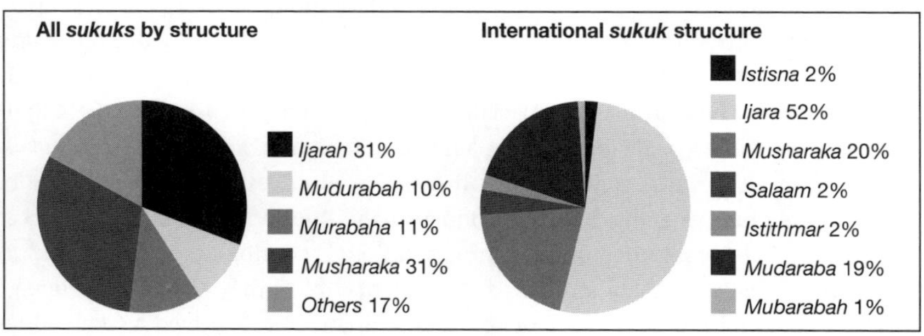

Data as at January 31 2009. Chart created from data sourced from: Securities Commission, Malaysia, Quarterly Bulletin for The Malaysian Islamic Capital Markets, *Zawya –* Sukuk *Monitor, Bloomberg, Liquidity Management Centre – Global* Sukuk *Table, Global Investment House – Global Research – List of* Sukuk *(2001-2007)*

As early as the 1990s, Malaysia introduced a series of measures to develop *sukuk*. The diagram below shows how other countries have caught on to this trend and how the global *sukuk* market is geographically split, together with the currency denomination for international *sukuk* structures – in addition to the Malaysian ringgit, the US dollar is the preferred currency of denomination.

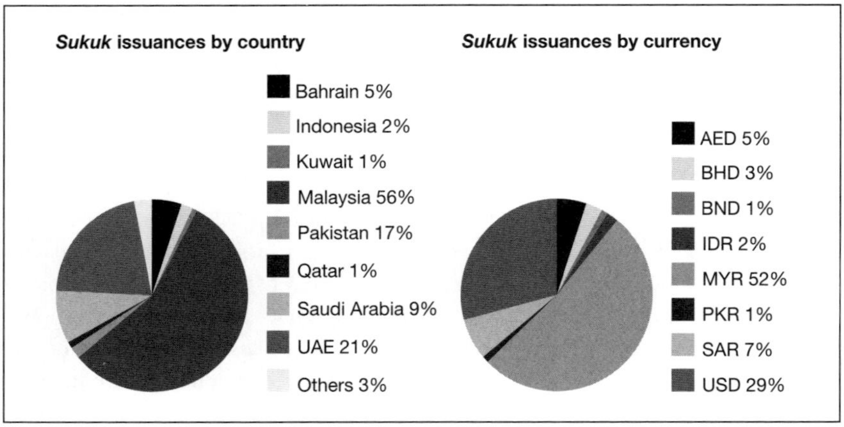

Data as at July 31 2009. Chart created from data sourced from: Securities Commission, Malaysia, Quarterly Bulletin for The Malaysian Islamic Capital Markets, *Zawya –* Sukuk *Monitor, Bloomberg, Liquidity Management Center – Global* Sukuk *Table, Global Investment House – Global Research – List of* Sukuk *(2001/2007)*

Following Malaysia's example, countries such as Saudi Arabia, Indonesia, Pakistan and, to a lesser extent, the United Arab Emirates have developed a local currency *sukuk* market relatively successfully, despite capital market activity in these countries (except Malaysia) being non-existent or fairly limited. This all serves to encourage corporate and sovereign issuers to use capital markets to raise liquidity or funding.

One interesting aspect of *sukuk* is that most issues to date – both Islamic and conventional – have been subscribed by institutional investors, including corporate houses, insurance companies, pension funds, mutual funds, hedge funds and banks. This can be explained by the fact that *sukuk* yield superior returns which would otherwise be unavailable, especially to banks which buy *sukuk* on a 'held to maturity' or 'available for sale' basis. The main reason for banks' active role in the *sukuk* market has been surplus liquidity, assisted by high oil prices for Gulf banks and booming economies generally. The reduction in bank liquidity and 'mark to market' issues have led treasury departments of institutional investors, especially banks, to avoid investing in exotic or structured instruments unless they are clearly prime grade.

During the last decade or so, Islamic finance has received a tremendous boost, mainly due to a basic desire for Muslims to conduct their affairs in an ethical manner compliant with their beliefs. The driver from *Sharia* scholars, their supervisory boards and Islamic institutions in structuring *Sharia*-compliant instruments, including *sukuk*, has been to encourage the migration of investors from conventional to Islamic finance, thereby gaining critical consumer mass. That said, *Sharia* scholars have different views as to the degree to which pragmatism or flexibility can be employed. This is a recurring issue in the context of Islamic finance being regulated in a conventional – debt-driven – regulatory paradigm. One school of thought maintains that strict compliance to *Sharia* must be observed. However, this view will not help the Islamic industry to develop and prosper, because a total migration to the Islamic banking and finance system, which is not consumer debt driven, is too dogmatic a condition to progress. The key point is that Islam is open to intellectual differences of opinion and, put simply, can easily provide pragmatic responses on issues – moderation is a virtue in Islam. If *Sharia* authorities have so far tolerated irregularities, or '*mafasid*', with earlier *sukuk* issuances, and at a time when there were fewer Islamic banks, now is a bad time to revisit this.

2. AAOIFI ruling

The structuring of *sukuk*, especially those based on *mudarabah*, *musharaka* or *wakala*, has been the focal point of discussion for various *Sharia* forums, including the AAOIFI. While a healthy debate has started to support or counter the 2008 AAOIFI ruling, one must fully understand the finer points of discussion between the various schools of thoughts under the Islamic jurisprudence, which is why some confusion has arisen. While *Sharia* scholars agree that Islamic banking and finance should follow *fiqh* (Islamic jurisprudence),[1] they have formed their own opinions. This is mainly why confusion exists in the Islamic banking and finance community, which tends to rely heavily on *Sharia fatwa* (rulings by *Sharia* scholars) when either structuring or simply participating in Islamic transactions. Accordingly, Standard & Poor's, for instance, has emphasised the need for greater standardisation in Islamic banking, especially pertaining to *Sharia* interpretation and the regulatory framework for the emergence of an integrated global *sukuk* market.

The *sukuk* market needs to have a definitive position on critical issues such as:

- 'real business' considerations – in other words, the extent to which *sukuk* structures (which rest on investing in business or enterprises) rely on real business viability; and
- whether it is acceptable to underwrite any investment risk by 'putting' assets to the *sukuk* obligor and whether there needs to be a fully perfected registered transfer of assets for *sukuk* structures which rely on a sale structure.

Sharia scholars, with their knowledge base, and the banking and finance community, with its market and product knowledge, should join efforts to create *Sharia* standards. A healthy domestic and international *sukuk* market and a refined

---

1 *Fiqh* (Islamic jurisprudence) is based on the *Quran* and *Hadith*. The *Quran* is the divine revelation revealed to Prophet Muhammed PBUH). '*Hadith*' refers to the oral traditions relating to the words and deeds of Prophet Muhammed PBUH. '*Ijtihad*' is a technical term of Islamic law that describes the process of making a legal decision by independent interpretation of the *Quran* and *Hadith*. '*Ijma*' is the consensus of the community of Muslims. '*Qiyas*' is the process of analogical reasoning by which new rulings are derived from existing rulings. A '*madhab*' is a school of Islamic law. In Sunni jurisprudence there are four *madhabs* (*Hanafi, Maliki, Shafi'I* and *Hanbali*), whereas in *Shia'* jurisprudence the main *madhab* is *Ja'fari Fuqaha*, which is expert in Islamic law.

use of structures will emerge once the Islamic banking and finance community reaches consensus on core issues.

3. Real businesses

One of the basic commercial principles of Islamic finance is the objective to protect capital. Islamic financial institutions are almost always prohibited by *Sharia* scholars and their *Sharia* supervisory boards from entering into any investment or transaction which is not financially viable – speculative ventures are discarded. Therefore, the premise of taking a *fatwa* beyond the stage of a mere seal of approval from *Sharia* scholars into its real business application requires closer inspection of the business or enterprise underpinning an investment or partnership *sukuk* structure (ie, *mudarabah, musharaka* or *istithmar wakala* (investment agency) structures).

4. 'Putting' investment risk

The AAIOFI's main area of contention is not whether *sukuk* are *Sharia* compliant, but rather the underlying structure itself and the use of the purchase undertaking in non-*ijarah*-based structures, where the person acting as *sukuk* manager (ie, managing partner, managing agent or investment agent acting as *mudarib, musharik* or *wakeel*) provides a purchase undertaking.

The primary cause for concern for the AAOIFI is the validity of 'attaching' a purchase undertaking to a partnership structure so as to create a fixed-income security, structurally.

The use of *Sharia*-compliant liquidity facilities to structures such as *mudarabah, musharaka* and *wakala* to guard against the inability to make periodic payments (due to timing mismatches or for any other reason) was also the focus of the AAOIFI's ruling. The practical effect of the AAOIFI's ruling is that the *sukuk* market is now constrained by limited structures available to create the much-needed depth of primary *sukuk* issues, yield curves and, consequently, a deep secondary market.

5. Ownership and transferability of assets

The constraining effect of the AAOIFI ruling is also exacerbated by the question of the form of ownership transfer for *sukuk*. The Islamic Financial Services Board (IFSB) has issued the Capital Adequacy Requirements for *Sukuk*, Securitisation and Real Estate Investment under IFSB 7 – Published Standards.[2] While the AAOIFI's focus is on *Sharia* requirements relating to ownership and transferability of assets under *sukuk* structures, the IFSB standard addresses the capital adequacy requirements for *sukuk* and securitisation. The purpose of the IFSB is to provide clear guidelines on the asset recognition criteria, especially for Islamic asset-backed securities (ABS).

A discussion of the IFSB standard is helpful to highlight how form of ownership considerations remain an issue for definitive restitution. The IFSB distinguishes between three types of *sukuk* structure:

- ABS – Islamic ABS are similar to conventional ABS. They expose the *sukuk*

---

2 IFSB 7 – Capital Adequacy Requirements for *Sukuk*, Securitisations and Real Estate Investment of January 2009.

holder to losses due to impairment of the asset (or cash flows) and the credit risk is essentially based on the underlying value of the asset (or cash flows) and not that of the obligor.

- Pay-through structure – any *sukuk* structure whereby the income generated from the underlying asset is paid to the *sukuk* holder through the issuer and where the obligor has issued a purchase undertaking will constitute a pay-through structure. Usually, such structures are based on transactions where the obligor undertakes to purchase *sukuk* assets on maturity or following a default event at a pre-formulated exercise price. The exercise price is drafted so as to return principal and profit. In such cases the primary risk is the obligor's creditworthiness.
- Pass-through structure – in a pass-through structure an entity different from the obligor executes the purchase undertaking.

It is necessary to understand the above distinctions because most *sukuk* are asset based. The IFSB recognises that from a *Sharia* perspective, subject to independent interpretation of jurists in their own jurisdiction, four key criteria are to be considered in order for a sale under a *sukuk* structure to be classified as a true sale:

- A transfer of assets should not be construed as a secured loan structured to avoid bankruptcy or insolvency proceedings by the court or other competent authorities;
- The bankruptcy or insolvency of the obligor must not affect the assets that have been transferred to the *sukuk* holder via the issuer;
- If *sukuk* holders or the issuer elects to have assets transferred to it outright, the assets must then be transferred; and
- The sale must be free and clear of all prior overriding liens.

Form of ownership considerations need focus to ensure that *Sharia* requirements are not confused with legal true sale requirements if the commercial deal does not require a true sale. Of course, the need for focus is not merely an academic matter – if, for example, a sale requires registration under local laws and fees are payable for that registration, then the economic viability of the *sukuk* is called into question. A conventional bond involves no such issues. Therefore, questions as to the competitiveness of the *sukuk* market are raised if such issues are not clearly dealt with.

It is possible that controversies surrounding *sukuk* could result in the development of a hybrid structure between the current *sukuk* structures and true asset-backed transactions. The hybrid would involve a put being made to the *sukuk* obligor and, if the obligor failed to pay, the *sukuk* assets would be open to sale in the market, with any shortfall in market price recovered being the subject of the obligor's indemnity obligations.

The *sukuk* market is young and is facing the teething issues typical of early-stage product development. Key challenges include the following:

- a consensus on *sukuk* structures among scholars globally;
- greater clarity in transaction structures, with increased standardisation and

reduced complexity;
- a more predictable and *sukuk*-friendly legal framework;
- harmonisation and standardisation of *sukuk* issuance regulations;
- better education of issuers and investors about *sukuk* and *Sharia* compliance;
- centralised information in which all data can be publicly accessed;
- development of active local debt capital markets to increase domestic participation;
- a focus on substance over form;
- a more liquid secondary market;
- the offer of multi-currency *sukuk* with a greater distribution network;
- an active domestic market and globally integrated international markets;
- ease of accessibility of local investors in both primary and secondary markets; and
- product innovation, with a focus on developing alternatives for controversial products.

It is clear that the *sukuk* market is entering a seminal stage in its development. Adverse market conditions, coupled with intellectual differences of opinion on *sukuk* structures, are hindering the development of the *sukuk* market. Along with pricing and geographical considerations, traditional distribution networks for *sukuk* must increasingly consider the extent to which a potential investor will agree (or refuse) to purchase *sukuk* on the basis of the structure adopted. All involved in the industry should take a step back, recognise the demands of financial institutions and issuers alike and rise to the challenges that those demands present. At a time when the markets are volatile, it is important to provide non-contentious *sukuk* structures so that striking the balance between investor appetite and issuer demand is not unnecessarily overshadowed by complex debates on *Sharia* compliance. Those familiar with Islamic jurisprudence will recognise that intellectual differences of opinion are a virtue. The Islamic capital markets must never lose sight of the fact that they are all about raising capital on an ethical basis. There is no difference of opinion on that from any quarter – this much is certain.

Glossary

Al-Wadi'ah: In contemporary Islamic finance, a deposit held by a deposit-taking financial institution for the depositor.
Amanah: Trust. The contract of *amanah* gives rise to a fiduciary relationship and duties.
Amwal: Wealth. In a business context, *amwal* means wealth that is contributed as capital in a partnership. Plural: *maal.*
Ameen, also spelled *Amin*: custodian or guardian.
'Aqd: A contract.
'Aqd sahih: A legal contract.
***'Arbun* (*urboon* or *arboon*)**: Down-payment paid in advance; a non-refundable deposit paid by a buyer retaining a right to complete a sale.
Arkan: The elements or essential ingredients of an act, without which the act is not legally valid.
Awad: Compensation or counter-value.
'Ayn: A tangible (physical) asset.
***Bai'* (also *Bay'*)**: Sale. Commonly used as a prefix in referring to different types of sales: *muajjal* (credit sale), *murabaha* (cost-plus agreed and disclosed profit sale), *tawliyah* (sale at cost) and *wadhi'ah* (sale at loss).
Dain: Loan or debt.
Dhaman: Liability.
Dharar: Harm, damage.
Diminishing *musharaka*: A form of *musharaka* financing developed in recent years where the share of the financier in the *musharaka* is purchased by the customer periodically and in scheduled amounts.
Faqih: Jurist specialising in *fiqh.*
Fard: Obligatory.
Fatwa: A legal verdict or pronouncement based on *fiqh*, given by a *Sharia* scholar or a *Sharia* board.
Fiqh: Islamic jurisprudence.
Gharar: Uncertainty, chance, or risk; ambiguity and uncertainty in transactions.
Hadith: Sayings and practices of the Prophet Mohammed (peace be upon him). Plural: *ahadith.*
Halal: An act or product that is permitted by Islam.
Haq: Legal right.
Haram: An act or product which is unlawful or prohibited in Islam.

Hawala: Transfer of liability.
Hibba: Gift.
Ijara: A lease – literally means 'to give something on rent'.
Ijmaa: Consensus.
Istisna: Sale of an asset to be produced.
Kafalah: Guarantee.
Kafil: Guarantor.
Maisir: Gambling. Literally means getting something too easily.
Makrooh: Disapproved of, but not prohibited.
Manfa'ah: Usufruct.
Mudaraba: Akin to a silent partnership or investment trust management, with the *rab-ul-maal* providing capital of the *mudaraba* and the *mudarib* using its skill and enterprise in investing that capital.
Mudarib: The person who provides entrepreneurship and management of a *mudaraba*. *Rab-ul-maal* are the investors or providers of capital of the *mudaraba*.
Mufti: One who passes verdicts.
Murabaha: Sale at cost plus agreed and stated profit.
Musharaka: Partnership or joint venture.
Qabd: Possession.
Qard: A non-interest bearing loan.
Qard al-Hassan: A loan given for a good cause.
Riba: Interest or usury.
Rab-ul-maal: A person who invests in *mudaraba*.
Salam: *Sharia*-compliant forward contract.
Sharia: (Literally, 'the way to the fountain'). The principle from the *Quran* and *Sunnah* to guide Muslims in the good conduct of their lives and for the good of the community as a whole.
Sharikat al-'aqd: A partnership created through contract as opposed to co-ownership that may be the result of, for instance, a joint purchase.
Sharikat al-jabr: Mandatory co-ownership arising by operation of law, such as inheritance.
Sharikat al-melk: Co-ownership that may be the result, for instance, of a joint purchase.
Sukuk: In contemporary Islamic finance, a trust certificate of entitlement deriving from a *pro rata* undivided ownership of one or more assets. Loosely termed an 'Islamic bond'.
Sunna: The practices and sayings of the Prophet Mohammed (peace be upon him), as documented in *Hadith*.
Takaful: Islamic insurance.
Thimma (zimma): the capacity to accept obligations and duties.
Tijaarah: Trade. Act of buying and selling.
Ulama: *Sharia* scholars.
Ummah: The Muslim nation.
Wa'd: Promise; used in the context of purchase undertakings and sale undertakings.
Wajib: Compulsory.

Wakala: Agency.
Wakala al mutlaqa: Absolute power of attorney.
Wakil: An agent under an agency (*wakalah*).
Waqf: Endowment. A charitable trust.
Zakat: Muslims' wealth tax: a Muslim must pay 2.5% of yearly savings above a certain threshold.

Note: transliterations of Arabic lexicology and terms vary. Readers should therefore look to phonetic similarities to determine what term is intended.

About the authors

Shibeer Ahmed
Partner, White & Case LLP
sahmed@whitecase.com

Shibeer Ahmed is a partner in the global projects department of White & Case LLP and has expertise in both Islamic and conventional banking and project finance.

His experience includes advising project sponsors, commercial banks and development finance institutions on energy, power and transport infrastructure (including private-public partnerships) projects in Western and Eastern Europe, the Middle East and Africa.

Mr Ahmed has wide experience of advising on Islamic financings. His Islamic finance experience includes advising Islamic banks and development finance institutions on the Djibouti Port Project (the first Islamic project financing benefiting from a MIGA-World Bank Group political risk guarantee); advising Islamic banks on the conventional and Islamic co-financing of the Engro Fertiliser Project in Pakistan; and advising Islamic banks on the Gulf Cement Project in Qatar. He has also been involved in the *Sharia*-compliant power, petrochemical and real estate financings in Saudi Arabia.

Rahail Ali
Partner and global head of Islamic finance,
Hogan Lovells (Middle East) LLP
Rahail.Ali@hoganlovells.com

Rahail Ali is the global head of Islamic finance at Hogan Lovells. He is an acknowledged expert on Islamic finance, reflected in numerous accreditations from leading industry and legal journals, as well as his top-tier rating in various directories. Mr Ali has worked on many of the most innovative and high-value Islamic finance transactions closed to date, including 'jumbo' syndicated financings and inaugural *sukuk* issuances for sovereigns, IFC (World Bank Group), Emirates and Petronas ("Rahail Ali is arguably the leading figure in the *sukuk* market" – *Legal 500 EMEA*). Mr Ali is regularly consulted by leading publications as well as banks, governments and regulatory authorities, and is a member of Her Majesty's Treasury's Islamic Finance Experts Group.

Manuela Belmontes
Associate, Maples and Calder
manuela.belmontes@maplesandcalder.com

Manuela Belmontes's main areas of practice are international capital markets, structured finance and Islamic finance. She has worked on a number of Islamic *sukuk* transactions and other Islamic compliant financings, conventional debt offerings and debt issuance programmes, as well as bespoke securitisations for clients based in the Middle East, Europe and North America. Ms Belmontes also has experience working on a variety of Cayman investment funds including hedge funds, mutual funds and private equity funds, advising investment managers and administrators, and advising on general corporate and commercial matters, including joint venture arrangements.

Ms Belmontes joined the Dubai office of

Maples and Calder in 2007. Before that, she worked for Turner & Roulstone in Cayman, Clifford Chance LLP in London and Blake, Cassels & Graydon LLP in Toronto.

Debashis Dey
Partner, Clifford Chance LLP
debashis.dey@cliffordchance.com

Debashis Dey is a partner in the international capital markets practice of Clifford Chance LLP. He is currently based in the firm's office in Dubai, the United Arab Emirates. Mr Dey specialises in complex financings that access the domestic and international capital markets, including Islamic finance *sukuk* issues, conventional bond issues and securitisation. His recent high-profile work includes some of the largest, most complex and innovative *sukuk* structures done in the Middle East and North Africa region. These include *sukuk* issues by Sorouh Real Estate PJSC, Tourism Development & Investment Company PJSC and others. Mr Dey also led the capital markets team responsible for structuring the aircraft *sukuk* sponsored by GE Capital, the largest international *sukuk* ever issued by a US corporate.

Roger Fankhauser
Senior associate, Hogan Lovells (Middle East) LLP
Roger.Fankhauser@hoganlovells.com

Roger Fankhauser is a senior associate in the Islamic finance team at Hogan Lovells in Dubai, and is recognised by SIX Swiss Exchange as an expert and knowledgeable representative of issuers. Dr Fankhauser has been involved in advising issuers and financial institutions on all legal aspects of issuing and listing equity and (conventional and *Sharia*-compliant) debt securities on the Australian Stock Exchange, London Stock Exchange, Nasdaq Dubai and SIX Swiss Exchange.

Since joining Hogan Lovells, Dr Fankhauser has worked on a number of *sukuk* transactions, including the issuance and listing of the first *sukuk* issued from Turkey and the $100 million *sukuk* due 2014 issued by the International Finance Corporation. Dr Fankhauser has also advised issuers and dealers on conventional bond transactions and the establishment of euro medium-term note programmes.

Rafe Haneef
Chief executive officer, HSBC Amanah Malaysia
rafehaneef@hsbc.com.my

Rafe Haneef is the chief executive officer of HSBC Amanah Malaysia and is also responsible for Islamic global markets in Asia-Pacific. Since 1999 he has helped to develop *sukuk* and Islamic structured and project finance at HSBC, ABN AMRO and Citigroup. He has worked on a number of notable *sukuk* deals.

He was previously head of Islamic banking for Citigroup Asia in Kuala Lumpur, responsible for developing Malaysia as a regional Islamic finance hub for Citigroup.

Before joining Citigroup, he established the global Islamic finance department at ABN AMRO in Dubai, and was in charge of the Islamic wholesale and retail businesses for the group. Previously, he was with HSBC Amanah in London and Dubai.

Mr Haneef read law and *Sharia* at the International Islamic University in Malaysia. He was admitted to the Malaysian Bar and practised law in Malaysia, specialising in Islamic finance. He then pursued his LLM at Harvard Law School and subsequently qualified to the New York Bar.

Tahir Jawed
Partner, Maples and Calder
tahir.jawed@maplesandcalder.com

Tahir Jawed has unrivalled experience in the offshore structuring of Islamic finance products and was involved in the first *sukuk* issue by a Cayman company to be listed on NASDAQ Dubai, as well as inaugural *sukuk* issues to be listed on other worldwide exchanges. His expertise covers swaps/derivatives, general corporate and investment and private equity funds, including funds which comply with Islamic principles.

Mr Jawed joined Maples and Calder in Cayman in 2000. He is managing partner of the Dubai office, where he has been a partner since 2005. He previously worked for Clifford Chance LLP in London, New York and Dubai. He is named as one of the 20 most prominent lawyers in the Middle East by *The Brief* magazine and is also ranked as one of the best lawyers in the United Arab Emirates by *Best Lawyer* magazine.

Mustafa Kamal
Legal adviser, Al-Yaqoub Attorneys & Legal Advisers in association with Hogan Lovells
Mustafa.Kamal@hoganlovells.com

Mustafa Kamal is a legal adviser in the Jeddah office of Hogan Lovells. He has worked with clients across a number of jurisdictions on a wide range of Islamic finance matters, including some of the largest *sukuk* transactions and Islamic project financings to date. Before joining Hogan Lovells, he worked with international law firms in Saudi Arabia and in the United States. Mr Kamal holds a JD from the University of Maryland, United States and is qualified as an attorney at law in Maryland, United States.

Sema Kandemir
Associate, Hogan Lovells International LLP
sema.kandemir@hoganlovells.com

Sema Kandemir is an associate in the capital markets practice of Hogan Lovells in London. Ms Kandemir joined the firm in 2005, where she worked in the capital markets team in London, frequently acting for trustees and paying agents in conventional capital markets transactions. She spent almost three years in the firm's Dubai office, primarily focusing on Islamic and conventional debt capital markets, before returning to practise in London.

Ms Kandemir has been involved in a number of recent high-profile *sukuk* transactions, including for the government of Bahrain, the PETRONAS Global *sukuk* and the IFC Hilal *sukuk*, the first debt capital market product cleared and settled entirely in the Middle East.

Moinuddin Malim
Chief executive officer, Mashreq Al-Islami Finance Company; head of Islamic Bank Division, Mashreq Bank PJSC
moinuddinm@mashreqalislami.com

Moinuddin Malim has vast experience of Islamic banking, stretching back nearly 20 years. He leads Mashreq Al-Islami, which acts as originator of deals and a product house serving the entire Mashreq banking group across regional markets and providing a full range of *Sharia*-compliant products and services to meet the retail and wholesale banking needs of its clients.

Previously, Mr Malim was the managing director of Dubai Islamic Bank (DIB) for asset management and capital markets, where he successfully arranged a number of *sukuks* with a total value of $9 billion and Islamic investment funds. During his tenure, DIB established its credentials as Best Global *Sukuk* House (Euromoney) and Best *Sukuk* House (Banker Middle East), and topped the Euromoney lead tables in 2004 and 2005, plus other awards.

Mr Malim has also worked with the International Investor as senior partner, running the group's investment banking activities in the United Arab Emirates and Qatar. His Islamic career started in the early 1990s with Al Baraka Banking Group.

Yavar Moini
Head of Islamic banking, Morgan Stanley
yavar.moini@morganstanley.com

Yavar Moini is head of Islamic banking at Morgan Stanley and is based in the Dubai office. He has 16 years of banking experience, 12 of which have been spent in the Islamic finance industry. He has led the Islamic financial services group at Ernst & Young Bahrain and headed Islamic structured products for Dubai Bank and Islamic banking at the National Bank of Dubai. Mr Moini has served on the board of Bank Islami Pakistan and has been a part of the UK government's Islamic finance experts group.

While at Morgan Stanley, Mr Moini has been involved in landmark transactions such as PETRONAS's $1.5 billion five-year *sukuk*, which is one of two largest global dollar straight *sukuk* to date; Tabreed's Dh1.7 billion mandatory convertible *sukuk*, which was the first mandatory convertible *sukuk* in the United Arab Emirates; and Tamweel's $220 million mortgage-backed *sukuk*, which represented the first true sale securitisation in the United Arab Emirates.

Mark Morris
Senior associate, Latham & Watkins LLP
Mark.Morris@lw.com

Mark Morris is a senior associate with Latham & Watkins LLP. He has over five years' Islamic finance experience advising governments, corporates and financial institutions on a wide range of Islamic finance transactions. Mr Morris has advised on Islamic equity funding structures, multi-source and wholly Islamic project financings, *Sharia*-compliant syndicated debt and Islamic asset finance transactions in the United States, Asia and all Gulf Cooperation Council jurisdictions.

Mr Morris holds the Islamic finance qualification issued by the UK Chartered Institute of Securities and Investment and is named as one of the world's leading Islamic finance practitioners in the 2008 and 2010 editions of *Expert Guides*, a Euromoney publication.

Imran Mufti
Partner, Hogan Lovells (Middle East) LLP
Imran.Mufti@hoganlovells.com

Imran Mufti is a partner with Hogan Lovells, based in the Riyadh office of its associate firm, Al-Yaqoub Attorneys & Legal Advisors. He has practised in the Middle East for more than eight years, primarily concentrating on the areas of Islamic capital markets and structured finance. He is a regular speaker at conferences and seminars which focus on Islamic capital markets. Mr Mufti holds an LLB (Hons) from the University of London. He is qualified as a solicitor in England and Wales and an attorney at law in New York.

Daniel Rankin
Senior associate, Hogan Lovells (Middle East) LLP
Daniel.Rankin@HoganLovells.com

Daniel Rankin is a senior associate in the capital markets practice of the Dubai office of Hogan Lovells (Middle East) LLP. His practice in Dubai primarily focuses on the areas of capital markets (debt and equity), funds and regulatory issues. Before joining Hogan Lovells in 2007, Mr Rankin was with a major Canadian law firm.

Mr Rankin's work in the Islamic capital markets has involved transactions such as the first-ever *sukuk* buy-back for Dubai Islamic Bank, the PETRONAS global *sukuk* (IFN Corporate Finance Deal of the Year 2010) and the IFC Hilal *sukuk* (the first capital market product cleared and settled entirely in the Middle East).

Stuart Ure
Senior associate, Clifford Chance LLP
stuart.ure@cliffordchance.com

Stuart Ure is a senior associate in the international capital markets practice of Clifford Chance LLP. He is currently based in the firm's office in Abu Dhabi, the United Arab Emirates. Mr Ure specialises in structured finance and conventional and Islamic debt capital markets transactions. His recent work includes the *sukuk* issue by Sorouh Real Estate PJSC; acting for Tourism Development & Investment Company PJSC in relation to its global medium-term note programme and trust certificate issuance programme; and acting for Qatar Telecom QSC in relation to its global medium-term note programme.